Laughter and Tears

JOHANNA'S STORY

by Irene Powell

Order this book online at www.trafford.com
or email orders@trafford.com

Most Trafford titles are also available at major online book retailers.

Printed in the United States of America.

ISBN: 978-1-4120-9423-8 (sc)
ISBN: 978-1-4669-7822-5 (e)

 www.trafford.com

North America & international
toll-free: 1 888 232 4444 (USA & Canada)
fax: 812 355 4082

To Johanna,
the dearest and best friend anyone could ever wish for.

Also to Alan, my husband,
without whose practical help and support this book
could never have been written.

INTRODUCTION

It all began in 1926. I was born on 16th. June that year, and my face crumpled in fury at the injustice of being thrust into a cold new world. With my first gasp of air I began my fight for survival and independence.

Of course at that moment all that really mattered was that I was alive. I had arrived into the world and announced it with a gutsy yell. My parents, Ali and Henk Hanenburg named me Johanna, meaning, "God is Grace".

Would my life live up to such a name? What would the future hold for me? Fortunately at that time I had no way of knowing the hardships, pain, joys and triumphs to come. Only one thing was certain. There would be laughter and tears in the years that lay ahead.

CHAPTER ONE

My father, Henk, had been brought up by an aunt and uncle following the death of his own parents when he was just three years of age. Home for him had been in Freesia in the north of Holland. His uncle was a baker and he and his wife took good care of the young orphan hoping that one day he would follow into the bakery business. However Henk had other ideas and when he was seventeen he left to take up an apprenticeship as a barber. During this time he met Ali and it soon became apparent that this was the girl he wanted to marry.

Ali came from a large family with nine brothers and sisters. Her parents were strict, religious, hard working folk who ran their own furniture removing business in the old centre of Amsterdam alongside the canals.

Eventually Henk passed his exams and became a barber. The couple found a rented property in which to live, with a front room that could be used as a barbers shop. They got married and life seemed perfect. Then I arrived! Nine months and six days after their wedding. A honeymoon baby had not been on their agenda.

Our house in Amsterdam was typical of most in the area. It was tall and narrow and divided into separate dwellings on each floor. We lived on the ground floor to enable my dad to use the front room as his shop. His name was proudly painted on the front window and the red and white pole denoting his trade was fixed by the side.

Behind the shop was a large room, which my parents used as their bedroom, but which also doubled as the best "Sunday" room. There was a small kitchen with the bare basics, table, chairs, large sink and cold water. Running the length of the building was a corridor with several cupboards. Originally used for storage these later became "bedstees". With wide shelves fixed to the walls and a thin mattress on top they became the place for children to sleep. As more children came along additional shelves were installed making them a little like English

7

bunk beds and then the next cupboard along would be changed into "bedstees". Eventually we had little storage space but several "bedstees"! Doors were opened at night and conveniently closed during the day and this was a typical Dutch custom in many households especially in the city.

Outside there was a small paved yard and a flight of stone steps leading up to two doors. One door led into another flat and the other to flights of wooden stairs leading to three more floors of similar flats. The main front door had an electric bell and the names of the residents were listed to the side. Unfortunately the door had to be opened manually by pulling on a rope on the individual landings.

The area itself was quite prosperous with a large population of Jewish people who became regular customers of my father. All the rows of properties were similar and it was a busy street with lots of small shops, a milk factory, bakers, delicatessen, grocer and removal firm. There was also a laundry where the richer folk took their best clothes to be washed and ironed. Not a place my family ever frequented. To one side of us was a garage where it seemed they would repair anything on wheels whether it was a pram, a bicycle or in later days a motor car.

There were many families living in the street so there was no shortage of children running around, in fact living opposite was a family with five sets of twins - all girls! The next door neighbours were tailors by trade making all sorts of garments by hand. As a toddler I was sometimes lifted over the wall and taken into their house were I would sit in the middle of their huge table playing with all the lovely coloured buttons whilst they sewed all around me. If I was very good I would be given a sweet or half a biscuit. This was a luxury and a treat my parents could seldom afford to give me.

I suppose the first really memorable event I can recall is the birth of my first sister Esther when I was aged two. I was amazed by how tiny she seemed but other than that I couldn't really understand what all the fuss was about. She seemed to cry a lot and mother would breast-feed her. Always inquisitive I decided if it was good enough for this new baby I wanted some too. I tried it. Yuk! She could keep it.

My hair was blonde and straight. Esther's was blonde and curly. She was the pretty one so everyone said. Mother used to put an enormous bow in my hair in an effort to keep it from falling all over my face. The bow was bigger than my head. Esther, of course did not actually need a bow as her lovely curls stayed just perfect. One day we were put into the playpen together whilst mother got on with her chores. I was enraged. Esther was wearing one of my dresses. My favourite pink one with the embroidery. I was too young to understand the economics of pass me down clothes. It was the first of many for all of us but I can still vividly recall the feeling of injustice that "she" had what was "mine". I guess I had a lot to learn.

My parents were deeply religious and I was brought up strictly. My father especially lived by the rule "spare the rod and spoil the child". By nature I was inquisitive. I always had to know the why, where and how of everything. It was not in me to accept the exasperated answer from a parent saying, "because I say so". I always had to push that little bit further and still ask "why?" I had a hunger and a thirst for knowledge, meaning and understanding of everything around me. Some might say I haven't changed in that respect! For my parents struggling to bring up a family in cramped conditions, with little money and in years to come enduring hunger and hostile German occupation my stubbornness and constant questioning of everything must have sorely tried their patience. I was to become all too familiar with my dad's rule of punishment.

At the time of my childhood and indeed throughout my life in Holland religion played an important part in the lives of most people. It was a very Protestant country and although there were some "town" and Roman Catholic schools most children went to the Reformed Church schools where religion was very much a part of the daily curriculum.

So it was at the tender age of three I was taken to school for the first time. The nursery section was part of the main school. It had just two big rooms and outside there was a sand pit and an area for playing games. Each day began at 9 a.m. and for the first forty five minutes we had a Bible story, prayers and a hymn. This was the pattern right through school even when I was older. School was to become my solace in the years to come. At school I could reach for the skies and expand my knowledge, broaden my horizons and realise there was another world outside the constraints of life at home but for now I was content to be just a three year old happily playing in the sandpit and eagerly waiting to learn how to read and write.

The years passed. I got used to being told to "look after Esther" and then having to take her to school with me but now there was another baby for me to mind. My brother Jan was born when I was five. My father was delighted to have a son. I couldn't understand what all the excitement was about. It was just another mouth to feed and there seemed little enough to go around anyway. The house was getting cramped. I already shared a "bedstee" with Esther and now another cupboard had to be changed to make room for Jan. Still, a boy was something different, something new. I didn't know much about boys! He was quite different to Esther. He never demanded attention. He was a quiet child. Even as he got bigger he never seemed to move and make a noise. I can still see him in my minds eye sitting on the step wearing a knitted jumper and trousers. He was about eighteen months old and he just sat and sat and sat. I decided boys were very boring. At least I could fight with Esther!

By now I was much more aware of my surroundings and the things going on in life generally. I had left nursery school with its sandpit, seesaw and swings. I had progressed from colouring, cutting out and pasting. Although I wouldn't admit it I secretly missed all the singing and teacher telling us a story but life in the "bigger" school held much more interesting things for me. I had learnt to read and write and books then, as now, were a wonderful source of interest and inspiration. I couldn't get enough of them. Sometimes on sunny days the teacher would take us for a walk to the nearby park where we would collect, draw and study the different types of trees and plants. This was also a favourite lesson. I loved being out in the open and enjoyed being able to recognise different types of trees by their leaves. Drawing them was not such a pleasure. Art was never my strong point and although I could clearly see the difference in shapes and size somehow my end result always looked the same - a green oval.

School attendance was from nine until noon, then from

two until four Monday to Saturday but we had Wednesday and Saturday afternoons off. It was on those days that I noticed my life was different to many of my classmates.

The Hanenburg family was growing. Another sister, Leni had been born and my role as surrogate mother and general dogsbody had increased. Whilst my friends were playing outside on sunny summer days with their tops and whips, skipping ropes and skates I was usually inside doing one of my seemingly endless chores.

With hindsight I can see how hard my parents worked and how they struggled to cope and make ends meet. My father's day began at 7 a.m. when he opened his shop to his first customers and it was usually 10 p.m. before he again closed the door. Each and every regular customer had his own set of towels with a number embroidered in the corner. These were kept in drawers with corresponding numbers. When a customer came into the shop he received his own clean towel each time no matter whether he came in for a haircut or a shave. For mother, this meant endless washing. There was of course at that stage no washing machine and no hot water. Pans of water had to be boiled on the stove and then poured into the big sink. All those towels had to be hand washed every day, starched, hung outside in the yard on fine days or hung across ropes in the kitchen when it rained. Then they had to be neatly pressed, folded and stored back in the appropriate drawers. There were also the white coats that father wore and woe betide my mother if there was a single hair left on anything that was supposed to be clean. My father would inspect them regularly.

In addition to all the laundry Mother of course had to prepare and cook the family meals, although even at that time, before the recession had really hit, our main meal was usually just potatoes and vegetables. There was rarely any money for meat except perhaps for a tiny piece on Sundays when if we were lucky there might also be a semolina pudding with a little bit of fruit in it.

Another daily job for my mother was to hang the blankets, bedspreads and pillows out in the fresh air each morning. Carpets and rugs would also be taken outside and beaten then the paths and steps would all be brushed clean. She also scrubbed the steps for a neighbour - just to earn a few extra cents each day. All this was usually done before 8 a.m. and not to do it was considered a lack of duty and laziness. Such a thing could never be said of my mother.

So it was that even at a young age I had the job of dusting, running errands and looking after the younger children. As I grew older peeling the potatoes and vegetables, scrubbing the steps and helping to keep the shop clean were also added to my list. Homework was considered by my parents as less important than getting my chores done and often I had to get up at 6 a.m. to do the school work I had no time for in the evenings.

Religion, duty and obedience were the cornerstones of our lives. Unfortunately I wasn't always too keen about any of them. At each mealtime my mother would begin by thanking God for our food. At the end of each meal my father would read a passage, often a lengthy one, from the Bible and my mother would again pray. Often we children would be squirming in our seats wanting to leave the table but one look from our father or a crack across the knuckles from the large wooden spoon he kept to hand would be sufficient to keep us glued to our seats.

Another child was born. My mother said each child was a "blessing from the Lord". I thought it was just another mouth to feed and another one for me to look after. They named her Ellie. She would become very special to me.

On Sundays at 10 a.m. we would all go to church. For me it always seemed the longest day of the week! The morning service began with a hymn then the creed was said, a psalm was sung, more hymns and Bible readings then a sermon for forty five minutes - that was just the first part - after more hymns and long prayers there would be another forty five minute sermon before the final hymn and prayer. The whole service lasted about two and a half hours. We all sat near the back and were given strict instructions to be polite and respectful to everyone, to sit quietly and not fidget. We were told to be especially polite to the men wearing suits, as many of these people were father's customers!

Eventually the service ended but we still had to wait around outside while the "grown ups" stood chattering and discussing the sermon. Then we walked home for lunch. If only that had been it for the day! Later in the afternoon we had to go to Sunday school and then another service in the evening. Any spare time in between could only be used for religious games. It was "The Lord's Day" and we were not allowed to play outside, read ordinary books or play with our few toys. Instead, Father would make up games using the Bible and seeing who could remember certain stories, or answering a Bible quiz.

Sometimes men in dark clothes would appear during the evening. They were from the church and came to discuss religion with my father. Several years later my mother began attending a different church one that wasn't quite so strict. My father wasn't happy about it at all and really I think my mother was very brave to go against his wishes. The men in suits became more frequent visitors arguing that Father should make Mother attend their church but amazingly she stood her ground. She argued that they all believed in the same God and the same salvation through Jesus. Eventually though they wore her down and she compromised by going to both churches, choosing the one that had the best preacher on any particular Sunday. As I got older I was also allowed to go to church with Mother and if there were any discussions about sermons or which was the better church I always took her side.

Life continued but there were some changes that seemed amazing to me. Our next door neighbours moved to a bigger house and I was sorry to see them go. They had always been kind to me and over the years my mother had been grateful for the outgrown children's clothes they had passed on for us. One day we were invited to visit them. In our own home we had no heating except for an anthracite stove in the big room where my parents slept and which doubled as the best room. This stove would be lit only on Sundays if it was exceptionally cold. Now in the new house of the tailors I saw gas fires for the first time. I watched enthralled as they turned a switch and these special white things gradually turned red and warmth came out. I couldn't believe it. It was like watching a real live miracle!

One day Father told us he had a special surprise in store for us. One of his customers would be arriving in a motor car. We ran to the window to watch. No one else in our neighbourhood had a car and we felt so proud that one should come to our shop.

Another day a big box arrived and inside was a large

13

wooden thing. The neighbours gathered around to watch. I tried to imagine what it could possibly be. It was round with a big handle that moved backwards and forwards. Mother kept me guessing but she was bursting to tell me. I had never seen her so excited. It was her first washing machine. She was so proud. No more washing all those towels by hand.

At 6 a.m. each morning we would hear the swish, swish of the new machine. The hot water still had to be lifted from the stove and poured into the machine. Then a handle was pushed backwards and forwards which turned a paddle inside moving the clothes around. When Mother considered the clothes to be clean enough she lifted the lid and the towels were placed one by one through two rollers. By turning another handle these rollers squeezed the soapy water out. By repeating the whole process with clean water for rinsing, the washing was then completed and the water allowed to drain out through a hole at the bottom. It certainly saved my mother's poor wash worn hands but compared to our electric "do all" machines of today it was still a lot of hard work. It took them a long time putting aside a little each week before they were able to pay off the cost but it was considered well worth it.

Not all our extended family struggled financially and often those living in the country would send potatoes and vegetables to us. Similarly when an aunt whose husband had died visited us with her numerous children Mother would gladly share with them what little we had. Her way of doing things as always ruled by the Bible "Feed the widows and orphans and look after the poor" she would quote to me when I complained they were eating our food when we had little enough for ourselves. I wasn't sure I'd ever get the hang of this religious stuff!

I was growing up fast - too fast according to Mother as she had a hard job finding second hand clothes for me. In junior school we worked more and played less but I didn't mind that. Instead of walks to the park there was a big P.E. room with wall bars, swings and ropes. I loved climbing up the ropes and being extra careful not to burn my hands on the way down.

There were no school uniforms and boys and girls were all in the same class. Often I was teased because my clothes were too small or rather shabby. Once I remember a girl laughing and telling everyone I was wearing her cast off dress. I was mortified but instead of running away as some would have done I stood my ground and loudly protested that it was not hers, my mother had just bought it from the same shop.

There were about thirty six children in each class. Two girls or two boys to each desk, which had an inkwell in the middle. Many a time girls behind me took hold of my long blonde plaits and dipped them in the inkwell. Although not my fault it would cost me a good thrashing when I got home.

The windows of the classrooms were long and high and opened either by sash cord or with a long window pole. It was tempting to look out at the sunshine in the summer but I was never one to daydream for long. There was so much to learn and I wanted to know it all. I especially loved our Geography lessons. The big wall map would be unrolled and the teacher would tell us about other countries, provinces, capital cities, rivers and Bible lands. I soaked it all up like a thirsty sponge. Would I ever get to see any of those seemingly far away places? I think that was the beginning of my longing to escape and find out what life, customs and other places were really like.

Science also excited me. My questioning mind longed to understand how things worked and to try to understand principles like gravity. Even now I still want to know how things work. Someone says of me "We just flick the switch and accept the light comes on but Johanna has to know why."

My least favourite subject was needlework, which I hated. There was embroidery, darning and patching. We had to make pillowslips and tablecloths. Then there was the dreaded knitting. We had to knit a long piece and then the teacher would cut a hole in it so that we could learn to pick up the stitches and repair it again! Only after that was perfectly done could we then make a cloth bag, embroider it and be proud of our very first handbag.

Summers always seemed to be sunny and warm. When the chores were done Mother would send me off with all the younger ones to the park with the stern instruction to look after them all and not come back until 6 o'clock. She would give me a big bottle of water and a few sandwiches but always she would make me take my dreaded knitting. I was supposed to do twenty lines and she would check on my return. If it wasn't perfect she would undo the lot and make me start again. How I resented it. It wasn't fair. All the others could run around and play but I had to be the one responsible for them all and sit knitting.

One day Leni was being really troublesome so my mother told me to take her out in the pram and go for a walk. It was a lovely, warm, sunny day and all the other kids in the road were playing. There was a Spanish family living at the end of the street and they all loved babies and young children. As I walked past, one of their children was playing on skates. I stopped to chat for a minute and she began making a fuss of Leni. Suddenly I had an idea. If she would let me borrow her skates for a while I would let her borrow Leni. We both thought it was a good deal so I happily left my sister with her and skated off down the road and round the corner.

I was having the time of my life. It was wonderful to be whizzing along. Freedom. No little hands clutching at my skirts, no noses to wipe, no responsibility. I felt exhilarated. I don't know how long I skated around the district but obviously longer than I should. I returned to our street to look for the girl with whom I'd left my sister. She was nowhere to be seen. I knocked at the door of the Spanish family and returned the skates but was not allowed to speak to the girl. I was scared stiff. My Mother would kill me that's if my Father didn't do so first. I began to panic. I searched everywhere I could possibly think of. Suddenly I remembered God and prayed, "Dear God please let me find my sister."

The minutes went by and I went rushing from place to place looking in every corner although not really knowing why she should be in any of them. I tried bargaining "Dear God, please let me find my sister and I promise I'll never swap her for anything ever again." Reluctantly I had to admit my prayers were not being answered and trembling with fear I went home. As soon as I walked through the door my Mother asked where Leni was. I can still hear myself saying "I swapped her for a pair of roller skates, just for half an hour, but now I can't find her". Mother went hysterical and began shrieking

"Where is she? Where is she? Dear God, bring her back. Don't let anything happen to her".

I stood dumbstruck. It's not often I am lost for words but that was certainly one occasion. Mother left the room and I stood there alone wondering what to do and what would become of me. A few minutes later Mother returned, gave me a hefty walloping and told me my sister was safely asleep in bed and had been home for ages. She made me promise to never do such a thing again. I was more relieved than I could ever put into words and I gladly made the promise, which of course I kept - well, for a while anyway!

Wintertime in Holland was quite magical. It would be bitterly cold, often ten or more degrees below freezing. The canals all froze over and people would go skating on the ice. My father had a pair of skates and sometimes when he wasn't looking I would "borrow" them. I loved skating and the fact that I didn't have many opportunities for it only made it seem more fun. One day, early one winter the ice had just appeared on the canals and I was determined to go skating. Mother had said the ice wasn't yet thick and hard enough but I had seen others skating and wanted to join them. When no one was looking I took Father's skates and headed off to the nearby canal. There were quite a lot of people already skating and I quickly rushed to join them. I loved it when we joined hands and skated really fast, the last one in the line being pulled around in a big arc but that day people were mainly skating individually.

I was happily going up and down the canal when suddenly there was a loud crack and the next thing I knew I was up to my neck in freezing water. Struggling for breath and seriously impeded by my wet clothes and heavy skates I began thrashing about but somehow managed to haul myself out of the water and back onto the ice. Meanwhile my Father's skates had come loose and were lost to the bottom of the canal.

I was dithering and my teeth were chattering. People around kept shouting to me to run home as fast as I could before I froze to death. That's just what I did. Ran and ran the mile or so back home. My plaits were frozen, my clothes were stiff and my legs and hands hurt so much with the cold. I rushed through the door panting for breath and scared. Mother took one look at me and gave me a good thrashing before telling me to get out of my wet clothes and go into the kitchen to warm up. I was forbidden to go out again for weeks.

Winter of course also brought St. Nicholas. In Holland, Christmas Day was always a religious day, a day to remember the birth of Jesus and nothing to do with exchanging presents. St. Nicholas is the patron saint of children and legend says he rides on his horse over the roofs of the houses listening through the chimneys to see if boys and girls are being good. Then, on 4th December he arrives by boat into Amsterdam centre before riding his white horse in a parade through the streets. He is dressed as a Bishop with long red robes, a mitred hat, long white beard and carrying a shepherds crook. He is accompanied by his "Black Peters" his helpers whose task is to punish naughty children. Black Peter is dressed in Black puffy knee length trousers, black stockings and black pointed shoes. His black shirt with wide sleeves is embroidered in red and he wears a black beret with a feather in it. In his hand he carries a long pole for chastising misbehaved children. Everyone loves to go and watch the parade and the Black Peters throw sweets to the waiting children.

Later that night before the children go to bed they hang up their stockings by the chimney. Below, they place their shoes in which they put some hay and a carrot for St. Nicholas' horse. By next morning they will find their shoes are empty.

On the evening of St. Nicholas, 5th December in most houses where there are children a knock will be heard on the door and a black hand will appear throwing sweets to the waiting children. The father of the household will have dressed up as St. Nicholas and will come in and ask each child to come and sit on his knee. He will ask if they have been good and remind them of the times when they have been naughty, enlisting a promise of good behaviour in the coming year. He will then give each child their presents.

As children we eagerly awaited the 5th December and were delighted with whatever small gift was given to us. As the recession and the war years later took hold there would be some years when our parents were unable to provide even a small present but their faith and prayers were answered. On such occasions there would be a knock on the door and outside we would find a box with brightly wrapped parcels each bearing our individual names. We were not left out after all. We never discovered who left those presents for us but as children we learnt to be truly grateful. As Mother often said, "God moves in mysterious ways"

CHAPTER TWO

The recession was beginning to make life ever more difficult. Throughout Europe people were being laid off work. Without jobs there was no money and without money no food. In Germany Adolf Hitler thought he had the answer. He set the men to work again building roads, constructing bridges and repairing buildings. It seemed a good idea. Morale lifted and the people were able to feed their families again. His popularity increased rapidly. Sadly, at the time, most of those people had little idea how it would all end.

Many men in Holland were out of work. Although Father still had his shop he had lost a large number of customers. Some of the more wealthy Jews still came in regularly but the ordinary men got wives and girlfriends to give them a haircut and a shave at the barbers was a luxury few could afford.

As the lack of money became a real problem the churches gave food coupons to the poorest families. These could be exchanged in certain shops for basics like bread, margarine and cans of fatty pork, which tasted awful. Once again it fell to me to go with our coupons and queue for these items. I felt deeply ashamed that we had to resort to such things and made excuses to friends about where I was going.

Each day on my way to school I passed a sweet shop. I would stop and look in the window at all those goodies. My mouth would water as I imagined how wonderful they would taste. We had an aunt who visited occasionally and she would sometimes give us a few sweets. Oh, nothing ever tasted quite so good and I was an expert at making just a couple of sweets last a whole week or more. Something I can still easily do today!

However, we had another aunt who was not quite so charitable. I recall her telling Mother,

"If they have jam on their bread they do not need sugar in their tea."

I was furious and shouted

"How do you know what children need? You haven't

even got children yourself."

That little outburst cost me another good thrashing and a stint in the dark broom cupboard. Still, it was worth it just to see the look of horror on my aunt's face!

About this time I was often sent to other relatives who lived in quite a wealthy part of Amsterdam and for whom food shortages and lack of money had not yet become a problem. In exchange for a guilder, which of course I had to pass to Mother, I would help with the dusting and washing up especially when they had guests for dinner. The best part of it all was that my aunt would always give me little bits of food and any leftovers. A few years later during the Hunger Winter I would be more than grateful to be able to lick out any remaining food from the cooking pots.

In 1939 my brother Henk was born. He was to be the last addition to our family. There were now six children. He was a tiny baby and small enough to fit in the bread basket. I had noticed Mother putting on weight but when I questioned her she told me it was due to nerves having to put up with me. When the new baby arrived I took a chance and again commented that it was strange she had a big stomach, went away, came home with a baby and her stomach was flat again. Her answer was it was due to the fact she'd had a rest from me. I was then thirteen and that was as much as I would ever be told about the birds and the bees!

When Henk was about eight months old and sitting in his high chair he somehow managed to lean forward and pull a pot of freshly made tea over himself. He was badly scalded and had to stay in hospital for a while but fortunately no permanent damage was done.

I was no stranger to hospitals. My sister Ellie had been born with a birthmark down one side of her body. From an early age I had been the one to take her to the hospital each week for laser treatment to her face. I think this was one of the reasons I always felt protective towards her and we shared a special bond, trusting and looking out for each other. Many were the times she would cover for me when I was doing something I shouldn't, or comfort me when I'd received a thrashing. Similarly when she was feeling cold and vulnerable she would come into my bed and ask to snuggle up to me.

Father began listening to the "secret" radio station. He met with the men of the church and started to attend political meetings. He began to think the Germans were doing things better than the Dutch. After all, their men had work and could feed their families. There were arguments at home and the strain of every day living began to take its toll. One day when Father was out at yet another meeting and Mother was again left alone to cope with the family she snapped and went outside with a brush in her hand and broke all the windows in the pigeon loft my father kept. Whilst probably getting rid of some of her anger and frustration she badly cut her wrists. The local chemist could do nothing so once again I paid a visit to the hospital this time for Mother to have several stitches put in her wounds.

Even though the recession was making life difficult for everyone there were still the lighter moments. Whenever I had the chance I used to play out in the street with my friends. We would enjoy skipping, hopscotch and marbles. I had to watch out that Father never caught me playing marbles as he considered it undignified for a girl as in bending down I might show my knickers!

On one corner of the street was a "Brown Café" something unique to Holland. Although called a café, no food was ever served. Instead they were places for smoking, drinking and playing billiards. Many of the customers would leave very inebriated. My parents of course thought such places to be dens of iniquity. In our strict religious upbringing even the cinema or dancing were considered works of the Devil. Consequently we were forbidden to go anywhere near the Brown Café. It was a place of sin and sinners. What temptation! The fact that it was off limits only enhanced the appeal and I would strain on tiptoe to see through the windows. I wanted to see what sin looked like!

On Thursday nights I attended choir practice - well, I was supposed to. However the lure of a summer night and freedom often meant I would play truant and go off with some of the local boys to the park. I suppose I was a real tomboy at heart. I loved nothing better than collecting conkers and climbing trees, the taller the better. Many a time I caught and ripped my dress on a branch and would have to creep quietly into the house, surreptitiously find a needle and cotton and make a hasty repair. Perhaps all those sewing lessons in school had not been such a bad idea after all.

As a family we all continued to attend church each week. Father gave each of his children one cent to put into the collection. When the small bag on a short pole was passed around I was often sorely tempted to either not put in my cent or even to take some out. My mother still firmly believed "The Lord will provide" and told us so each day so I usually decided to do the right thing, put in my money and leave things to God.

I still loved school and considered it to be the best thing in my life. Often I would be severely thrashed for misdemeanours or put in the dreaded dark cupboard with the rats, which terrified me. However, for me, by far the worst punishment was to be kept away from school. On such occasions I would go round to a friend's house and copy up all the work I'd missed. Learning was so important to me.

One day at school I had been kept behind for too much talking in class, not an unusual occurrence! Whilst waiting for the teacher to come I noticed strange words on the blackboard. I had no idea what they were, what they meant or even in which language they were written. I knew there was a class after school where for a few cents pupils could learn English, German and French. I wished I could learn those languages but knew there was no way my parents could afford the extra money. I took out pen and paper and began to copy the list. The teacher caught me in the act and asked what I was doing. I explained, and he replied,

"If you are so interested why don't you come to the after school language classes?" Red with embarrassment I told her we didn't have even a few cents to spare. He was quiet for a moment then told me if I agreed to tell no one at school he would allow me to come to the extra lessons free of charge provided I promised to work really hard. I was stunned and could scarcely believe that someone would do this for me. It was all I could do not to hug him on the spot. Instead I promised fervently to work as hard as I possibly could.

Mother was not too pleased when I told her. I think she felt ashamed that she could not afford to pay. However, she realised how much education meant to me. As a girl of eleven she had missed some schooling herself because she had to deliver bread to the rich people in the big houses to earn extra cents. She relented and said I could go. I began the next week and it was the beginning of my love for languages, which has stayed with me to the present day.

At school I was still teased by some of the other girls because of my poor clothes but I worked hard, got good results and although my reports often said I talked too much my teachers were always pleased with my work. Gradually the other girls began to see me for the person I was and not for the clothes I wore.

At home I still had a seemingly endless amount of chores to do as my brothers and sisters were considered too young to help. I developed the habit of doing my homework early in the morning, as I was often too busy doing jobs the night before. I had an uncle who was a milkman and in those days milk was delivered to the houses but not in nicely sealed bottles. Households left a jug outside the door and a note saying how much milk was required. The milkman then measured it out by the quart from his big urn. I made arrangements with my uncle to knock loudly on our door each morning at 6 a.m. when he delivered our milk. That was my signal to get up and do my homework from the previous night. Mother too thought this was a good idea saying my brain would be fresh in the mornings. Strangely I never minded having to get up early. Years later when milk came to the shops in funny shaped bottles with peculiar tops and labels saying the milk had been "double steamed" to make it last longer and kill off bacteria I thought it tasted horrible.

If milk was ever in our house long enough for it to go off it was never wasted. Mother would take a finely woven cloth and stretch it over a pan then pour the soured milk through the cloth. The watery part went into the pan and the rest stayed in the cloth. To this was added some salt and a few other things and it formed a sort of creamed cheese to spread on our bread. As a rare treat Mother would sometimes make "posh" coffee. This involved boiling the milk, beating it until it became frothy and then adding it to the rich ground coffee. Who needs cappuccino machines?

What little time my parents had to themselves was usually spent discussing religion, my father playing chess and my mother reading. Father had a Saturday helper in his shop when he could afford to pay him. His name was Jan and like Mother he was an avid reader. They often discussed books together especially those about other countries and how other people lived. I was eager to read these books too but Mother firmly told me that it was morally wrong to read books above my age.

The years were passing. The recession was so much worse. There were rumours about a possible war. People felt unsettled and no longer in control of their own lives. Many of Father's Jewish customers had fled to England or America. Jews from Austria and Poland began to arrive in Holland. It seemed the world was about to be turned upside down.

Without his Jewish customers Father's business was really slack. Those customers had often paid for "extras" - a shave, some cologne, powder, shampoo. Now there were only the basics. Each morning Father would give me the money to go to the baker and buy a loaf of bread so we could eat something before setting off for school. Many were the times now that I had to wait until Father had his first customer before he had that money. Then I would grab the cents and run as fast as my legs could carry me, get the bread, quickly cut a slice and eat it on my way to school.

I remember only too well that some days before school, I also had to go to the elders of the church and beg for some socks for myself or one of the others. I had to tell them it didn't matter if there were holes in them, we would mend them. I was mortified at such tasks, made worse because the daughters of some of the elders were in my class at school and often found out about my early morning visits.

On Saturdays there was a local market and towards the end of the day Father would give me a few cents to go there and see what fresh fruit and vegetables I could get. I would go around all the stalls checking the best prices and return to the stall where I could get the most goods for the least amount of money. Proud of my efforts I would return home perhaps with a bag of oranges and some vegetables, sure in the knowledge that at least we would have some vitamins that week.

Another shopping expedition was to a butcher selling cheap meat. He was by no means the local butcher. In fact I passed several other butchers en route. It was a good half hour walk in both directions and I often complained it must cost more in shoe leather getting there than we saved on the price of the meat. Mother did not agree!

Sometimes I'd sit in the corridor outside the shop and listen to the men talking of poverty, lack of work and food, the troubles throughout Europe, politics and always religion.

Life was so hard yet we all still went to church, believed in God, sang our hymns and read our Bibles but all the time we were getting thinner and thinner. On Sundays if we were lucky there would be a boiled egg for tea. It was divided between eight of us! Mother was a great one for quotations. Her favourites were "God will provide" and "Children are a blessing of the Lord but they cost you the buttons off your coat" I wasn't sure I agreed with the first but I did agree with the last part of the second.

Behind a cupboard in the kitchen were a family of mice. Sometimes we would see them hurry out and scamper away with any crumbs they may have found. We coped with the mice but the rats were a different matter. Father repeatedly asked the Landlord to do something about them but he never did. We feared the rats would bring disease so one day Father got some large traps and set them. Having caught several enormous rats he laid them outside on the pavement in front of the shop with a big sign saying they were a threat to his family and the Landlord was not prepared to do anything about them. With so many canals around rats were a problem to many people but at least Father tried to get rid of them.

There was an empty shop opposite. Another barber moved in and trade for Father became even worse. Both tried in vain to undercut the other but in many ways it was a hopeless situation.

People were beginning to become aware of the Jewish situation. Esther, because of her Biblical name had been a great favourite of Father's Jewish customers but now that same name was causing her to be picked on by others. One day some girls were taunting her. I had always felt she'd been the favourite of the family and so we were not especially close but I was not having someone bully a sister of mine. Without stopping to think I rushed to her defence and hit one girl over the head with a roller skate. Well, what are sisters for if not to stick up for each other?

Sometimes I would go out with my friends looking at the "posh" houses. Many of them had typical "half" curtains so we could see into the rooms inside. Especially at night they looked so cosy. Most had plants on the windowsills and we would stop to see which ones looked the best, imagining how we would have our own homes one day. Along the canals of course were houseboats and we loved to see how many of the people even had little "extensions" added, on which they too, would proudly display their plants. I remember from my visits to our more wealthy relatives there would often be a chenille cloth on the big dining table and in the centre would stand a plant in a large brass pot. The Dutch people have always taken pride in their plants and flowers.

Of course a trip to the flower market was a treat. We loved admiring all the bunches of flowers, their colours vividly contrasting with each other and I secretly vowed to myself that when I left school I would buy my mother a big bunch of flowers with my first wage packet.

All alongside the canals, trees were planted and window boxes on the tall houses were filled with flowers and so there was always a sense of nature and greenery despite being in the centre of a city.

I can vaguely remember my grandparents living in one of the big old houses. My grandfather had a kind face and a soft voice; sadly he died of throat cancer when I was only a few years old. My grandmother was a tall lady, hair tightly wrapped in a bun and black clothes high up to her neck and skirts down to the floor. She was strict and old fashioned in the way she brought up my mother and her siblings. The boys were put to work in the family removal business whilst the girls, including my mother went into "service" working as servants for the more wealthy families. This sort of arrangement was still prevalent as I was growing up, as I was to find out for myself in the not too distant future.

As I got older I was given additional chores to do on Saturdays - cleaning the windows, washing the paintwork and cleaning the living room. However, as Esther and Jan were now older they too had been given jobs to do each day so life seemed marginally easier. The others were still too young to help.

I was now attending senior school. I had passed the examination enabling me to go to the equivalent of an English Grammar School but my parents had refused to let me go. They had three reasons: - only children of the "posh" families went there and I would be out of place; they couldn't afford to dress me as well as the other children and finally I was just a girl and education was not so important as it was for boys! I was absolutely furious and felt life was totally unfair. However, despite my protestations they were adamant and I had no choice but to go to the equivalent of an English Secondary Modern School. I vowed I would work doubly hard and I would succeed!

I still loved school and continued to enjoy the challenges of learning new things. Everything that is, except Geometry. I couldn't seem to get the hang of it and certainly couldn't see the point to it. This was not helped by the fact that I didn't like the teacher. He had a habit of saying, "You can and you shall". I hated being told what I **had** to do.

There was another teacher whom I really liked. She taught French and Geography, two of my favourite subjects. Often whilst I was sitting eating my sandwich at lunchtime she would sit beside me asking about my life and telling me about life in France. I think she realised how difficult things were at home but she also knew how eager I was to learn. One day, unknown to me she went to talk to my parents and tried to persuade them to transfer me to the higher education school (the one they had previously said I couldn't go to). My mother said I was cheeky, argumentative, resentful towards the church and generally rebellious and she didn't see any good reason why I should be allowed to change to a better school. With hindsight I can see that she may have had a point! However, both the teacher and I were bitterly disappointed but she encouraged me to do my best at the school I was in and further my education at night school once I left.

This teacher continued to have a special interest in me. One day I had no sandwich for my lunch and she offered to go to her home nearby and bring one back for me. It looked delicious but when I bit into it I was horrified. What was all this yellow stuff? It turned out to be butter, which I had never tasted before! After that the teacher often brought a sandwich into school for me knowing I had so little to eat at home and I soon began to appreciate the taste of butter.

She continued to encourage me especially in French and suggested I go to her home on Wednesday afternoons when we had no school and she would give me extra lessons. Mother thought it unnecessary but agreed to let me go.

The first time I went to her house it seemed very posh. There were four flights of steps and the occupants names and numbers were written on little brass plaques. When I rang the appropriate bell I heard her voice calling me up and instead of a rope being pulled the door opened electronically. A very well spoken lady welcomed me and told me to go to her daughter's room along the corridor, promising to bring a tray of tea soon.

The teacher's room was beautiful with a high slanted ceiling, lovely bureau and furniture and expensive looking ornaments but to me the best of all was a wall lined with books. We started the lesson based on my schoolwork and then she began to tell me about her family and life in France. Over the coming weeks my French improved and I had a wider vocabulary and knowledge of the country whose language I was learning.

During the first summer holidays from senior school, this teacher had also arranged to take a group of girls cycling and staying in youth hostels for a week. The cost was not great but of course I knew there was no point asking my parents for the money and yet I longed to go. I had never been on a holiday. Not only did we not have the money, I didn't even have a bike!

One night I saw an advertisement in the local paper for additional summer help in a nearby ice cream factory. I had already begun collecting empty jam jars and selling them for a cent but the chance of a real job would surely enable me to get enough money for the trip. Boldly I went for an interview. I had just turned twelve years of age. When asked how old I was I told

29

them I was fourteen. The manager agreed to employ me and I was filled with triumph.

All I had to do now was to tell my parents. Firstly I had to explain that I wouldn't be able to look after the younger children the next day as I had to go somewhere but I might be able to get some extra money if I went. Amazingly they made no objection except of course to say that I would still have to do my chores.

I began at the factory the next day at 8 a.m. and was given a cap for my hair and an overall to wear. It was tedious and tiring work standing at a conveyor belt putting ice cream into cartons. Music blared continuously and the other girls were of course a lot older than me. They swore a lot and we had little if anything in common. Most of them had left school at the earliest opportunity with no interest in learning or indeed in anything other than their immediate environment. They kept asking how old I was and said if I was old enough to have left school why did I still have plaits in my hair? I said my father was a barber and wouldn't let me have my hair cut. Surprisingly they believed me.

At the end of the week I was given my wages. It wasn't much - two guilders fifty cents the equivalent of about eighty pence but I felt very rich. Two nights at a Youth Hostel cost two guilders and I was hoping to go for a week so I needed to keep earning. I was so afraid my mother would take my wages from me but when she asked how much I'd earned and knew that if I saved it all I would be able to pay for my own holiday she agreed to let me keep the job and all the wages.

One day the next week the manager called me into his office. I went with shaking knees trying to think what I could possibly have done wrong. He told me to sit down then asked me again how old I was. I said I was fourteen. He said he didn't believe me and asked the question again. I hesitated and he told me to tell the truth. "This is it", I thought, "He's going to give me the sack." Still, it was worth putting up a fight so I told him if I gave the true answer I was afraid that would be the end of my job. He said it wouldn't and somehow I believed him. Reluctantly I told him I was twelve. When asked why the job was so important to me I found myself telling him all about the school trip and my parents inability to pay for it.

He looked sympathetically at me and then to my surprise

asked if I was any good at sums. I told him I was quite good, that at least was true. He said he'd been watching me and knew I wasn't like the other girls. I didn't join in their vulgar language and songs, didn't boast of boyfriends, and just got on with my work. He thought I was capable of more than production work so suggested I work in the office where the pay was better too. I couldn't believe my good fortune.

He took me into the office and explained the procedures. All the ice cream delivery men had cards which they collected in the mornings and returned at the end of the day showing how much ice cream they had sold. According to that they were paid a wage plus a commission. I was to keep their time sheets and details of how much they sold and earned.

Six weeks later I received my final wage plus a bonus for working hard, and never being late. At home that night I counted and recounted my money. I was so happy. I had enough for each night at the Youth Hostel plus enough for food and drinks along the way. There was enough to give Mother a few extra guilders for food and even enough to buy a dress. A brand new one. My first ever! I can still remember it now. It was printed with lots of apples and pears on a pale beige background, a tight bodice and a flared skirt. I was so pleased with myself.

I borrowed a bike and during the last week of the school holidays I joined the group of seven other girls plus our teacher as we set off cycling between youth hostels. The weather was glorious, the scenery green and fresh, the company good and perhaps best of all was that glorious sense of freedom and excitement as I visited new places.

The teacher rode in front and we cycled behind in pairs, swapping partners and positions so we each had a turn at the front and back. We stopped and went walking, collected flowers and leaves to press and dry for the school nature table. In towns we studied important buildings. It was quite educational but also great fun.

Most of the Youth Hostels had just one big room with beds side by side. The teacher joked that as I talked a lot I should sleep in the bed next to her so she could tell me to be quiet and let everyone get to sleep.

In the morning we all had to share the cleaning duties,

brushing the floor and folding the bedding but it didn't take long and we were soon on our way again cycling about fifty to seventy kilometres each day. The teacher always had interesting information about the places we passed through and often we would stop at farms to buy food. I loved the heather fields we passed by and the pretty little villages beside the canals.

Sadly, all too soon the holiday came to an end but I had enjoyed every minute of it. I think my friendship with the teacher had strengthened too. Despite my constant talking and inquisitiveness I think she admired the initiative I had taken to earn the money and pay for the holiday myself. It had been a great week.

I continued to work hard and get good marks although my chattering often resulted in me being given "lines". If Mother ever discovered this she would immediately double the number I had been given. Sometimes I would sit in the toilet to write them so she would not find out. Once I remember thinking I would be clever and instead of writing all the hundred lines out time after time I just wrote it once and put ninety nine ditto marks down the rest of the page. My teacher was not amused. He trebled the amount I had to do. Well, you can't blame a girl for trying!

At home I suppose I often asked for trouble too. If something was forbidden I would have to do it. If others could have something, go somewhere, do something, say something; I didn't see why I shouldn't too. Many a time I went to bed crying after I'd felt the heel of my father's shoe on my backside for being cheeky or disobedient. At such times my little sister Ellie would often creep into my bed saying,

"Don't cry, I'll make it better."

During my twelfth year Mother decided it was time for me to attend Catechism classes at church. These took place each week and lasted for an hour. I resented the extra time taken away from me but have to admit I did get to air my own views. The instruction involved learning by heart huge chunks of the Bible and the Heidelberg Chatechsmus. The latter was divided into fifty two parts and the questions and responses for each week had to be learnt and repeated word for word. One such question was "What is our comfort in life and death?" The response was "Our comfort in life and death is that our body and soul are not our own but they belong to the Lord Jesus Christ whose precious blood paid for our sins".

Even as a child I had been unafraid to speak my mind and now as a twelve year old I was not about to just accept everything without question. Not for me the "Because the Bible says so" answer. I still wanted to know "why?" and was not prepared to just sit there and accept everything they taught us. When they talked about a God of love I questioned why He was allowing such awful things to happen in the world. When we were told about Jesus feeding the five thousand I wanted to know why He couldn't feed us!

Needless to say this was not appreciated by the church Elders, who reported my errant ways to Mother.

I began to think life couldn't get any worse but of course I was very wrong. Now, even before the war lack of food was a big problem. We had got used to doing without many items, shopping at the cheapest places, using the church coupons and even swapping coupons for things like cheese and meat for the more basics like milk and bread. Central kitchens were opened to feed the children most in need. Myself, Esther, Jan and Leni were sent to get a hot meal there each day. I hated it. I hated the feeling of being so poor it had become necessary for us to even be there. I hated the food. I hated the other kids there and the lack of order and discipline. Generally it was sheer bedlam with kids throwing food around, climbing on tables and generally causing havoc. On Fridays the food was just a plateful of cooked barley. Sometimes we secretly stayed away but that just meant we went even more hungry and had nothing to eat. Mother somehow discovered this and agreed she wouldn't send us anymore but the alternative at home didn't seem much better.

Instead of barley we got a plateful of brown beans, which I absolutely hated. Somehow I just couldn't manage to swallow them. One day Father got so mad with me he took my plate still with the beans on it, wrapped it in newspaper and took it with me to school. He spoke to the teacher then in front of the whole class I was made to eat the then cold beans. I heaved and heaved as they got stuck in my throat. The other kids laughed and jeered at me and I silently vowed that one day I would get my revenge. My father and teacher lectured me on the value of food and how grateful I should be for it. I felt so sick and degraded. Eventually my plate was empty. The teacher took it, wrapped it in the newspaper and told me to take it home at the end of the day and never to let it happen again. To waste food was a sin. A few years later I suppose I would have been glad to have even a spoonful of brown beans but I didn't know that at the time.

Life at home was becoming more and more fraught with tension. There was so much political and social unrest in the country and with over forty different political parties the streets were filled with campaigners and billboards. There were lots of debates and demonstrations, which sometimes erupted into street fights. Father was leaning more and more towards the National Socialist Party who like Hitler, were promising more employment, better welfare and less poverty. My mother was against them. She would say,

"Listen to what they've done to the Jews who are God's people. They are being hunted down and persecuted."

Father would always argue back saying how many of his customers were Jews and they were the ones with the money to flee so where did that leave him? No customers, no money to put food on the table. He wanted a good life and a good business. He had hopes and dreams but with each child and each year nearer the war those hopes had disappeared.

I listened to these constant arguments between them and often in later years wondered why they had such a big family but then I could always hear my mother's voice saying with each additional child that, "children are a blessing of the Lord". To have prevented such births was not something they would have contemplated. I could cope with the poverty - after all, I had known little else throughout my life but what I hated most was that in the not too distant future I would be robbed of my most precious thing - the chance to continue my education.

Mother went out cleaning for other people to get some extra money for food. Talk of an impending war was on everyone's lips. Despite having invaded some countries, Hitler had said in a national radio broadcast that he would never invade the lower countries like Holland, but as a nation we began making preparations, just in case.

Bomb shelters began to be built but the major defence

plan involved the dykes. If we were invaded the dykes would be broken and with the centre of Holland then flooded the Germans would be unable to cross the water line to reach Amsterdam. It apparently hadn't occurred to the Government that the Germans might come by boat!

In Germany the persecution of the Jews had already begun. Many had been taken for slave labour in the salt mines. Some had fled to Holland thinking they would be safe. Their young girls were employed as servants in the rich households. However, knowing they were desperate for shelter and had nowhere else to go many of them were treated badly and forced to work long hours cooking and cleaning for little more than a pittance. The wealthier Jews in our district began to leave for other countries where they thought they would be safe. As yet no one quite realised that to be Jewish meant you were unlikely to be really safe anywhere in Europe.

During the winter we suffered terribly from the cold. With little food in our stomachs and no money for coal we would huddle together in our bedstees with our coats on top of the blankets for extra warmth. In really desperate weeks Mother would be given the leftover bread from the church communion. This she used to fry just to be able to give us something warm to eat.

On 10th May 1940 we were all called into the main hall in school. The announcement was made that the Germans had broken their word. They had known our plans and had indeed arrived in their boats. Within five days Holland became an occupied country and German soldiers were everywhere.

CHAPTER THREE

When the occupation began I was just one month away from my fourteenth birthday. Esther was twelve, Jan nine, Leni six, Ellie three and Henk just one year old. Fortunately the younger ones would remember little of the war, occupation and hunger winter still to come.

The day after the Germans arrived I saw countless numbers of Dutch soldiers walking dejectedly through the streets saying to everyone,

"She's gone. We can't believe she's gone."

I wanted to know what they were talking about and asked my mother who had gone. The answer shocked me. The Queen of Holland had fled the country. The Government had gone with her. I will never forget the look of dejection on those soldiers faces. They had seen hundreds of their fellow countrymen and others lose their lives already and now they handed in their guns saying brokenly,

"What's the use? There's no Queen and country left to fight for, they've abandoned us." Some days later the German tanks entered Amsterdam.

The National Socialists welcomed the invasion. They knew that in Germany, Hitler had set the men to making roads and some thought that when they came to Holland they would do the same and there would be jobs, and money for food once again. They saw the Germans as rescuers who would take Holland out of the recession, provide a new economy and better social conditions. How mistaken they were!

Not everyone shared those views but in Amsterdam the people accepted the arrival of the Germans without too much protest. In nearby Rotterdam however it had been a different matter. Rotterdam had resisted and the result was the total bombing of the city leaving it little more than a mass of rubble and countless numbers of people dead. Just five days after the initial invasion Holland realised it was too small to take on a country the size of Germany and we had no choice but to accept the occupation of the foreign power. We were to learn to our cost that occupation meant more than just lack of freedom it would result in further hardship and brutality.

However, as a fourteen year old I was quite excited by it all and quite unaware of the impact it would have on my life. More and more German soldiers poured into Amsterdam and I was surprised to see that some of them were women, well, girls really, only a few years older than myself.

The National Socialist Party grew in strength and formed a children's organisation similar to the Hitler Youth Movement in Germany. Their children joined, together with the children of parents who happened to be German by birth. The uniform was a navy skirt or trousers, pale blue blouse or shirt and an orange tie. I thought they looked really smart. I suppose some of their activities where similar to those of our Guides and Scouts and they seemed to get to do all the things I wanted to do. There wasn't even any fee to pay. I asked my parents if I could join but the answer was a very resounding and unanimous "no". My mother said they were friends of the enemy and against God. One day I tagged on behind as they proudly marched through the streets following their brass band. Unfortunately a neighbour saw me, told my mother and I got a good hiding.

Undeterred, I was still fascinated by them and envious of all the things they got to do. I secretly went to their office and explained that I wanted to join but my parents were against it. The man in charge gave me a uniform, which I used to hide at a friends house, and I loved being part of the group and joining in the organised games, swimming, sports and marching. Of course I took an awful risk. I was well known in the area. Mother especially, had several sisters living nearby and I had lots of cousins. People were used to seeing me going to the shops and taking my younger brothers and sisters out for walks and to the park. Inevitably someone told my mother they had seen me wearing the uniform and marching with the group. Mother said it couldn't possibly be me as I had been forbidden to join. My secret was never discovered. Luck seemed to be on my side for once.

I was fascinated to hear the German language being spoken all around me and my yearning to learn soon enabled me to pick up phrases. I think because of my blonde hair and long plaits, some of the soldiers thought I was German and occasionally they would speak to me and give me a sweet. I didn't dare tell my parents. To have anything to do with the Germans was definitely asking for trouble but then I was never one for avoiding that.

Some Sunday afternoons I would manage to escape from the house telling my parents I needed to go for a walk to collect leaves for a school project. Secretly I would meet some German girls I had got to know who were glad of someone to befriend them. I tried to learn more and more of their language and an extra bonus was the biscuit they sometimes gave me. However, having done this for a few weeks my mother became suspicious and insisted I take my young sister Ellie with me on these walks. I think she reckoned with Ellie in tow I couldn't get up to anything I shouldn't. However she hadn't counted on the special bond Ellie and I had. We continued to meet the German girls and Ellie never betrayed me. We never told lies. It was true; we had been for a walk and collected leaves and flowers. We were just economical with the truth about who else accompanied us!

As the Germans made their presence known there was obvious resentment. Sometimes on the way to school we would see dead German soldiers floating in the canals. When Dutch men threw them over the canal bridges, the weight of their boots made swimming impossible and drowning was inevitable.

The Germans had taken over some of the schools and hotels, cinemas were closed, blackout and curfew were imposed. They had raided our homes and taken all the brass doorknobs and metal dishes to melt down and use for ammunitions. Bicycle tyres were taken from us, and radios had to be handed in to have the short wave taken out so preventing any English news being received. Most of the time there was just German music on the radio.

Some people dared to keep a spare radio hidden beneath floor boards and would listen to "Germany Calling" full of German propaganda or "Here is London" the BBC giving programmes in Dutch from the Dutch Government now in hiding in England. We resented them so much. It was alright for them. They had the money and the means to escape leaving their fellow countrymen to live under German occupation. I think that was when I truly realised that often in this life there is one rule for the rich and another for the poor.

However, amazingly in the midst of all this I was about to embark on one of the happiest episodes of my life, a treasured and magical eight weeks that is firmly imprinted on my memory. During the **First** World War some Austrian children who had really suffered hardship had been invited to Holland to recuperate. Now, Austria wanted to reciprocate and had invited Dutch children aged over eleven to spend the summer in Austria. It had been organised by the Socialist Party and had the approval of the Germans. Unfortunately because of that it meant many Dutch people, including my mother, disapproved it of. Despite this Father applied for places for Esther and myself and I was overjoyed when we were accepted. Mother continued to have nothing to do with the arrangements and even refused to sew name tapes in all our clothing. Not to be deterred, I did it myself.

As the time for our departure drew closer I was becoming very excited but I noticed other people were beginning to treat me differently. Girls at school no longer wanted to talk to me. People I had known all my life would walk past both Mother and I in the street without saying "hello". It was then I discovered that many people considered that to go on this holiday to Austria was a way of collaborating with the enemy. Whilst hurt by their rejection nothing was going to dampen my enthusiasm and anticipation. I was going away from everyone. Freedom! A new adventure and perhaps best of all, a chance to see another country. I could hardly bear to wait the last few days.

The big day finally arrived. We met at the school and were divided into groups before setting off for the train. At the station music was being played and our special train was decorated with streamers and balloons. Amidst loud cheering and much waving of hands we eventually set off on our journey accompanied by Dutch teachers and leaders. On board there were biscuits and lemonade for everyone and each station we passed through had a brass band playing for us. We felt like royalty.

At the Dutch border our own teachers left us and were replaced by Germans. Many were from the Hitler Youth Movement and others were schoolteachers who during the school holidays had been given the choice of either spending four weeks with the Dutch children or three weeks working in a factory. They were all very kind to us.

Soon we came to the River Rhine and for the first time in my life I saw hills and mountains. I gasped in awe. I had never seen anything so beautiful. I pressed my face hard against the window afraid to miss anything of this wonderful new land and its magnificent scenery.

It was a long and in some ways tiring journey but we eventually arrived in Salzburg where banners and a big band welcomed us to Austria. I couldn't believe it. I was actually in another country, somewhere I'd only heard or read about and a place no other person in my family had ever been to. Other trains began to pull into the station bringing even more children from different parts of Holland. We were again divided into groups according to our final destinations. Esther and I were in different groups and I didn't see her again until we were once more back home in Amsterdam. Some children were upset at being separated from their siblings but I was just too excited for that. My final destination was to be a hotel in St. Wolfgang and twenty seven other children would be accompanying me.

We began the final part of our journey and once again I was enthralled by the beauty of my surroundings. We passed pretty lakeside villages, saw a steamer crossing the lake and up on the mountains I could see what I thought to be steam. I was told it was from a train going up the mountain on cog wheels. I was mesmerised and couldn't wait to see and learn about all these new things.

At last we arrived in St. Wolfgang and a German lady called Marianne led us through narrow streets of white painted houses many of which had elaborate pictures of landscapes, farmers or saints painted on the side. Many people waved and spoke to us as we passed but their German sounded different to that which I had heard at home. I noticed with interest the lovely white cotton blouses with wide sleeves the ladies wore and their brightly coloured full skirts with little aprons over. They all looked so clean, fresh and happy. The men wore short leather trousers with straps over their shoulders. They had hats with a little feather in the side, which I thought looked a bit like one of my fathers shaving brushes. I had never seen anything like it!

The hotel, which was to be our home for the next eight weeks, seemed huge to me and very "posh". There was a very grand marble staircase and when our coats and luggage were taken from us we were led out onto a large balcony overlooking the garden, vineyard and lake. On the balcony were tables, beautifully set ready for the meal that would soon be served to us. We were invited to sit down and a feast appeared before our very eyes. There was soup with "dough balls" different to anything I'd ever had before but very nice. Next there was sausage, red cabbage and potatoes. Then, unbelievably there was even a pudding. It was great. I thought I had died and gone to Heaven!

After the meal the leaders introduced themselves and explained that they would be taking us for walks, swimming and games. There would be plenty of books to read, games to play, pictures to colour and songs to sing. Food would be plentiful, there would be no chores to do and we were to have no worries, just enjoy a lovely holiday.

We were then taken into the huge kitchen and introduced to all the staff before being taken upstairs to unpack. We each had our own room. I couldn't believe it. I had never even had my own bed before let alone my own room. Now I had a bed, wardrobe, cupboard and washbasin in my very own room. The only thing we had to share was the bathroom. No problem.

As I lay in my bed that night I truly thanked God then pinched myself just to be certain it wasn't really just a dream.

The days stretched seemingly endlessly ahead of me. Days of swimming in the lake then lying in the sunshine to dry off; long walks collecting flowers along the way and hikes in the mountains where we paddling in freezing but crystal clear streams.

One day as a treat we were taken up the mountain in the cog wheel train. I watched from the window as the train was slowly pulled up the track. At the top was a corner aptly named Heaven and Hell. If you stayed to the right you were in "Heaven" with glorious views, move to the left and there was a 3,000 feet drop. We stepped very carefully.

We had a picnic lunch that day and then went in search of

the edelweiss flowers. Custom said that if a boy really loved you he would go to the edge of "Hell" and pick you an edelweiss to prove his love. None of our boys took up the challenge. I loved being so high up. The air was crisp and pure and I felt I could just reach out and pluck a fluffy white cloud. I wondered if I stepped out onto one of them would I sink to the ground far below? I felt on top of the world. Nothing could ever beat this moment. Looking down I could see the town, the lake and the steamer crossing it but at that moment they could all have belonged to a different planet. How I wished I had a camera but instead I was determined to commit every detail to memory so I could describe it all when I returned home. They say nothing lasts forever and much as I wanted to stay I eventually had to join the others on the very long walk back down the track to our hotel. It had been a very special day.

Twice a week we were given cards to write to our parents back home. We were also given a little pocket money to spend on souvenirs. I spent ages looking in shop windows trying to decide what to buy. To have my own money and to choose how to spend it was something I could never have imagined.

I never ceased to be amazed at all the food we were given, much of which I had never before tasted. There were sausage rolls, crisp white bread rolls, fresh strawberries, cakes, biscuits and even chocolate. We were encouraged to eat as much as we wanted and before we went to bed we were even given some supper.

Some of the girls were homesick but I was just glad to be away and I had made lots of new friends. In some ways I felt I was experiencing the innocence and freedom of childhood for the first time and yet in other ways sharing "girly" talk and secrets made me feel I was grown up.

We went to the local market and saw wild strawberries for sale. They tasted delicious on their own but the cook in our hotel made a special pudding with them, which tasted out of this world. She suggested a few of us take big tins and go out collecting the fruit ourselves adding that we could then sell it in the market. It seemed a good idea and we were able to earn extra pocket money this way.

With more money in my pocket than I had ever had

before, except for the time I worked in the ice cream factory, I went into the town and bought myself a necklace with an edelweiss inside a glass pendant, some little pens, picture postcards and small presents for my parents, brothers and sisters. To be able to do this gave me so much pleasure and satisfaction.

I was always looking for adventure and one day I suggested a few of us swim across the lake to the other side. It looked quite a long way but we were all fairly good swimmers so I didn't think it would be a problem. The others agreed. It was a perfect day with blue skies and warm sunshine.

We ran down to the lake and into the water. Setting our sights on the distant shoreline we began to swim. Inevitably it was a lot further than we had expected. Part of the way across we found ourselves tiring and had to float on our backs for a while to regain our strength. It was one of those moments when it's difficult to decide if it would be quicker and more sensible to go forwards or to return the way we had come. I was sure we could still make it across and so we began to swim again. After about three hours of swimming, resting and swimming again we eventually arrived exhausted on the other side. We just flopped on the shoreline whilst we regained our strength.

No one voiced the question as to how we were to get back but I think we were all secretly scared at the prospect. Having rested for a while and dried off in the sunshine we began to explore and scrambled up the hillside but it was densely wooded and very steep. We began to walk around the lake in the hope of finding a path that we could take to walk back to the hotel, but if such a path existed we didn't find it.

By now we were all beginning to feel hungry, thirsty and more than a little scared. We rested a while longer and then decided we had no option but to swim all the way back across the lake. We gathered pieces of flat wood to use as floats in case we became too weary and then we reluctantly left the safety of the shore and entered the water once again.

The sun was shining brightly and reflecting off the lake into our eyes but we tried to keep focused on the opposite shore. Many times we had to stop and rest. We were exhausted and had to keep encouraging each other as one by one we came to the point when we felt we could go no further.

Eventually we hauled ourselves out of the lake onto solid ground. The swim back had taken even longer than when we went but at least we were all back safely.

Back at the hotel we were severely reprimanded but I think even that was tempered because they could see how exhausted we were. However, that was not then end of the matter. What we hadn't realised was that whilst we had been in the cool water the sun had been blazing down on us and we were badly sunburnt and covered with blisters. The local doctor was called out to check us over and we were kept in the shade for a full week afterwards and told never to be so stupid again. I think we had all painfully learned our lesson and would not be repeating it.

Our time continued to be spent enjoying good food and lots of fresh air. We all grew stronger day by day and I wanted it all to last forever. The local girls taught us some German songs and I was so pleased I couldn't wait to sing them to my parents. Unfortunately when I returned home I was forbidden to sing them or to demonstrate my newly acquired German phrases of which I was so proud.

In the grounds of the hotel there was a small cinema. I had never been allowed to go to watch a film and so it was yet another new experience for me. The nephew of the hotel owner ran the film shows and I became one of his favourites. He used to let me go up into the projection room and look through the window to the screen. I watched many films from there and also the newsreels showing how at that time the Germans were winning the war. It didn't bother me that sometimes they showed the occupation forces in Holland. That was all in another life somehow. All that mattered to me was that I was in Austria, which I loved.

The weeks sped by and September came around all too quickly. I begged the owner of the hotel to let me stay, assuring her I would cook, clean and do anything if only she would keep me there and not return me to Holland. Her sympathetic eyes told me she understood but she had no alternative but to let me go.

A couple of days before our agreed departure date I was talking with a group of friends and we were all saying how much we wanted to stay in Austria and not return home. With all the fervour and hotheadedness of a typical fourteen year old I suggested we run away and hide until the day after the train had taken everyone back. I had thought it all out. If we saved some rolls and bits of food from our meals during the next couple of days, ate the wild berries and fruits growing on the hedgerows we could easily survive a few days. We could go up into the hills where no one would find us, and return after the train had left for Holland. It all seemed so simple and foolproof! I never considered the worry and trouble such action would cause others.

My seven friends agreed with the plan and so for the next two days we began to assemble our stash of food. We each packed a small bag and on the afternoon before we were due to leave Austria we climbed up into the mountains.

At dinner that night our absence was noted and the staff began to question the younger children. They realised we had run away and informed the police. Search parties were set up and after checking the town some of them began to climb up into the hills and mountains looking for us.

It was getting darker and colder. We were wearing only thin summer dresses and no coats. Despite the food we had brought we were all beginning to feel hungry. Why did the mountain seem so beautiful in the sunshine but now it appeared dark and unfriendly? We heard voices approaching and we stupidly tried to climb even higher up the mountain. There was still snow on the peak and it was really cold. We were more than a little frightened.

Somewhat inevitably I suppose, we were eventually found, wrapped in blankets and brought back down the mountain to the warmth of the hotel, none the worse for our adventure. However we were all disheartened and even though we had been cold, hungry and afraid we were still sad that our plan had failed. The police gave us a stern telling off and the local doctor was called out again to check we were alright.

I sobbed uncontrollably. The local people could not understand why I didn't want to go home. In between sobs I tried to explain that if someone has only experienced poverty, hunger and hardship they do not miss the better things in life for they have never known them. If they then experience freedom, plentiful food, warmth, happiness and good things they have no wish to return to empty stomachs and drudgery. They could offer no answer or consolation.

A close check was kept on us for the last two days in case we tried to run away again but all too soon we were packing our suitcases, saying tearful goodbyes and making our way to the railway station. The Austrian and German people had been wonderful. They had loved and cared for us beyond our wildest dreams. I would never forget them. I was leaving the only place where I had ever felt truly happy. I vowed that someday I would return.

We boarded the train with heavy hearts. Even the playing of the brass band and the waving of so many friends could not bring a smile to my face. My sister Esther was also on that train. She had stayed with one family and had been absolutely ruined. She was wearing a beautiful Austrian dress and in her suitcase were lots of new clothes and presents that had been bought for her. Apart from the few presents I had bought myself for my family I had nothing but if I'd had a hundred suitcases of new clothes and gifts I would have gladly exchanged them for a life back in Austria. Esther was looking forward to going home. I was dreading it.

In Amsterdam our parents were waiting for us as the train pulled into the station. My mother had tears in her eyes and was obviously overjoyed to have us back. I felt no such emotion. I remember going into the house thinking how small everything seemed and how narrow the corridors were. That night in my tiny cupboard "bedstee" I wept silently for all I had lost.

I hated being back home. I hated everything about life. I hated the lack of food, the petty restrictions and the endless chores. How I missed the pure, clean air and the spectacular views of mountains and lakes.

Out in the neighbourhood and at school everyone knew where I'd been and they refused to talk to me. They considered me a fascist because I'd gone to enemy country. I coped by throwing myself into my school studies and holding in my heart the precious memories of those wonderful eight weeks. No one could ever take those memories away. It had been the happiest time of my young life.

Eventually the girls at school began to realise that I was not to blame for going away and they began to be friends with me again. I remember a day in the winter of that year when it had snowed heavily and a thick layer was already on the ground. A group of us passed some German soldiers standing outside their barracks. For sheer devilment we began throwing snowballs at the soldiers. The one I threw hit one of them square in the face and he gave chase. I have never run so fast in all my life. That was one stunt I never repeated.

We were all so cold and our clothes were pitifully thin and worn. To try to give us some extra warmth we lined our jumpers and even our socks and underwear with newspaper. With little money to buy food Mother was beside herself with worry. Almost day by day she could see her family getting thinner and thinner. Only Esther seemed to fare better than the rest of us. With her lovely blonde curly hair she was very pretty and had many rich friends who often gave her something to eat when she visited their houses.

Some Dutch girls started to go out with German soldiers. They were harassed, jeered and often ostracised for it. It was seen as a betrayal of their country and fellow citizens. When Holland was eventually liberated many of those girls were quite cruelly punished and forcibly had their heads shaved. Such were the consequences of "fraternising with the enemy."

Meanwhile the Germans had stepped up their efforts to make life ever more difficult. All the men aged between eighteen and forty five were rounded up and forced to go to work in Germany to replace their own men who were fighting. If they went "voluntarily" they were sent to work in the factories but if they resisted they were put to slave labour in the salt mines, which often lead to death.

My father went to the North of Germany and was set to work in a torpedo factory. It was hard knowing that they were making missiles which could be used against their own people. He lived in a camp with three hundred other men and they were paid a small wage. Although they were allowed to write and could have occasional short visits home it was difficult for all the families.

On more than one occasion Father came home without permission. He travelled any way he could, catching lifts from passing lorries and even a milk float! At such times we had to hide him making sure no one was aware of his presence. Once he went to a secret meeting with some other men and was nearly caught by the German soldiers. After his first visit home he took back with him his barbers tools and was able to cut the hair of the other men in the camp so gaining a little extra money to send home to us.

Despite this we were always short of money, which in turn meant shortage of food. The church helped out by giving Mother a couple of guilders each week. It wasn't a lot of money but she was more than grateful for it and it was sufficient to buy a loaf of bread, some margarine and maybe a little sugar or jam.

During the occupation the Germans said children could leave school at fifteen years of age provided they went to the Labour Exchange and began work immediately. The night before my fifteenth birthday is one I will never forget.

There was a ring on the doorbell whilst I was doing my chores. One of the Elders from Father's church had come to see Mother and she showed him into the "best" room. He was a man I neither liked nor trusted. He owned a huge furniture store in the wealthy part of Amsterdam. He always liked to feel his own self-importance and took delight in people shaking his hand and asking his opinions. Like so many of the elders in Father's church he always appeared to me to be smug, pompous and self-righteous. I decided to eavesdrop to discover why he had come.

He told Mother that as I was to be fifteen the following day I should leave school and earn some money. His wife was looking for a servant and he said I would suit the job perfectly. To be fair Mother said I loved school and she was happy for me to do my final year and gain my certificate. The elder argued it was unnecessary for a girl to finish her education and insisted that the right thing to do was to make me work for his wife starting the next day. He then played what he thought was his winning card. If I didn't go to work for his wife he would stop the extra two guilders Mother received from the church each week.

I was furious. That was little short of blackmail. Who did he think he was, barging in here and saying what I should be doing? How dare he tackle Mother like this whilst Father was away? The man had two sons at university who were noted for wasting money and fooling around yet he had the audacity to bully Mother and expect me to give up my education. All my hatred and frustration burst to the surface. I threw open the door and stormed in.

I hit him. Mother stood ashen faced and shocked to the core but I wasn't finished yet! I came out with swear words I'd never used before. I called him everything under the sun. I told him in no uncertain terms that education was my life, the only part of it in which I was happy. I reminded him that I'd already had to give up the opportunity to go to the better senior school because my parents thought it would prove too expensive and there was no way he was going to stop me finishing school. I can hear myself ranting

"I will not have my education taken from me. Never. Not by you, the church, God or anyone else!"

He turned on his heel and left.

Mother grabbed me, belted me severely and put me in the darkened cupboard until I'd calmed down. Eventually she let me out and admitted that although she was angry with me she also felt sad and humiliated. I was still adamant that I would not leave school and threatened to leave home if I was made to go and work for "that creep of a man". There was silence between us for days. How I wished I could have discussed it all with someone but I felt there was really nobody who would truly understand how I felt.

Mother decided to write and ask my father for his opinion. I vowed that if he said I had to go and be a servant I would definitely leave home and find myself a job, even if I had to work for the Germans. Thankfully it didn't come to that. Father came home on a quick visit and although there were many heated arguments between us he finally, grudgingly agreed to let me stay at school for my final year. I was so relieved I could have hugged him, but that was something else we didn't do.

That Sunday in church I had the greatest satisfaction looking at that pompous elder and knowing I had won. If anyone could have read my thoughts I would probably have been struck by lightning or something equally drastic. From that time on I began to find even more fault in the church, the sermons, the people and religion in general. I even tried hating God Himself. I vowed that once I reached eighteen I would have no more to do with any of it.

Unfortunately I still had the dreaded catechism classes to attend each week and I became even more disruptive. They were held in the elders meeting room - the place where they decided who should be given extra money. I looked around at the posh room with its comfortable chairs and the huge Bible at the front. I felt like tearing it apart. I felt it was all so hypocritical. I disagreed with everything they taught us and took delight in saying so. One night they were teaching about predestination - that we are chosen to be saved even before we are born. I said I didn't believe that. I was told to be quiet but took no notice and eventually I was told to leave. I dared not go home too early or Mother would question me so I went on a "ring and run" spree - ringing doorbells then running away and watching the puzzled expressions on the people's faces as they opened their doors only to find no one there. It beat catechism class any day.

I suppose it was inevitable that Mother would soon find out. The following evening the minister of the church called at the house. When the bell rang Mother called out,

"Who is it?"

On hearing the reply she invited the minister to come up but he said,

"No. I've no time. I just want to tell you about Johanna."

I shouted,

"Don't bother Mother. He's only got time for those in the rich houses who offer him a glass of wine and a cigar. He knows he'll only get a cup of tea here and it's beneath him to come in."

That of course cost me another hefty beating. Would I ever learn to keep my mouth shut for self-preservation?

With Father away in Germany we no longer needed nor could afford the shop and so we moved to another flat on the west side of Amsterdam. It was up six flights of stairs, not ideal with six children but it was slightly bigger as it had one big bedroom and a further small one, together with a kitchen, bathroom and living room. Having a bathroom for the first time meant we didn't have to wash in the kitchen. All six children slept in the one big room but at least we were in proper beds and not "bedstees" although we could not manage the luxury of one to a bed.

Unfortunately the move meant me having to go to a different school as we now lived too far from the one where I had been so happy. Now I was faced with attending a school ruled by my father's very strict Reformed church. I was not looking forward to it .We went to see the headmaster who informed us that there was no room for me in the year I should have joined but looking at my records he thought that if I continued to work hard I would probably be able to keep pace with the students a year ahead of my age. He also agreed to let me take the exams at the end of that year although warned that because I was younger than everyone else my grades may not be as high. It was certainly worth a try and I was determined to succeed.

At this point the Germans still appeared to be winning the war but life was getting harder for the Dutch people. Many commodities disappeared as the Germans took them and sent them back to Germany for their own wives and families. France, Belgium, Austria and Poland were all occupied and the Germans took food from all these countries for their own use. Often Mother would find some food available but she didn't have enough money or coupons to purchase it. People traded their ration coupons. One week Mother would trade our cheese coupon and try to buy eggs. The next week she would trade the egg coupon and try to buy cheese. More and more German soldiers appeared. Gas, electricity and water were cut off for long periods. The rules imposed by the Germans increased and failure to obey would often result in instant shooting.

Life at home continued to be harsh. I was outspoken, inquisitive, thirsty for education and none of these traits seemed to endear me to my parents. In retrospect I suppose I deserved many of the beatings I was given although not the severity of them. One such incident had grave consequences.

My father was on a short home leave from Germany. As usual I wanted to go out and Mother had given me yet more chores to do. I was sick and tired of being used as little more than a servant and angrily said so. I told them I wished I could be away from them in a children's home where the kids were better

51

off than me. Father grabbed me, took off his shoe and gave me a good hiding saying that would teach me to be so ungrateful.

The next day at school, where all the teachers belonged to Father's strict church, one of them made a sarcastic comment about my shabby clothes. Instead of accepting it as I usually did I lifted my skirt and showed him the imprint and bruises left by Father's shoe on my thighs. I shouted,

"How dare you mock me? You think you're all so good. Well, this has been done by one of you holy ones. You know, the ones who love the Lord and their neighbour as themselves."

He took me out of class to an empty room and questioned me as to why it had happened and how often it had happened before. I told him - "all the time". I think he was quite shocked and promised to deal with it.

I was scared what would happen. Some of the elders of the church came to see my parents who told them I was naughty, disobedient and that I showed no respect for God or the church. However, although the elders agreed I needed discipline and sometimes punishment they said what was done to me was too severe and in future I should not be beaten with a shoe only smacked by hand. My parents agreed and for a while it stayed that way but it was not the end of the matter.

At school news that I was being beaten was openly talked about. I was still going secretly to the Youth Movement and someone there reported the fact that I was being ill treated at home. Mother and I were called to the Juvenile Court and subjected to rigorous questioning. They asked me if I was beaten regularly. What were the dates? Was I always left with bruises? The questions seemed endless. I told them I often had bruises but couldn't remember specific dates as it happened all the time. Amazingly I somehow just took it all in my stride. I knew I gave cheek and answered back. I knew there were things I was forbidden to do but I did them anyway. I knew that when I did something wrong and was found out I would get beaten. That was just our way of life and I accepted it. I think in a way I thought it was normal.

Mother was questioned too and told how as parents they had promised God to bring me up in the discipline of the church. The result was that a Court Protection Order was placed on me.

An officer would be assigned to keep an eye on me and ensure I was no longer being beaten. As from then, my parents were forbidden to beat me and only allowed to punish me by keeping me in. I left court wondering how on earth the person would ever know what went on behind our closed doors.

I was now approaching my sixteenth birthday and would leave school officially after taking my final exams in the summer. I had worked as hard as I could and was hopeful of good results. We had about fourteen subjects including typing, English, French and German. It's strange looking back how some of the most trivial things stay in your mind. I remember the half hour oral examinations in languages. In the English I wanted to say the ceiling was low but couldn't recall the right word so I said it was not high. In the German I was questioned about the war and submarines. I didn't know the vocabulary for those things either so I told the examiner those questions were more for boys. Amazingly he agreed and changed the questions to ones about books, nature, food and clothes. My mother had difficulty in finding the ten guilders for the examination fee, finally having no alternative other than to take out a loan for that amount and now I was afraid in case I failed and her money would be wasted.

The time waiting for the results was nerve wracking. Eventually I learned my fate. I had passed. Not with tremendously high marks but considering I had taken the exams a year early I was very pleased with myself.

I was asked what job I would like to do and for some reason the first thing that sprung to mind was nursing. I had no idea why I should have said that, as I'd never even considered it before. However, such a job was out of the question as there was no money for me to continue into higher education and a career. Any additional studies would have to be at night school in my own time. According to German rules I left school on a Thursday and had to have a job by the following Monday. I went to the Labour Exchange. There were lots of jobs I would have liked but I did not have sufficient qualifications. A large department store wanted trainees so I went for an interview, was accepted and scheduled to start on the Monday. A new chapter of my life was about to begin. Where would it lead me?

CHAPTER FOUR

Promptly on Monday morning I arrived at the Beehive Department store. I was both nervous and excited. I was sorry to have left my school days behind and yet I was looking forward to being a part of the "adult" world and earning some money. I was also secretly hoping that being a full time worker might mean less chores to do at home and perhaps some freedom to do and see the things I wanted.

The store was quite a "posh" one situated in the heart of the main Amsterdam shopping centre. It had six floors and sold everything you could possibly imagine from clothes to furniture. I was told to report to the haberdashery department.

It was quite a large department with a good range of fabrics, buttons, bows and zips. The other girls all seemed to be very friendly and the supervisor was kind to me. Once a week I had to go upstairs for a training session to learn all about the different fabrics - where they came from, how they were made, the difference and benefits of linen, cotton, nylon wool etc. We were also trained in how best to serve and advise the customers and how to handle any difficult ones! I really enjoyed learning all this. However, we were told not to sell anything to the Germans unless it was already on view. If they could not see a particular item, even if it was under the counter, we were to say we did not have any left in stock.

On the shop floor I put my training to good use and became popular with regular customers, especially the Germans. Many of the other girls disliked serving them but it made no difference to me and I was glad of the opportunity to practise my German.

At the end of the first week when I received my pay packet I was delighted. At last I would have money of my own to spend on whatever I liked. On the way home I bought a big bunch of flowers for my mother and looked forward to being able to give her some of my first wage. I should have known better. Not for me, the kind gesture of giving to Mother. Instead, she took all my wages and gave back to me just enough to cover the return tram journey to work. I was no better off and felt so downhearted. I had seen the pretty dresses the other girls wore, the nylons, the makeup and I had been so looking forward to being like them.

However, life had taught me never to give in and so instead of using the tram to get to and from work I walked instead. It took about an hour each way but at least in doing that I was able to pocket the fare and have a little money for myself.

The girls I worked with were always talking about fashion, new clothes, boyfriends and going out. How I wished I could be a part of that lifestyle. It was not long before they began to wander why I did not join in those conversations. It was difficult to explain how strict my parents were and that apart from going to church and catechism classes I was not allowed to go out very much. However, when I was sure they would not betray my trust I told them that whenever I had the opportunity I secretly went to the Youth Movement. I think they began to feel a bit sorry for me and decided to play a part in promoting the "new Johanna".

At that time I still wore ankle socks. All the other girls wore nylons. One day they gathered round me and asked why I still wore socks. I explained I had never had nylons and really never had the money for such a luxury. They were amazed and encouraged me to buy a pair helping me to choose the best colour. I was so proud. Unfortunately I couldn't also afford to buy something to keep them up so I had to make do with two pieces of elastic. This was not always successful and sometimes they slipped down and wrinkled around my ankles. Not a pretty sight!

Next on the agenda for transforming me from a school girl into a "young lady" was the art of makeup. I had never seen my mother wear makeup and was sure she would not approve but one lunchtime when the girls gathered around and said they were going to "make me up" I happily went along with the idea. The transformation amazed me although I must confess I wasn't sure I liked the "new me." The lunch break was over just as the girls finished and so we all went back to work. By six o'clock when it was time to go home I had forgotten I was still in full war paint and walked home as usual.

On arriving home the evening meal was ready to be served and I took my place at the table. My father was home on a visit from Germany. Mother said grace and began to serve the food and I was just about to pick up my first mouthful when Father rose from the table, came over to me and grabbed me by the neck forcing my head up.

"What's all this filth on your face?"

Without waiting for an answer he pulled me up and dragged me into the kitchen. Taking a hard nailbrush and the tin of Vim he scrubbed and scrubbed at my face.

"I'll teach you to look like a prostitute in my house," he yelled. "If you ever do this again I'll cover your face in boot polish".

Oh, how my poor face hurt. It was so red and raw for days after. I have never used makeup from that day to this and the girls in work never suggested it again.

One day whilst I was working in the store I became aware of a man watching me. I had seen him before and each time he never bought anything just stared over at me. I mentioned it to one of the other girls who thought he may be a store detective. Plucking up courage I went across to ask him why he was watching me. He explained he was from the Child Protection office and as I was under their care until I was eighteen he was assigned to check up on me periodically to ensure I was not covered in bruises. I thought it a pity he had not been around when my face was red and raw.

During my time in the department a female German Officer came in requesting a beige skirt zip for her uniform. In accordance with store rules I told her we had no more zips in stock. She was obviously concerned and in real need of a new zip as she asked if we had one in any other colour. Again I had to say "no". Dispirited she turned away. When I was sure no one was watching me I went after her and speaking quietly in German I told her that I may be able to get the zip but it would have to be done secretly and I wanted something in return. I knew the Germans had food coupons, which they could exchange in their own shops and I bargained for some bread coupons in exchange for the zip. She agreed and we arranged to meet at a certain place after I had finished work for the day.

All went according to plan. We met, she paid for the zip and in addition she gave me some bread coupons. Now all I had to do was pass myself off as a German girl. On the long walk home I knew I would pass a German bakery and so began rehearsing in my mind what I would say. Only the Germans were allowed into these special shops and only Germans had these special coupons. It was imperative that the shopkeeper believed me to be German. If my subterfuge was discovered I would be in serious trouble.

I approached the shop and tried in vain to stop my knees trembling. I pushed open the door and in what I hoped was my best German I wished the shop keeper a polite good evening and requested a large loaf of bread, handing over the coupons as if it was something I did every day. Thanking her once again I walked slowly out of the shop when in fact what I really wanted to do was run for my life. I'd done it. I was over the moon.

I couldn't wait to get home with my prize. Dashing up the stairs I called out,

"Hey kids, look what I've got."

They all came running. Mother looked at me in disbelief. She knew instantly it was German bread and was horrified at what I'd done. She said,

"I will not touch it. I am disgusted. You have traded with the enemy."

We children had no such hang-ups. We were just glad to get some extra food and hungrily ripped it apart and ate it in huge chunks. Bread had never tasted so good!

After about nine months working on the shop floor I was transferred to the statistics office upstairs. I was reluctant to leave my friends in the department especially as the girls in the office were not so friendly towards me. They disapproved of me speaking to Germans especially in their own language and did not like the fact that I went to the Youth Movement. Such behaviour was considered unacceptable and disloyal to our own country.

I enjoyed the challenge of the new work. I was responsible for checking sales receipts, department figures and working out which items sold best. In the office I got a longer lunch break and I did not have to work on Saturdays. I also got an increase in my wages. Eventually most of the girls began to accept me and became more friendly. All except one, who attended the Salvation Army and continued to think my involvement with the Youth Movement inappropriate.

During this time I started going out with my first boyfriend. His name was Wim and he worked in the same store as me. He was a quiet boy and very polite. We used to spend our lunch times together and he would tell me of his love of painting and how he dreamt of visiting other countries some day. I would tell him of my time in Austria and describe the beautiful mountains and wooden houses. For my seventeenth birthday he painted me an Austrian scene - a picture that still hangs in my home to this day!

At last I was beginning to feel I had a life of my own. By saving my tram fare each day I was able to buy a few new dresses and my mother was allowing me to go out a little more. I still loved learning and went to night school to further my education and improve my typing and shorthand skills. I wanted so much from life and I was prepared to work hard to achieve it. To this end I applied, took the necessary exams and was accepted for a better job as a telegraphist with the Post Office.

My new position had many benefits beside the obvious one of more money. The hours were irregular so no one at home could keep a check on me and know whether I was going to work or going out! The post office had been taken over by the Germans but quite often for reasons they did not explain we would suddenly, without warning be given a few hours or even a whole day off and yet we were still paid as though we had worked those hours. Our positions had to be covered during the evening and over night so we were given special white arm bands to prevent us being shot when we were out on the streets travelling to or from work during curfew. I, of course, took full advantage of this often staying out visiting friends long after curfew had begun.

The work itself involved learning all about the instruments, which were different to typewriters and had different spacing between the characters. We were never allowed to look down at the keyboards and had to continually take exams each time becoming faster and more accurate. Some of the girls worked the Morse code but I thought that seemed less interesting, just pushing a machine a bit like a big stapler up and down in a series of dots and dashes.

Working on the telegrams was much more fun. Many of them were being sent from the Germans in Holland to places in Berlin, Paris and Belgium. In quiet moments provided there were no supervisors around I could "talk" via my machine to other operators in other countries and receive their messages back. I loved it. I learned about their way of life and what was happening in their country. Unfortunately, unknown to me, all the tapes were kept and checked and it was not long before my additional activities were discovered. I was lucky not to lose my job but as punishment I was made to work Sundays with no pay. I did not mind at all. It meant I didn't have to go to church and I got to know other girls on other lines. Instead of conversations via our machines I asked them to write to me. That was the beginning of many pen pal friendships, some of which are still in existence today.

The girls at work knew how difficult home life was for me and some of them knew a family who were "German friendly" who were looking for a lodger. They took me to meet them. We liked each other immediately and discussed how much I could afford to pay for a room and food. A price was fixed and I could move in straight away. I was thrilled. A room of my own with the freedom to come and go when I wanted with no parents asking questions and wanting to know everything.

I went home that night packed my bags and told Mother I was moving out. She tried hard to persuade me to stay but I was not about to change my mind. I left without a backward glance and also without leaving an address. At last I was away from home. I had my own room in a comfortable house, enough food to eat and best of all my freedom. I had to do my own ironing and help with the washing up but that was all. I could go out in the evening with no questions asked and actually have a life to call my own.

The euphoria lasted all of five days. My parents arrived at the house. They had asked the post office to give them my new address and now they stood at the door, Mother with tears streaming down her face, pleading with me to return home. I refused to let them in and so we stood on the doorstep for an hour arguing. I told them they only wanted me back to do the housework and take my wages. Mother said she wanted me back because that was where I belonged and what God wanted! Eventually the owners of the house persuaded me to try again at home but they suggested to my parents that they allow me some extra money and freedom and stop beating me. They said they would.

Very reluctantly I returned home the next day. Mother said "Thank God" and promised life would be better. It was, for a couple of weeks and then everything returned to the way it had always been. "Where have you been? What have you been doing? Who have you been with?" Have you cleaned that room, peeled those vegetables?" I was too tired to fight the battle any more. Instead I found new ways of being more secretive.

I was enjoying receiving letters from pen friends in several different countries but my parents always insisted on seeing them and this made me angry. They were addressed to me and I felt I should be the only one to open and read them. A friend at work suggested I get my letters sent to her house and it seemed a simple and effective answer. Unfortunately, because we were often on different shifts it became a problem collecting them. Then I discovered that for ten cents per letter I could have them delivered to a newsagents. At last I thought I had outwitted my parents. The system worked well for quite a long time but then my parents became suspicious that there was no more mail being delivered to the house for me. I still do not know to this day how my father discovered my arrangements but the lady in the shop told me he had come in and said if she continued to collect letters for his daughter who was under twenty one years of age he would report her to the police.

Sometimes I felt the whole of life was against me. Why couldn't I live in a normal family and have the freedom my friends had? Still, I was not to be daunted. I found another newspaper kiosk willing to receive my letters.

One day I had collected a letter on my way home from work and was sitting in the toilet reading it (that was the only place I could get some privacy). Suddenly the door was pulled open and my father tried to grab the letter but I was too fast for him and darted past, running from the house. To my amazement Father gave chase. I was not going to let hum get the better of me. As I ran I tore up the letter and began stuffing it into my mouth, chewing and swallowing it! Two streets later I was out of breath and Father caught up with me.

"Give me that letter," he demanded, red with anger and exertion.

"No" was my short reply.

"I'm your father, do as I say. You are under age and I'm responsible for you."

"Well, you'll have to make me sick if you want it because I've swallowed it."

He forced open my mouth and could see the tiny remnants of paper still inside. He gave me one quick blow with his hand and stormed away. I learned that even the toilet was not a safe haven and in future read my letters away from the house.

My German was improving and sometimes I met with a German soldier. We were not really going out together, we just enjoyed each other's company and talking. We became great friends but of course it was a dangerous liaison for me and yet again I put myself at risk of being caught "fraternising with the enemy." Much as I hated the war and the German occupation of my country I could see that many of the soldiers, mostly not much older than myself were merely boys who back in their own country had similar families, jobs, lives and dreams just as the rest of us. One day he was moved on and I really missed him.

Occasionally on a Sunday when Father was home he and I would ride on our bikes to visit some relatives of his who lived in the country. They were obviously quite wealthy and lived in a big house. They even had a pony and trap. I used to enjoy going, as they would always give me some sweets and plenty to eat. Father usually left with a bag of food for the rest of the family too. Three aunts lived together in the house and they all went to different churches, which I thought very peculiar. The eldest was very strict and old fashioned and not surprisingly she went to the same type of church as Father. The middle aunt went to a Baptist church, something I'd never heard of and the youngest aunt was an officer in the Salvation Army and worked in one of their children's homes.

One particular Sunday this youngest aunt went across to the organ and began to play and sing. The words sounded religious but the music was lively and cheerful. I asked what it was she was singing. She laughed and said,

"It's a hymn of course."

"We don't have hymns like that in Father's church. They are all slow and miserable. Where did you learn that one?" I asked.

She explained to me that these were songs she sang in the Salvation Army and if I liked them perhaps I should go to one of their meetings. I had seen the bands of the Salvation Army in the park and on street corners where they preached but although I liked their music I hadn't realised they were a church!

One Sunday evening a few weeks later when the thought of yet another boring two and a half hours in Father's church was too much I announced I was going instead to the Salvation Army. Predictably there was uproar from my parents. I pointed out that one of Father's relatives went so why shouldn't I? Eventually Mother relented and said I could go. It was a long walk into the centre of Amsterdam and when I reached the place I was a rather afraid to go inside. Instead, I stood in the porch listening to the singing. It sounded great. So joyful. I had never heard anything like it in a church in all my life.

I had no money for an offering and was wondering if I should just turn around and go back home when a lady appeared and said,

"Hello. Please, come inside. You're most welcome".

Stunned, I looked at her. Since when had a church made anyone welcome? Not in my experience. I decided that as I'd walked all that way I might as well give it a try. I went inside. It didn't look like a normal church so I sat in the back row in case I needed to make a hasty retreat.

It was totally different from any church service I'd ever known. It was lively, interesting and happy. The band played and the hymns were great. Someone stood up to give what they called a testimony saying how God had changed their life. Then a woman gave the sermon. A woman! My father would have had apoplexy at the very thought. I couldn't believe the time had passed so quickly and I was sorry when the service came to an end. I had never enjoyed church before. This was a totally new experience!

Back home I was questioned and enthusiastically told them all about it. Father forbade me to go again. When had that ever stopped me? I waited a few weeks then went again.

Life under German occupation had become more oppressive. Anyone who was Jewish had been forced to wear the Star of David on their sleeve and they were discriminated against. There were only a few shops in which they were allowed to go. It was forbidden to assist them in any way. One day, on my way home from work I passed an elderly Jewish lady who stopped me and asked if I would go into the greengrocers and buy some vegetables for her. It was a shop Jews were not allowed into. I hesitated. I knew if I was discovered helping a Jew I would be severely punished, perhaps even shot by the Germans. I looked at the old lady and suddenly the words of the Bible came into my mind - "In as much as you have done it for one of the least of these, you have done it for Me." I made my decision. Taking her money I quickly went into the shop and bought her vegetables. Outside once more I gave them to her then ran all the way home. My legs were trembling. It was one thing going against my father or even being ostracised by my fellow countrymen for being friendly with the Germans but to do something expressly forbidden by the occupying forces was in quite a different league.

Warplanes continued flying over Amsterdam and especially at night we could not tell if they were German or British. We lay in our beds rigid with fear praying they would not drop bombs on us. Many of the battles took place over the sea and the sky would be bright with searchlights. We hoped that if any British soldiers baled out they would be picked up by the Dutch Resistance and taken underground to safety before returning them to Britain and their squadrons. Those found by the Germans suffered greatly. Huge pieces of aircraft often fell around us and strangely people would pick up the smaller pieces and keep them as souvenirs.

There was even less food available, fewer men were at home to work and there were frequent executions in the streets. If the Germans found one of their soldiers dead they would take seven Dutch people and publicly kill them in retribution.

Then the persecution of the Jews was stepped up and they were rounded up like animals. Men, women, children, the elderly it made no difference. They were taken away. They just disappeared. Those same trains, which had been decorated with balloons for my trip to Austria, now took thousands of Jews away to unknown places. Few of them would survive the horrors that lay ahead.

For the rest of us the war continued its relentless hold. Thousands had lost their lives. Countless numbers had lost limbs, sight and hope. Whole cities had been wiped out by bombs and still Hitler was forging ahead but for those of us in Amsterdam we had still to face what was perhaps the greatest testing of the war. It was now October 1944 and we were approaching what would be known throughout history as The Hunger Winter.

CHAPTER FIVE

The recession had swept through Europe for several years and like people in many other countries we had become accustomed to the lack of employment and subsequent lack of money for food. However, we now faced a new challenge. Lack of money was not the greatest problem. Even those with limited income found themselves without food as shortages became more and more widespread and the shelves in the shops became empty.

There was always the "Black Market" of course where those who had plenty of money could still get hold of essential and occasionally even luxury commodities but this was not an option for most people. Someone discovered that boiled tulip bulbs made a reasonable alternative to vegetables but after a while even these became scarce and were then only available on the black market at the astronomical price of forty guilders for just one pound in weight. Daffodil bulbs were not so versatile and those who tried to eat them found to their cost that they were poisonous.

The only reliable source of food was from the soup kitchens, which were set up across the city. I would go with my sister Esther and stand in the long queues, often for several hours. Sometimes Esther fainted and was taken inside and immediately given some free soup. I tried to faint too but could never manage to make it look realistic! Eventually we would reach the front of the queue, hand over our coupons and the soup was then pumped into our bucket, covered with a cloth to try to keep it warm and we began the half hour walk back home again. The soup was made of frozen potatoes and sugar beet but if we were really lucky some days a few vegetables may have been added. It was pretty tasteless but at least we had something hot in our stomachs on those days. Often I would desperately long for a piece of bread to go with the soup and would beg Mother for some. More often than not the answer would be that she had none and I can still vividly remember saying,

"What, not even a crumb?" to which she replied,

"No. Not even a crumb."

Hunger became a way of life.

Every day in the street we would see pitifully thin people walking around but it was not long before more and more people developed grotesquely swollen bellies, ballooning out with hunger oedema. Most mornings we would find bodies lying in the gutter of the street, dead from starvation. There was no wood available for coffins or boxes. There were no horses and carts to take the bodies to the cemetery and so the Germans instructed all bodies to be taken and stacked up inside some of the churches. The smell was indescribable!

During this time my father had decided to return to Holland. A lot of the time the German soldiers were in their barracks but they regularly went on raids descending on a particular area or street and searching every house looking for Jews, people in hiding, anyone working for the Underground Movement or men who should have been working in Germany. We often had to hide Father.

During the day Father would go out across the polder into the countryside to cut the hair of those working in the Underground Movement and sometimes he would deliver illegal and forged documents for them. He would not receive payment as such, for money had little value when there was nothing in the shops to buy, but he would be given a half pint of "blue" milk. This was milk from which all the fat and the goodness had been taken out and in normal times would have been given to the pigs. It was not a lot but we were grateful for anything.

One day Father was returning home from one such expedition when he was suddenly ambushed by a German soldier with a gun. Knowing he would be arrested or even shot for being back in Holland he retaliated with the only weapon he had - the bottle of milk. He crashed it over the head of the soldier and pedalled his bike away as fast as he could. It was a very lucky escape.

Once, during one of the unannounced raids in our street the Germans took away one of our neighbours. We had known he had leanings towards Communism but he was just an ordinary man. After the war had finished he returned and showed us the holes in his back where he had been tortured with a red-hot poker in their endeavours to discover what he knew about communist activity. He had known nothing.

One evening our doorbell rang and when Mother went to see who was there she found a small food parcel beside the door with some extra food coupons inside. This was repeated several times throughout that awful winter. We never discovered who left those parcels but we nicknamed him St. Nicholas. At the end of the war the man responsible for them came to say he was going away. He still did not give his name, only that he worked for the Underground Movement. We were more grateful for those parcels than he could ever know. Often, they appeared just as we were at our lowest when perhaps we had not eaten for a couple of days. My mother's faith that "The Lord will provide" was certainly fulfilled through that man.

The weather seemed particularly harsh that winter. I suppose the frailty of our bodies and the lack of food added to our inability to produce any body heat. Any coal or wood for burning had long since disappeared and we huddled together in what flimsy blankets and coats we could pull around us. The cold still seeped into our bones.

One day, my little brother Henk then aged about five, had gone out to play. He had climbed up the dyke outside our house and onto the railway to try to find any bits of coal the engine drivers might have thrown out. Suddenly we heard a gun shot and realising Henk was missing Mother screamed

"Oh God, don't let that be my little Henk."

We all rushed out but to our immense relief Henk was coming towards us struggling to carry a small bucket filled with coal. As the train had approached the German soldiers on board had seen Henk and some other boys and had fired a shot to frighten them away. Henk had lain flat on the ground but not before the Dutch engine driver had seen him. Stopping the train the driver had got out and asked Henk what he was doing so near the railway. Explaining that he wanted some coal for his family the kindly driver had quickly filled his bucket before continuing his journey. We were filled with a mixture of thankfulness for the coal, relief that Henk hadn't been shot and amazement that he should have considered the task in the first place!

Soon after this episode Jan and Henk went for two weeks to stay with some family friends in the north. Mother made Jan promise he would not let his little brother out of his sight for even a moment. They arrived back safe and well having had a great time.

The winter continued to take its toll. Thousands of Dutch people died of starvation and the piles of bodies in the churches mounted higher and higher.

The transport system had all but ground to a halt. There was no fuel for engines so even in the north of Holland where the farmers could still provide meat and crops they had no means of getting their goods to the markets and cities.

My father's church decided something must be done to try to at least save the children from starvation. They contacted farmers in the north who belonged to the same type of church and arrangements were made for them to care for some of the children. At least at the farms they would have sufficient food. All this was done in secrecy so that the Germans did not discover the plans. After much whispering and planning the night for their departure arrived.

Myself and Esther would not be leaving as we were considered old enough to manage the situation but Jan, Leni, Ellie and Henk were taken to the church late at night on the appointed day. The only way to get them out of Amsterdam was by boat and the parents were not allowed to know exactly where their children were going to. They would have no contact, no letters or news of them until the day they returned home and no one knew when that might be. It must have been incredibly hard for the mothers to say goodbye to their youngsters even though they knew it was to be for the best.

The night the children left was a Friday and we had been told to listen carefully in church on Sunday morning and we would be given a secret message to say that all the children had arrived safely. We had a couple of anxious days wait.

On the Sunday the church was packed with worried parents. It was not unusual for informers working for the Germans to be in amongst church congregations, mingling with the people to try and pick up any useful information. They also

68

listened intently to the sermons and sometimes preachers would be imprisoned or sent to concentration camps for teaching something the Germans had forbidden or considered anti war propaganda.

Our minister had considered and prepared his sermon carefully. He spoke about the Israelites crossing the Red Sea and his text was "They landed safely on the other side." That was the message we had all been waiting for. Our children had arrived safely. We truly thanked God.

On a less spiritual but more practical plane the evacuation of the children meant there was more soup to go around the rest of us. The children had gone but their ration books had stayed behind and so we were able to get more food. They say every cloud has a silver lining but the house seemed strangely quiet and empty without them.

Despite the extra coupons we were still desperately short of food. Many people were going on what had now become known as "The Hunger March", a long walk that passed by the farms in the north where some meat and vegetables were still available. Esther and I decided we would join them.

We had heard that the farmers would take anything valuable in exchange for food. We looked around our house and decided we had nothing of value with which to trade. In desperation, when Father was not looking we took some of his shaving soaps and hoped they would be acceptable. Mother kept a few carrots and beetroot in the loft - her real emergency rations she called them - and in the early hours I crept into the loft to take a few to eat on the way.

Our plans were made and so leaving a note to say we had gone on the hunger march we crept out of the house at 6 a.m. The first part of the journey was easy. We took a ferry across the river. On the other side I noticed the German soldiers were stopping everyone before they got back on the ferry. Any food they had was taken from them. It was heartbreaking to see. People had walked for days to barter for food and now that precious food was being taken from them again. Many wept inconsolably. I considered not going any further. It seemed futile. Then my stubborn nature rose to the surface once again. I would not be beaten. The Germans would not get the better of me. Somehow I would manage to get some food back home for my parents.

We began the long walk. It was bitterly cold and our clothes were inadequate for being outside for such a prolonged length of time. On and on we walked. Lunchtime came and we shared a beetroot between us. By mid afternoon my feet were blistered and it seemed more comfortable to walk bare footed so I took off my clogs. It didn't really help.

As evening approached we neared some farms and our spirits began to lift. We stopped at the first one and asked if they could spare some food. We offered the shaving soap. They didn't want to know. Disheartened we walked further and stopped at another farm. The answer was the same. Silver or gold was worth trading, shaving soap was not.

I was never normally one to give in but I began fighting back the tears. I was cold, hungry, tired and my feet were now bleeding. Why did life have to be so hard? We walked some more and stopped at a few more farms but all to no avail. It was now dark and we faced having to spend the night in the open unless someone took pity on us.

I remembered the visit Jan and Henk had to a farm in the area and prayed we might find it. Surely they would take us in? Another door was closed against us and this time my tears fell freely. I didn't know what else to do and the security of home seemed so far away.

We planned to knock on just one final door and then if that failed find somewhere sheltered, perhaps beneath a tree, where we could curl up for the night. It was now nearly eight o'clock and we had been walking for thirteen hours. Esther knocked on yet another farm door and it was opened by a kindly looking lady who needed no explanation of our plight. She welcomed us immediately into her home.

Amazingly this was the very farm where my brothers had stayed not long ago. God must have heard my prayer after all. She gave us hot drinks and food and warm water to soak our tired and battered feet. She agreed to allow us to stay for three days provided we helped with the farm work and in return she would give us food to take home. She did not dare keep us any longer, as she would be punished if the Germans found out. Gratefully we accepted her offer and soon fell fast asleep. It had been an exhausting day and we had walked about thirty miles.

During the next three days we helped press the rapeseed into oil. It was hard work and long hours but we were well fed for our labours. All too soon we had to face the long walk back to Amsterdam but at least we had a large bag of vegetables to take with us.

Eventually we arrived at the ferry crossing and saw to our dismay that the Germans were still searching and taking food from everyone. A little way off I took all the vegetables out of the bags and stuffed them down my trousers! Fortunately having lost so much weight there was plenty of room and as there was elastic around the bottom hems I was hopeful nothing would fall out. I told Esther to keep quiet and not to say a word and practised once again in my mind my best German phrases.

As we approached the soldiers I greeted them in German and commented on what a fine day it had been. They assumed I was German and so let me pass on to the boat without searching me. Esther followed closely behind but even if they had searched her she had no food hidden.

At long last, weary but secretly triumphant we arrived back home. Mother was so relieved to see us. With hindsight it seems to have been a monumental effort just for the sake of a few vegetables but I suspect that unless someone has known what starvation is really like there is no way they can appreciate just how important even a tiny amount of food becomes.

CHAPTER SIX

I was still attending the Salvation Army church whenever I could and had become quite involved. Although by now they knew a little of my family background I always felt they accepted me for who I was as an individual and I loved their services. Enjoyment of church was quite a new experience for me! It was customary at the end of the Gospel service on Sunday nights to invite anyone who was not saved to go forward for prayer. I had watched many people do this but had no desire to be one of them. However, one particular night the Major was preaching from the Bible about the return of the Prodigal Son. It was a story I had heard many times before but something was different that night. It felt as though everything she said was about me. Gradually I felt as though God was speaking into my heart telling me that like the wayward son in the story, I too needed to return to my (heavenly) Father and ask His forgiveness for the way I had been living my life. I realised that everyone needed to be saved. It wasn't just for people who had committed big crimes like murder or theft, but to God, just the fact that we didn't put Him first, that we lived our lives without Him were things which separated us from His love and forgiveness. I realised that to God, things like hatred, anger, jealousy, unkindness and telling lies were just as bad as the so called big crimes. I knew without hesitation that God was asking me to turn to Him, ask His forgiveness and allow Him to become my Saviour and Lord.

At the end of the service I went forward and knelt at the Penitent's rail asking Jesus to forgive me and come into my life. This was not about religion; this was about a relationship with God. Afterwards I felt a peace I had never known before and I knew that my future was in His hands.

I went home after the service and told my parents I'd given my heart to Jesus. They were not impressed. My mother said she would wait and see if there was any change in my behaviour! When I said an officer from the Salvation Army would come to visit them soon the response was,

"Good. I'll tell her what you're really like."

I was scared and afraid my mother would be proved right, and that the Army would no longer want me but God had promised to hold me in the palm of His hand and I learnt to trust in Him.

Despite my parents disapproval I began to become more involved in the Salvation Army. I went to as many of the church services as I could, attended the weekly Bible Classes, the choir and other activities. Walking in the blackout for an hour to get there was not always easy and many times I fell over in the darkness, but nothing could curtail my enthusiasm. I wanted to win the whole world for Christ! I wanted to be a Soldier in His Army. I wanted to do everything, go everywhere, tell everyone that Jesus was the answer to life's questions and problems.

I applied to join the church officially by becoming a "soldier" but was told I must wait six months until the next training course began. I was impatient and wanted to start it right away. God had saved and forgiven me but He had a great deal to teach me in the way of patience and in that respect I was not such a fast learner! Eventually the months passed, I went on the training course and learned how to grow in my spiritual life, what the Army believed and how they worked.

I was so proud the day I became a Soldier in the Salvation Army. It was Easter Sunday 1944. I was sworn in under the flag and promised to stay faithful to God, keep the Army rules and obey the Creed. My only regret was that none of my family had come to share in the special service with me but I told myself that they had never approved of anything I had ever done so why should this have been any different? It still hurt though.

Some weeks later at the end of a service I was given quite a large piece of cheese to take home to my family. We never knew where it had come from only that several needy families were given cheese that day. It seemed like a taste from Heaven itself. We savoured every mouthful and hungrily devoured the very last and tiniest crumb. It was so long since we had eaten cheese and for a country like Holland, which prides itself on its cheese production, it was one of the things we had missed the most.

Another incident in the Salvation Army is firmly imprinted on my mind. During one evening service we were gustily singing one of the hymns when the door at the back of the church suddenly swung open and a German soldier stood there with his gun in his hand. The singing stopped abruptly and we stood rooted to the spot, frightened he was going to shoot at us. Slowly he made his way to the front of the church, gun still in hand. It was not unknown for innocent people to be shot indiscriminately often in retribution for something completely unrelated to them. Slowly he turned to look at us all then to our astonishment he laid down his gun and knelt in prayer. One of the leaders gently lifted him to his feet again and led him into a side room. Later we heard his remarkable story. He had been passing the church and had heard our singing. He stopped to listen and realised we had been singing one of his own mother's favourite hymns. Suddenly he felt God speaking into his heart and knew he could no longer go on fighting and killing people. He came to hand over his weapon and to surrender his life to the Lord. Late that night he was taken into the Underground Movement for his protection and subsequent return to his homeland. It was a reminder to us that God's love is to all people.

Rumours were rife that the end of the war was near. Those who had secret radios hidden under floorboards began telling of Allied victories in Europe. We lived in hope but our daily lives and struggles remained the same. Lack of food was still the major problem but the cold had also taken its toll on many of the elderly and those most vulnerable. All available wood had long since disappeared and even the railway sleepers had been pulled up. One night we were desperate for some fuel and I promised Mother that on returning from my late shift at work and under cover of darkness I would try to find even a few splinters of wood. There was total blackout of course and the only light was from the moon. I picked my way gingerly along the old tram and rail tracks gathering even the smallest splinters of wood. Suddenly I tripped and fell crashing against something hard. I remember thinking, "don't try to save yourself, just keep hold of the wood". That's exactly what I did but it cost me three broken ribs in the process!

Daily the undercurrents of excitement grew more noticeable. Hitler was about to be overthrown. The end of the war was imminent. Messages from the Underground Movement somehow spread around the city by word of mouth. We all hoped and prayed they were true and yet could scarcely believe that they might be.

One day we could barely contain our excitement when we were told the British Royal Air Force together with the Americans would be dropping food parcels because they had heard the people of Amsterdam were starving. We were to gather on top of any flat roofed buildings with as many Dutch flags as we could find! To describe the moment is almost impossible. We gathered on the roofs laughing and waving our flags as we craned our necks to see the approaching aircraft and listen as the drone of their engines drew closer. We watched in awe and wonder as packages began to fall from the sky and land on the flat rooftops. Finally the planes flew above us and it was our turn. Each family received a parcel. We shouted, cheered and wept many a tear in thankfulness.

Eager hands ripped open the packaging to discover the delights inside. There were packets of Jacobs cream crackers, a tin of cooking fat, bag of flour, chewing gum and a bar of chocolate. We smeared the cooking fat on the crackers and ate them. Every last crumb. Nothing had ever tasted so good not even the chocolate

The German soldiers realised the war was nearly over and two days later their country finally surrendered. The horrors of the past five years had at last come to an end but the cost in human suffering was immeasurable.

On that momentous day, 5th May 1945, everyone went to Dam Square in the centre of Amsterdam to celebrate. We were awaiting the arrival of the liberation forces and the atmosphere was electric. People were laughing and carefree, thankful to be alive and looking forward to the new era and peace but the Germans were not finished with us yet! Suddenly there was the sound of gunfire. All those hundreds of people, myself included, fell to the ground and covered our heads with our hands.

In a nearby hotel some Germans had decided their war was not yet over and they fired indiscriminately into the crowds over and over again. Eventually the gunfire stopped and slowly people began to dare to raise their heads. I stood up, trembling in fear and ran home as fast as I possibly could but many had been killed in that final act of defiance.

Over the next few days and weeks the liberating forces piled into Amsterdam and we were so grateful to see them. It is impossible to describe just how we felt. Throughout Europe people were celebrating the end of the war but for those countries who had endured occupation it was not just about celebrating an end to hostilities it was an all consuming relief that our lives and our countries were once again our own. We could fly our National flag, sing our National Anthem and rejoice in the freedom of our country.

The Canadians came in from one side, the British from the other. Their soldiers threw handfuls of chocolates and sweets to the waiting children often making us sing them a song as part of the bargain.

Suddenly people were free to share incidents, which for their safety they had kept quiet for five long years. We discovered that in the flat beneath us a Jew had been kept hidden. After liberation he came to visit us. He told us how he felt he knew each one of us. He knew our names, who was good, who was naughty, who laughed a lot, who cried a lot. He had listened to our daily lives, our discussions, arguments, laughter and tears. He had been encouraged by our singing and activity and he thanked us for helping to keep his spirits up which he attributed to keeping him alive. Of course we had no idea that he had been in hiding below us but he had been one of many kept safe in such a way.

Finally, after nine long months away my younger brothers and sisters were returned to the family. It was a joyous reunion all round. We were so relieved to see them alive and back amongst us. The boys had fared quite well and looked reasonably healthy but sent to a different home poor Leni and Ellie were still very thin. I can also vividly recall my mother's horror at the colour of Ellie. She looked as though she had not seen soap and water since the day she had left us. I was given the task of getting her clean again. It took days to get the grime off her.

Not everything was joyous in those early weeks of liberation. Girls who had been openly dating German soldiers were now cruelly rounded up, their hair pulled out or shaved off and black swastikas painted on their heads. Many were questioned, imprisoned or even executed. Feeling that they had betrayed their fellow countrymen by fraternising with the enemy aroused deep hatred in the hearts of many. Others who had helped the Germans in any way were similarly treated.

The Allies began helping to restore order. The town had to be cleared of rubble, bodies had to be taken from the churches for burial and everywhere disinfected. All Germans were made prisoners and taken away to enable the liberating forces to use their barracks. The Salvation Army worked with the soldiers in setting up soup kitchens, looking after the sick, elderly and homeless. At that time, because there was little electricity I was working only part time and so was able to offer my help with this work.

An English couple, Captain and Mrs. Ray had come with the Salvation Army from England to help supervise the work and I became friendly with them. One day Mrs. Ray told me she couldn't stand my noisy clattering up and down the wooden stairs in my clogs any longer and offered me a pair of brown sandals. With my black stockings it was not the most fashionable ensemble but I was so pleased to have my first pair of shoes since before the war and not to have to wear clogs any more.

Whilst working with this couple my English improved and when they asked to visit my family I was able to translate for my parents. Our friendship grew and whenever possible this kindly couple would visit my family bringing much needed and appreciated food and clothes.

Gradually life began to improve. Rubble was cleared from the streets and rebuilding began. Gas, electricity and transport systems were becoming more reliable. The homeless found shelter, the hospitals began to see fewer injuries and people began to pick up the broken threads of their lives. There was much work to be done but this was good news for it meant employment, wages and the ability to buy food and provide for our families once again. The future beckoned to us all.

I was becoming more involved in the Salvation Army. By now I had a uniform of sorts. No new uniforms were available but I wore a black skirt and jacket with a white blouse underneath and had been given an old "bonnet". I felt proud to wear the uniform but was often made fun of in the streets. At home it was cause for merriment too. One day I returned from work to discover my siblings had taken my uniform, filled it with straw, made a cardboard face and stuck my bonnet on top then tied this "figure" to the front railings. I could hear their giggling even before I saw the reason for it.

Being in the Army also meant that I lost many of my former friends, as being part of the Youth Movement and their activities was considered unsuitable for a Soldier. Other friends thought I had become "too religious" and were unimpressed by my new zeal for the Lord. They preferred the old Johanna who loved getting into mischief! My parents were in trouble too because I no longer attended catechism classes or services at their church and their leaders strongly disapproved of the Army.

Despite all of this I felt that with God I could endure anything and my love for Him and His work was my driving force. I suspect there was still a great deal of stubbornness on my part to show "them" that I would not give in but then that was one of the things God and I were working on together!

I wanted to share the Gospel with everyone and to this end I considered becoming a missionary where I could perhaps use my language skills. I started going out with a boy called Henk. He and his family were all in the Army and they encouraged me in my faith. Gradually I felt God leading me towards working full time in the Army and told the Major I wanted to become an officer. I still had a longing to be a missionary but told him I would also like to work with children or in one of the mother and baby homes but I was willing to do anything.

After some consideration he told me if I was really serious about becoming an Officer I would have to leave my job as a telegraphist and go to work in the Salvation Army Headquarters where they needed office help. It was not the answer I had hoped for.

I had a lot to consider. I really enjoyed my job at the Post Office and the money was good. If I went to work in HQ the pay would be much less which in turn meant less for Mother. She wouldn't be pleased. Also, I loved being with the Army in the centre of Amsterdam. I sang in the choir and at open air meetings. I went with them into public houses selling the "War Cry", the Army newspaper. From 11p.m. to 1 a.m. we went into the Red Light District talking with the prostitutes and drunks. Often we would take drunken men from the gutter and see them safely home. Then there was the work in the soup kitchens and with the homeless. If I had to go to work in HQ I would miss all this "action". Surely this was where God intended me to be, not in some stuffy HQ office?

I thought long and hard. I prayed and asked God for guidance. I talked it over with friends in the Army. Eventually I came to a decision. If I truly felt it right for me to become an officer then I had to be committed enough to take this first step.

I agreed to become secretary to the man responsible for choosing candidates to go forward into officer training. The applicants were all interviewed and it was my job to type up their confidential reports. I was horrified to learn how they had been questioned on all aspects of their lives including intimate details of their relationships. Anyone entering training was strictly forbidden to see or even correspond with a boyfriend or girlfriend during the whole of the twelve month training period.

Despite the drop in earnings and being out of the centre of Amsterdam I quite enjoyed working at HQ and became good friends with an English Commissioner. Many of the other staff considered him unapproachable because of his high rank but that made no difference to me. I thought everyone should be equal so sat happily on his desk whilst I ate my sandwiches at lunchtime. It was also another opportunity to practise my English. He kindly got me a proper second hand uniform from England with the "S" on the collar.

Our days in HQ began with a 9 a.m. prayer meeting before the daily work began. Missionaries often visited and told us of their work in far off lands. I loved to hear how they had started churches, schools and hospitals. I listened intently as they explained how little medical help was available and how by preaching the gospel and meeting the practical needs people were coming to know Jesus. Once again I felt God was urging me towards a special work for Him although I had no idea what that might be.

Finally, I was accepted for Officer training. As a result of the disruption of the war they were in desperate need of new officers and the training period had been reduced from twelve to six months. I would receive no money during my training and could have no contact with my boyfriend Henk either in person or by letter.

My parents thought I was mad to give up a well paid job to train without pay and they were furious I would have no money to give to them. My father told me not to bother coming home again until I could bring some wages with me.

The training college was a lovely building outside Amsterdam but I was totally unprepared for the host of rules and regulations! We had lectures in Salvation Army history and origins. We were taught how to conduct open air services, church services, prepare sermons and Bible studies. I had always loved learning but I confess I hated all this theory. I wanted to be out saving souls. In addition to this we had to spend at least an hour in prayer every day. I felt like a nun! Cooking and cleaning was done on a rota basis. The officers rooms also had to be cleaned by us.

Fortunately we did manage to "escape" sometimes and make the one and a half hour bicycle ride to Amsterdam where we were allowed to put into practise the things we had hopefully learned and conduct open air services. On one such occasion I was preaching and saw my mother approaching but when she saw me she turned and walked away. I tried unsuccessfully not to feel hurt.

On one particularly cold winter day we were cycling into the city and the sergeant had put me in the front of the group where the wind was at its worst. After a while I suggested we take turns to be in front but the sergeant disagreed. Undeterred I took myself off to the back. That was considered blatant disobedience and I was reported to the Major. I tried to argue my case on my return but was told in no uncertain terms that disobedience would not be tolerated.

My punishment was that on my only free afternoon I was to brush down all the cobwebs from the white ceilings. I did this vigorously; probably working off my frustration in the process and lots of white bits of flaking plaster and paint also came off the ceilings onto the chairs below. No one had told me to clean chairs so I happily left them covered in dust and paint! It took "them" longer to clean up the chairs than it had for me to dust off the cobwebs! I felt victorious. Not very Christian like I now admit but then God working in us is always an ongoing process. I still had a lot to learn from Him.

Some candidates could not stand the strict regimes and left before the end of their training. Others were considered unsuitable and told to leave. I hung on in there, probably by the skin of my teeth.

Towards the end of training we were sent for two weeks practical work and I was assigned to a mother and baby home where I helped with the cooking, cleaning and general care of the children. I enjoyed it even though it meant long hours and often tiring work.

Just prior to our final exams we had to write a report and say in which field of work we thought we were most suited. I said I thought I worked best with people on a one to one basis, loved being with children and babies but did not think preaching was my strong point.

The day the results of our final exams were given out I was terrified I had failed but amazingly that was not the case. A large concert hall in the centre of Amsterdam was booked for the presentations. It was one of the proudest days of my life. There was a big Army band and lots of singing and speeches. I had been chosen, because of my loud voice, to stand at the back and recite one of the "articles of war", the longest one. At the end of the ceremony we were told where we would be sent to serve. I was hoping to go abroad or to be sent to work with children but to my deepest disappointment I was to go and work in Groningen in the most northern part of Holland, for an elderly major who had the reputation of keeping her lieutenants as unpaid servants. I was dreading it but to refuse was not an option.

I had often thought as a child that I was used as an unpaid servant and now history was repeating itself. I was expected to do all the washing by hand including white tablecloths used for Sunday services. I prepared meals, washed dishes and generally kept everywhere clean and tidy. The house was opposite a railway line and as fast as I got everything clean it was covered in spots of dust and soot again. In between these household chores I was expected to visit the sick, run the youth work and Sunday school and generally rush to the major's every whim. I was not happy.

I was still in contact with the Commissioner and one day whilst I was feeling particularly fed up I wrote and told him exactly how I felt. His reply was not what I had expected. He said God had planted me to be a tree in the shade but I wrote back and said I'd rather be in the sun!

Eventually I was transferred back to Nijmegen, which was closer to Amsterdam, but again I was put to work with an elderly officer. Soon after my arrival she became ill and so I was left to continue the work on my own. I did not mind that. I went out visiting the sick, preaching in the open air together with the band and working amongst the children with youth activities and Guides.

Nijmegen was a fairly small town but there were a lot of Roman Catholics living there, something quite unusual for Holland. The children didn't quite get the idea of the Penitent rail or Mercy seat, thinking it was like their confessional and would often come to the front week after week! A new Captain was assigned to our area and she was happy to take me out visiting and preaching with her. We got on well together and at last it felt like I was really doing work for the Lord. Unfortunately it was not long before the captain was moved elsewhere and I was on my own again.

One day a letter arrived for me from HQ. They wanted me to put in writing that I was not seeing my old boyfriend Henk. I had given my word when I went into officer training that I would have no contact with him during that time. Once I became an Officer I knew it was forbidden for me to have a relationship with anyone other than another Officer and Henk was still only a soldier. I had not heard from him or seen him since I had begun my training. I had given my word and I considered that should be sufficient. I was filled with righteous indignation. How dare they doubt my word? They trusted me with souls they should trust what I said. I wrote and told them so!

Not surprisingly I was summoned back to HQ and told to

give account for my attitude. There was no way I was going to apologise. I suppose I have always had a strong sense of fairness and justice and I felt quite betrayed by their actions and mistrust. I resigned my commission and returned home to my parents.

I still attended the Salvation Army but was no longer an officer. Over the coming weeks they wrote many times asking me to reconsider but I was never tempted. Some months later they wrote and apologised for doubting my word and again asked me to reconsider but I was adamant I would not return. Perhaps it was pure stubbornness and pride on my part but if that was the case I was equally sure the Lord would sort me out in His way and His time. I still had my life in His hands and trusted Him to guide me where He wanted me to go.

I found a new job doing typing and bookkeeping and was soon promoted ensuring a higher wage and some additional and much needed money for my parents. One day I got chatting with one of the travellers in the office and he asked me out on a date. He was tall, blonde, and good looking. We got on really well and enjoyed each other's company but Mother wasn't happy about him and tried to make me give him up. He lived in Rotterdam and unknown to me Mother went to his hometown and made enquiries about him. I was furious when she told me what she had done but less so when she said he was a married man with two children! I could hardly believe it. All his work records showed him to be a single man. I confronted him with what I'd discovered and he admitted it was true, the only difference being he was recently separated. I felt very let down but amazingly we continued to be friends, but no more dates.

Some other people I remained friends with were Captain and Mrs Ray. They said that Holland was about fifty years behind the times in relation to their strict religious ways. They suggested I work in England or join them working in refugee camps in Germany. This was something I had never thought of. I said I would think and pray about it.

Gradually I began to feel that God was calling me to help the work in Germany. The people at the Salvation Army where I now attended also felt it was God's timing and purpose and they gave me a small amount of money to take with me. All I had to do was gain the necessary permits, one to leave the country and the second to allow me to work in Germany.

I wrote several times to the Salvation Army headquarters in The Hague requesting written permission to work for them in Germany but my letters were never answered. I made other enquiries and was advised that if I got a letter on official Army paper saying there was a job waiting for me in Germany there was a good chance I would get the required permit. The Rays sent me an official request to go and work with them and finally those papers were passed. As far as the English were concerned I was free to work in Germany. However, at that time no one was allowed to leave Holland without an official exit permit, which was only given in exceptional circumstances. I had no papers to actually allow me to pass the official border crossings from Holland into what was at that time a part of Germany still under English control. There was only one answer. If I couldn't get the required legal papers I would have to find another way out of Holland and into Germany.

I contacted my married traveller friend who of course had a car, and persuaded him to drive me one night to a quiet part of the border that was not patrolled. With my heart thumping in my chest and not knowing what lay ahead of me I left the safety of his car, picked up my small suitcase, hugged him farewell and pushed my bike across the border as quietly and unobtrusively as possible. I was terrified searchlights or soldiers would suddenly appear but the only noise was the muffled sound of my feet. Just a few more steps and I would be in Germany where hopefully, Captain and Mrs Ray would be waiting for me. I was just twenty two years old and about to walk into an unknown future.

CHAPTER SEVEN

I skirted the side of the field and found an opening out into a lane. It was dark and incredibly cold. I kept praying, "Please God, let the Captain and his wife be on the road waiting for me." My heart felt as though it was beating a hundred times faster than normal. I could hardly believe I was actually in Germany without a permit and still expected searchlights or soldiers to appear at any moment. By the light of the moon I made my way down the unfamiliar lane and after what seemed like an eternity, but was probably only about five or ten minutes, I could just see the outline of a jeep partly hidden in the bushes.

To my immense relief Captain and Mrs. Ray appeared and greeted me with huge hugs. As quickly and quietly as possible we loaded my things into their jeep and set off towards my future home. They told me they would explain fully over the weekend what my work would involve but for the moment all I had to do was sit back and relax. I was so thankful to have arrived safely and to be with them once again. The rest was in God's hands.

It was a long drive to their house in a place called Herford and the first thing I noticed about the house was that it was enclosed by wire fences and gates because it was occupied by the British in German territory.

After a light supper I was shown upstairs to a comfortable bedroom, advised to get a good nights sleep but to be ready by 8 a.m. sharp the next morning. The Captain had very briefly told me something about their work but most of it was a mystery to me. They talked of refugees, but where had they come from and why? So much had happened in Holland during the war that often we had been unaware of what was happening in other countries. What sort of work would I be doing? How would I communicate? These and many more questions buzzed around in my mind but eventually I fell into an exhausted sleep.

Next morning I went down for breakfast and tried my best to speak English. After a short prayer meeting and service I was taken around to see the work. I understood most of what was being said to me but concentrating on the constant English was hard work in itself. Some of the staff employed were German and it was a relief to be able to listen and talk with them. My German was better than my English!

In the afternoon we went by car to Munster and then to a tiny place called Greven where I would be living and working. Again, the house was surrounded by wire fencing and gates. I was taken inside and welcomed by the other workers. A Major from Kent was in overall charge of the work there and she seemed very nice. Her assistant was from Scotland and my first impression of her was that she was a bit stiff and starchy! She was in charge of everyone in the house. The others were Katy from Denmark, Olive from Canada and Suzie from Wales. Although they all spoke English to me I was totally confused by the different accents and wondered if I would ever understand anything any one of them said to me!

I was taken upstairs and shown my bedroom. It was a long, light room with a huge big window and a deep window ledge, which I knew would be perfect for displaying my photographs. There was a bathroom opposite, which we all shared, and a small garden outside. I unpacked my few belongings and went back downstairs. Soon after the Rays left to return to their own house and work in Herford. I felt a momentary feeling of fear. What had I let myself in for?

The next morning after our usual prayer meeting and service I was introduced to my driver! I could not believe it. Me, with my own driver! I wondered what my family would make of that! He was Polish and had an unpronounceable name so I called him Fred. We got along fine together despite the fact that he spoke very little Dutch, German or English and I spoke no Polish. It is amazing how you soon learn to communicate in signs and drawings when all else fails.

The Major accompanied Fred and I as we went around the camps for which I was to be responsible. There were two large refugee camps, one with 2,500 people, the other with 3,000. There was also a V.D. Hospital, a children's hospital and perhaps strangest of all - a castle holding Yugoslavian Generals. All of these were to be in my care. It was a daunting prospect and I had so many unanswered questions, not least of which was why all these people came to be there in the first place.

Next, I was taken to Munster to a huge German house, which was used as headquarters not only by the Salvation Army but also the Church Army and other voluntary welfare organisations. I was introduced to the General in charge and given an outline of the work I would be expected to do and an insight as to how the camps were run. It did little to prepare me for the reality I would face the following day.

I was taken to the stores and issued with my uniform. It consisted of a navy skirt, tie, jacket and beret worn with a white blouse. On the sleeve of the jacket were the initials CVWW (SA) denoting I was with the Civil Voluntary Welfare Workers (Salvation Army).

On the journey back to my new home I reflected on all I had learned that day and wondered not for the first time if I was up to the enormity of the task ahead. I reminded myself of a favourite Bible verse, "I can do all things through God who strengthens me".

Each morning began with breakfast then a short time of prayer, Bible reading and worship. We were expected to take turns reading aloud. I was very conscious of my poor English and asked them to correct me when I said something that was not quite right. Then we set out for our various duties. The others also had the supervision of similarly sized camps to mine. It shocked me when I realised just how many refugees were in Germany at that time. The days were long and in the evening our daily reports had to be written in English, which I found quite difficult. There was little free time but the challenge and opportunities afforded to me by my work made it so worthwhile and we shared our experiences and learned from each other how to deal with particular problems.

On my first day of work Fred drove me to the camp at Bocholt - "home" to 2,500 refugees. We drove up to the main office and I introduced myself. The camp was under the authority of the British Army on the Rhine and the commissioner was in charge of many British soldiers and looking after the camp as a whole. Most of the personnel were English so at least I could speak with them if I encountered insurmountable difficulties.

Knowing that 2,500 people were living at the camp I expected perhaps hundreds of barracks but that was not the case. I was shown into the first barrack and was horrified at the sight. Beds were not just two high, as in bunks, but stacked up four or even six high. I quickly counted the many sets of these "bunks" and found there were not three, four or five, but ten sets down each side of the relatively small barrack. I was appalled. There were, in this barrack alone, about one hundred people living in the most cramped conditions and I later realised the other barracks were the same. Each bed had a small pillow and a dark blanket. There were just a few small cupboards for personal possessions, totally inadequate for the number of people, so most of their belongings were just piled on the bed or in heaps on the floor. There were fairly primitive wash facilities at one end consisting of a shower, toilet and several washbasins.

Suddenly my eyes were drawn to some red writing on the wall. The language was Dutch. Mesmerised I walked across and almost recoiled in horror as I read, "If you ever come here, tell my mother I am still alive." It was followed by a name and a date. I didn't understand. Slowly, I turned to the commander and asked who had used these barracks before the refugees came and he replied,

"It was a prisoner of war camp used for Jews from Holland, Belgium and France."

I told him what was written on the wall and he was not surprised. I walked slowly down the length of the barrack and saw many similar messages some with addresses still visible; others had been painted or scratched over. How many previous occupants of this barrack had survived the war? How many ever got to be reunited with their families? I felt an unbelievably deep sorrow. What did it matter what nationality a person was - we were all human beings created by one God. I looked around at the sea of faces before me. What would happen to these people? Would they ever see their own country, homes and loved ones again?

Later, I learned that most of the refugees had feared Russian oppression and had fled from their Eastern Bloc countries towards the West, Germany being the first country they reached. Sadly, they found that the West was not all they had hoped it would be and unable to find employment or homes they had been forced to seek refuge and shelter in the refugee camps. I would get to know many of their individual heartbreaking stories in the months ahead.

Fred drove me to the second camp at Anhaus where there were 3,000 refugees. It was a similar situation to Bocholt. Next on my list were the two hospitals, one caring for the children who looked painfully thin and fretted terribly for their mothers but they were well cared for and the hospital was well equipped. Finally we went to the castle at Coesfeld where several Yugoslav Generals were in hiding from the Russians. Even though the war was over they knew if they returned to their homeland someone would find them and they would be shot. It struck me as somewhat strange. These men lived quite comfortably in a castle in beautiful grounds, which even had a lake, and yet despite these comforts they were still exiled from their families. The effects of the war obviously had on-going repercussions.

I soon settled into my work and began to get to know the other people in the house. Each morning after prayers Fred would collect me and drive me to whichever camp or place I wanted to go.

Once a month a train loaded with tinned foods, clothes and shoes would arrive from England or America. I had to make a list of everything and sort the clothes into different groups according to size, age, sex etc. I would go around the camps seeing who was most in need of new clothes or shoes and trying to find the items most suitable for them.

It was at such times that I got to know many of the refugees personally and even though we did not speak the same language some of them had learnt a little German and we were then able to communicate.

Many were women with their children. Their husbands had either been killed in the war or taken prisoner. They came from Poland, Latvia, Estonia and other Eastern Bloc countries often fleeing from harsh Russian domination. Some had relatives who had managed to emigrate to America, Canada, Australia or New Zealand and they lived in daily hope that a letter would arrive one day asking them to join those relatives in their new distant homes. With such a letter it was possible for them to emigrate too.

There was just one major hurdle. The authorities at that time would allow a woman travelling without a husband to take only one child with her. Many of the women had more than one child, and the weighing in the balance of continuing to live in a refugee camp or the possibility of a new life far away was one that posed a real challenge to some of them.

Consequently there were those who were prepared to give up one or more of their children. Plenty of German couples had lost children in the war and those same couples were now prepared to "adopt" a child from the camps. It was of course illegal and money was not important. To the mothers on the camp, desperate for extras like coffee or cigarettes such items would be sufficient payment. It was not so much that they did not care for their children, most just wanted a better life for them all. They thought a child "adopted" by a German couple would have a good quality of life in Germany and by keeping only one child themselves they would stand a better chance of being allowed to emigrate. Such "adoptions" were often organised by the German staff working in the camps or by the small number of men living in the camps who had been fortunate to find work locally. It was a desperate situation.

All names and numbers of people in each barrack were checked frequently and so it was not difficult to discover when a child suddenly went missing. It was part of my job to try to find these missing children and reunite them with their mothers. It was painstaking work searching through records, checking local schools and doctors and when the children were found, there were often tears for both families.

By the time I arrived in Germany many of these children had been "adopted" quite some time before and when I finally traced them the new parents understandably were reluctant to let the child go. The real mother was often sorry she had allowed the "adoption" and was glad to have her child back but occasionally mothers still considered their chances of emigration would be hindered with more than one child and did not want them back again.

I remember one case in particular. An elderly German couple had taken in a Polish child. They had "paid" for her in clothes and food. The child was happy, loved and well cared for but the law insisted such an "adoption" was illegal and therefore it was my job to restore her to her natural mother. The Germans were frantic and begged me not to take her away. They listed all the items they had "paid" for her. I went away and collected all those same items again and took them to the couple. Still they would not release the child. Eventually I made them realise they had no legal right to the child and I took her away with me. I left that elderly couple in tears. The mother was not pleased to have her back. She wanted to emigrate and now with the return of her second child she knew she would not be allowed to. She too wept tears - of frustration. The poor child was caught in the middle of an impossible situation. I felt like that too!

The law did not seem fair. Perhaps these children were better off with German families than living in a refugee camp? What kind of a mother would give her child away? They were questions to which there was no easy answer. It was not our place to judge. Who can tell how any of us would react when life seems at its worst and our situation unbearable?

Food at the camps was basic and consisted mainly of soup and bread with occasional supplements when we received extra from England. The refugees would line up at the central kitchen and receive their daily rations. However, mainly because of the overcrowding, epidemics of childhood illnesses like measles and scarlet fever would suddenly become rife and on such occasions all those in contact with the illness would be confined to barracks and huge canisters of soup left at the door of the barracks for them to divide amongst themselves. The empty containers would then be collected and thoroughly washed and disinfected to prevent the spread of infection. During these epidemics I still used to visit the people because I thought in their sickness that was the very time they needed me most. I never became ill myself and felt sure it was due to God's protection.

The children in the camps received no schooling and after a while I began to organise games to try to stimulate and occupy them. Often they would follow me around between the different barracks and sometimes I felt like the Pied Piper. One such child was a little Polish girl named Luzia. She had spent six months in a tuberculosis hospital where she had learnt to speak some

German. She came with me whenever she could and became a great help in translating for me to her fellow Polish refugees.

Regular medical inspections were made at the camps and on one occasion I had to tell the doctor that rats were becoming a problem, which in turn would lead to disease. The camp had previously been used by prisoners of war, and it was not uncommon to find human remains and skeletons, which the rats found tasty! He agreed to send in a team of rodent exterminators. It certainly helped but we found it was a recurring problem.

I had been accepted by the refugees as a friend and despite the language barrier many came to share their problems with me. Some received messages from their hometowns saying their families had been punished because they had escaped to "freedom". The guilt they felt was unbelievable. They told me of the families they had left behind - parents, brothers, sisters - but even though they had been driven hundreds of miles from home they were sure they would never want to go back to live under Russian oppression. However the price of their freedom was great and they missed their families so much.

One day I met a young man in the camp. He was just nineteen years old and had come from a large family. He desperately wanted to become a doctor and avidly studied the few medical books he had been able to bring with him. That day he had received a letter from home. The authorities were demanding his return. He must become a soldier. He did not want to return but knew if he did not go back there was every chance his father would be killed as punishment. If he still refused they would kill his mother and then there would be no one to take care of his younger brothers and sisters. I spoke to the camp commander who agreed that he should stay and have the opportunity to study and maybe emigrate. A week later I went to see that young man but he had gone back to save the lives of his parents even though he knew he would probably be killed himself. What a waste. We never heard of him again. I often think if he had only had the opportunity to study and become a doctor he could have helped so many people.

There was another lady, a head teacher, but because she had refused to teach communist propaganda her life had been endangered and she had been forced to flee her country. She longed to be able to emigrate but had no one to sponsor her. She was desperate for some books to read and said she would be grateful for anything. There were many people in similar circumstances. I spoke to the commander and my colleagues and together we were able to get quite a lot of books, even exchanging our cigarette coupons to buy some new ones. We took them round the camps and my teacher was so thrilled with the two she chose. She hugged and kissed me and her eyes were brimming with tears of thankfulness. Such small things meant such a lot to these people. I could now understand how in prisoner of war camps one book was divided up page by page, read and passed on to someone else. When you have nothing, even a little becomes precious.

I still continued to take clothes and shoes into the camps and they were received gratefully but gradually I noticed a difference. Many of the clothes were being carefully unpicked and redesigned into traditional national costumes especially for the children. The people wanted to dress in their own style. It was as though they needed a reminder of the people they were and where they had come from. They were so proud of their achievements and organised mini fashion parades! I was very impressed. Soon we began gathering the children together and encouraging them to sing their national songs. Other welfare officers visited the camp to see what we were doing and soon the idea of a special day of celebration was arranged.

After weeks of preparation the big day finally arrived and the excitement was tangible. The children had been scrubbed until their faces shone and they stood proudly in their "designer" national costumes. We had arranged a small stage, invited local bands, sold tickets and even had cakes and drinks. The children sang in their choirs and performed their traditional national dances. There was such a feeling of happiness and community spirit.

It was an occasion enjoyed by everyone and one that would stay in all our memories for a very long time. A day like that was a rare treat. It gave a great boost to their morale and also swept aside for a short time the boredom and desperation so many of them felt as one day merged into the next with little hope of the new life they had envisaged.

Easter was a very special time for the refugees and many of them were of Roman Catholic or Greek Orthodox faith. One year we managed to get a priest to come to the camp and he went around the people giving each a tiny piece of bread and saying,

"Christ is risen!"

"He is risen indeed", they replied

Later, we had managed to get a sheep and had roasted it in the open air. The people sat around and were given vine leaves. When the meat was cooked each person received a tiny piece of meat to roll in their vine leaf then, in groups of four they again said,

"Christ is risen!"

"He is risen indeed."

That made a big impression on me. Those people were so far from home, from loved ones, from all that they had once held dear and yet they did not forget the risen Christ. I thought of how rebellious I had been in my younger days and how I refused to say grace and thank God for the small amount of food we had and yet these people were truly thankful for this mouthful of food and all it represented and meant to them as a symbol of their traditional Easter celebration. I still had a lot to learn from God.

My colleagues and I went to an English speaking church in Munster and I remember one very special Easter service there. The church was filled with people of many nationalities and we sang a well-known hymn with the words, "Up from the grave He arose". The minister told us all to sing in our own language and we raised the roof! It was fantastic. I had a deep feeling inside me telling me that this was how it should be. God gave us language and voices and they should be united in praise of Him and not divided by differences. If only we could get that message across to the peoples of the world.

In addition to my work in the camps I visited the children in the two hospitals ensuring they were being taken care of and receiving the proper treatment and medication they required. Many of the children were orphans and looked forward to me coming, especially if I had a few sweets for them.

Each week I also visited the Generals in the castle to check they had sufficient food and had no medical problems. Many of them spoke quite good English and they were glad to have some one different to talk to. One of them gave me an English dictionary, which I still have today. If my visit corresponded with my lunchtime and it was in the winter I could often catch a precious half hour skating on the frozen lake in the castle grounds. It brought back memories of Holland.

Periodically there were meetings in Hanover for all the people working in the camps and it was good to share in the group church service and to exchange news and views with colleagues. We would have a short conference and a meal together before returning to our different areas.

We had occasional weekends off duty and sometimes I went to Dusseldorf to see how the work there was progressing. It was great to be able to drive through the countryside passing places I'd never seen before and admiring mountains and lakes. It made me remember Austria.

Dusseldorf gave me new experiences too. Firstly, there were so many shops. It was a while since I been in such a big city and it was wonderful looking at all the goods on offer.

Then, in the house where I was staying with fellow workers, I was offered some alcohol. I explained I was teetotal but they laughed and offered me "flavoured water". I took a gulp and found my throat on fire! I had just had my first and probably only taste of neat whiskey!

Just to the other side of Dusseldorf there was an amphitheatre producing the "Flying Dutchman". My friends decided to take me there too. Of course my strictly religious upbringing had also prohibited any association with theatres or cinema so this was to be another new experience for me. We sat in the open air but it was not too cold, although I was so mesmerised I am not sure I would have noticed such a minor thing. I sat transfixed. The words, the music, the atmosphere kept me spellbound. I had never seen anything like it and thought it was absolutely wonderful.

The next day we went on a leisurely drive along the Rhine. The scenery was beautiful. It felt a world away from the refugee camps and I felt suddenly sorry that so many of "my" people in the camps would probably never have the opportunity to see the things I was seeing that day.

All too soon it was time to return to work. I said goodbye to my friends but we promised to stay in touch with each other, which we did for many years. The bond of our work with the refugees united us and we never forgot the privilege, the laughter and the tears of our work in the refugee camps.

One day I was summoned to the Major's office and he asked if it was correct that my family were poor and that there were still five brothers and sisters at home. I told him that was true. He knew I was due for a short home leave soon and suggested that I go to the stores and pick out an outfit for each of my parents and brothers and sisters and take these clothes home with me. I was grateful for his thoughtfulness.

I went to the stores and picked out a lovely warm brown coat for Mother, a shirt for Father and warm jumpers for the others. There was a pair of fur lined boots which I was sure would fit Henk so I took them for him.

I was able to travel on the British military train, which went straight into Amsterdam without being stopped. This was just as well as without an official permit I would have again been in trouble at the border crossing.

When I arrived home and gave out the clothing plus small items of food and sweets I had been able to buy with my coupons my brothers and sisters thought St. Nicholas had come early! They were all thrilled.

Mother proudly wore her coat to church saying to everyone,

"Our Jos bought me this from Germany".

Father was saddened to accept what he considered to be charity.

Henk was so pleased and proud to have something to keep his little feet warm and was not bothered by the fact that the boots were really meant for girls!

I really enjoyed my time at home. It was good to see my family again, relax with them and share the things I was doing in Germany but soon it was time to board the military train to take me back to the work I loved.

On the journey back to Germany I thought a lot about my family and their continuing hardship. I thought about all we had come through together during the war years and especially the hunger winter. Then my thoughts turned to the refugees. They too had suffered and were in many ways still suffering. In Holland we had endured hunger and German occupation but at least we had still been in our own country, our own home. We had not been unwanted foreigners in a strange country, crowded into barracks shared with forty or fifty other families. I had a lot to be thankful for.

I soon settled back into my daily routines but I was mindful of the needs of my own family too. I was paid a small weekly wage of £1.50. I sent the 50 pence to my Dutch bank account and used the £1 for rations at the NAFFI buying food, drinks and clothes. Usually I swapped my cigarette coupons for extra food, which I saved and sent home to Mother.

The people in the camps amazed me with their courage and optimism. Often they would receive bad news from home, a long awaited letter would not arrive or their application for emigration was refused and yet still they remained hopeful.

They were so grateful for everything you gave or did for them. Nothing was insignificant whether it was an extra piece of clothing, a hair ribbon, a sweet or some extra food. Sometimes it was just a pat on the head, an arm around the shoulder, a hug, cheery "hello" or sympathetic ear. All these things meant so much to them and showed someone cared. Many of them had walked through Yugoslavia, Bulgaria, the Balkans, up over mountain passes and through forests to get to the safety of the refugee camps. They had suffered and lost so much.

Sometimes it was hard to know how to bring them comfort when I could not speak their language but a hug often seemed to do the trick. Also, I would place their hands together and put my own around theirs and pray. They could not understand my words but "Amen" is universal and they joined in this and knew in their hearts my concerns and love.

Sometimes I was able to arrange a church service in an empty barrack or even in the open air and a local Greek priest came to officiate. The people enjoyed these services and their spirits were always lifted.

After I had been in Germany for about two years things began to change. Many refugees in the Northern camps had been allowed to emigrate to America, Canada, Australia and New

Zealand and as these camps became more empty, refugees were transferred and smaller camps were amalgamated or closed. Now, the remaining camps were being handed over to the administration and control of the Germans. My camps had been closed and my work there was finished.

I had loved every minute of my time working amongst the refugees. They had so little and yet in many ways they had given me so much. Often their sheer determination had been an encouragement to me. God had indeed given me blessings in abundance as I had the privilege to work with these often forgotten people. I had met doctors, teachers, labourers and bin men but in the camps they were all equal. I was sad to leave them. I wished I could take them all home with me and give them a new and better life. That unfortunately was something I could not do but I prayed that God would lead and protect them in their future. I would never forget them.

The Major asked if I would be returning to Holland or whether I would consider working for the Red Shield? This organisation was a branch of the Salvation Army specifically called upon to support the British military in its work in several different countries. I had briefly worked voluntarily for them in Holland soon after the war, setting up soup kitchens, locating missing persons and generally helping to restore order. I said I would be willing to do this type of work again.

I had not bargained for the Major's next statement. He said the Red Shield were looking for someone to support the British military and their families in the Middle East. My heart stood still. Middle East! North Africa! In Germany if things had proved difficult I was near the Dutch border or indeed the borders of several other European countries. In the Middle East I could hardly hop on my bike and pedal home if the going got tough! I said I would think about it.

I had a long weekend leave owing to me and arranged to go home. I wanted to know my father's opinion. Although I often did not agree with him I considered he probably knew more about the current situation in the Middle East than I did.

Back in Holland I discussed the prospect with Father. After a while he suggested a very sensible option. Before I agreed to go I should ensure I had a written confirmation from the

British Army and Red Shield saying that in the event of an emergency evacuation from the area they would include me among their personnel and ensure I was brought out too. This seemed to be a good idea. Unfortunately I could not get this written agreement and the authorities said that in the event of hostilities their commitment was only to those carrying a British Passport. I decided not to take up the offer!

The Major then told me of another available position. A new captain would soon be arriving from England to take up duties caring for Royal Air Force personnel and their families in Rinteln on the river Weser. Unfortunately she spoke no German and needed someone who spoke English and German to assist her. This seemed a much safer idea and I readily agreed. Yet another chapter in my life was about to begin.

CHAPTER EIGHT

The new captain, whose name was Gladys, arrived from Blackburn in Lancashire. She had yet a different dialect for me to try to understand! I often wondered how my English really sounded as it was probably a mixture of that spoken in Kent, Scotland, Wales, Canada, Australia and now Lancashire. It was a miracle anyone ever understood a word I said!

We soon got to know each other and became great friends in the few weeks we spent preparing to go to Rinteln. Our new commission was to be totally different from anything I had done before. The town was in the middle of Germany, still in territory occupied by the British and we would be overseeing the canteen and married quarters for the Royal Air Force.

The drive to Rinteln took us through some beautiful scenery passing hillsides, rivers and small villages. We eventually arrived and took stock of our new home and work place. It was situated in a small village with just a few essential shops - butcher, baker and small grocery. All around was countryside, farmland and forests. On one edge of the village was a large building, which had now been taken over by the British. Inside was the main canteen, above were sixteen small flats used as married quarters for those airmen who had married German girls and opposite those was a larger flat with bedrooms, living room, kitchen and bathroom which was to be home for myself and Gladys. Nearby were houses also used as married quarters and the headquarters for the squadron. The main barracks were a few miles away.

The canteen could cater for four hundred airmen at a time. There were several German cooks, cleaners and helpers but the British now wanted the whole operation to be overseen by the Red Shield. Soon after our arrival an officer from the RAF headquarters told us more about the work involved and also the problems.

The number of men who came into the canteen could vary greatly. Sometimes several hundred would require feeding, sometimes only a few. The canteen was open all day and evening and the men were encouraged to use it as a community facility and call in just for a coffee and chat.

We were told to expect to receive phone calls saying military manoeuvres were about to take place and we would need to have sandwiches and hot drinks ready for a certain number of personnel, anything from a dozen to three hundred! For security reasons these manoeuvres were kept secret until the last minute so we would be given very little notice of the numbers involved. I thought this promised to be a logistical nightmare!

There was more good news to come! The officer told us that for some time it had been apparent that money and supplies were going missing and it was hoped we could sort this out too. He suggested that I pretend not to understand German and to keep my ears open in the hope I would discover who was responsible. Not bad for our introduction to the new job! It crossed my mind that our involvement was not going to make us very popular with the Germans working in the canteen. God certainly liked to give me a challenge.

The first thing that needed to be done was to take stock of all the supplies and I found quite serious discrepancies. I had taken the officer's suggestion and made sure all the staff were unaware of my ability to speak and understand their language. That in itself was difficult. My nature means that I usually breeze into a room with a cheery "good morning" to everyone and to remember not to say this in German was sometimes difficult. Other times the staff would try to tell me something and I had to practise looking blank, shrugging my shoulders and pretending I had no idea what they were saying. I was convinced that one day I would forget and reply in German!

All the supply cupboards were kept locked overnight with only the cook and ourselves having a key. How was such a lot of food going missing? We set specific traps, knowing the exact amount or weight of certain foods then checking it again first thing in the morning. Half of it would have gone. The cook was the obvious culprit but somehow we would have to prove it.

Feeling a bit like Miss Marple or Monsieur Poirot, I decided the only way to find out was to lie in wait. I can now admire the work of policemen who go on "stake outs". It is long, lonely and uncomfortable waiting! Eventually my patience was rewarded. The cellar man and boiler man appeared and using a key proceeded to calmly unlock the cupboards and help themselves to a variety of supplies. One of them said to the other,

"It doesn't bother me doing this. When you steal from the enemy it's not really stealing."

That amazed me. It was obvious that they still saw the British as being the enemy even though the war was over. I decided against being a hero and tackling them to the ground!

The following day I called the two men, plus the cook into the office. Their first surprise was when I spoke in German to them. The second was when I told them what I had seen the previous evening. At first they tried to deny it but soon realised that I was not to be fooled and admitted the continuing thefts. The three were friends and thought that if anyone suspected anything the cook would be the one questioned, but as he never actually took anything, (just provided the keys and always had an alibi), they would be able to get away with it. It seemed the local baker was giving them money in return for the goods so he could bake things he could not get with his rations. The military police were called, the men lost their jobs, new staff were employed and that was the end of that problem.

Part of our work was to ensure the smooth running of all the premises and supervising the work of cleaners, maintenance, supplies, cooking and just about everything else. However, we were also there to offer comfort, friendship and support to all the airmen and their families.

We started a church and were encouraged when quite a number of families began attending. We soon realised that activities for the children was something many of them missed and so to meet this need we hired a bus! Each Sunday this special bus made a one hour round trip of the whole area picking up youngsters from all the barracks and married quarters. We had a great time with them. We taught them Bible stories and choruses. We played games, had quizzes and a whole lot of fun. We got to know and love them all and it was wonderful when they told us about what they had been doing that week, or about their families or "home". So many of them had already been in several different countries and Sunday afternoons became a haven of stability for them where they could just have fun and forget their daddies were fighting a war or considered to be the enemy.

One day I developed toothache. The nearest army hospital or doctor was miles away and so reluctantly I went to a local German dentist. I only required a filling but he was not impressed by the state of my teeth. I suppose years without food and calcium had taken their toll. He also suggested I had a stomach problem! That was news to me but years later when doctors in England diagnosed ulcers I remembered the words of that German dentist.

People say it is a small world and that was proved one day when a young airman came into the canteen and recognised Gladys from their mutual hometown of Blackburn. He was unmarried and soon became a regular visitor to the canteen where he would stop for a chat over a cup of tea. Soon he began visiting us if he had a free weekend and sometimes took us out in a jeep to visit neighbouring towns or just to drive through the countryside admiring the views. It was so good to be able to see somewhere different.

We began to build friendships with many of the airmen and their families. Often in their free time they would come to the canteen always sure of a warm welcome, a friendly chat or a sympathetic and listening ear. Some were quite homesick and missed their families and the familiar things of home. Even those in married quarters still missed having parents or brothers and sisters around especially at certain times of the year like Christmas. It was our privilege to make them all feel they were special and not alone.

There were some women in the administrative offices of the R.A.F. and they often came into the canteen for a chat. One day two of them asked if I was allowed to use the military train and did I have any leave owing to me. I answered, "yes" to both questions. They then began telling me about the military holiday centres which they said were set high up in the mountains with beautiful views, good food and special cheap rates for military and red shield personnel. They invited me to go with them. It was too good an offer to refuse and another chance to see somewhere different. I requested permission and was allowed a

103

weeks leave. We arranged to go in April and I could hardly wait.

We took the military train to the Harz mountain area, which was truly spectacular. The centre itself was in a lovely old building, I had my own room and everywhere was warm and comfortable. The views of snow capped mountains reminded me of my time in Austria when I was a child. In the town were lovely shops, trees, parks and fountains. My friends borrowed a car and we toured around the area taking in the sights, visiting holiday resorts and appreciating the scenery. I could remember as a child always promising myself that some day I would travel and see new places and now I was in a different country and my dreams were being fulfilled.

One day as we drove around we came close to the Russian border and suddenly we were confronted by large warning notices telling us of that fact. Just further along on the Russian side we saw tall watchtowers, barbed wire and soldiers with guns. On "our" side were English soldiers and what we were seeing was in fact the beginning of what was later to become the Berlin Wall. It was so sad to see people on either side of the "new" border looking longingly to the other side and wishing they could cross as they had always done before. This was the new Germany. Where once it had been one country, now it was divided between east and west. It was yet another startling reminder that although the war had ended there were many repercussions and ongoing problems.

Sadly the week ended all too quickly and we had to return to Rinteln. I thanked God for the blessings of these new friends and all the wonderful places I had seen. I thought back to my very first holiday with my teacher and school friends when we had cycled through different parts of Holland. That had been a real adventure. Then I remembered that very special time in Austria and how I had not wanted to return home. Now I had not only been allowed to work in another country but I had also been able to spend a holiday there. My desire to see other countries and places was as strong as it had ever been. The world was a big place and I was looking forward to seeing more of it.

Not long after my return to work I received a letter from the Salvation Army missing persons service. During the war, one of my mother's brothers had disappeared and although presumed dead I had requested the army to try to find out for certain and also what had happened to his wife. We knew he had married a kind, hardworking German girl who had been a servant to some rich Dutch people. After the war she too disappeared. The part of Germany from where she originated was now occupied by the Russians and so we knew she could not have gone back there. Now, the army had located her in a small village just outside Hanover. I wrote to her and arranged to visit on my next free weekend.

She met me at the train station and took me to where she now lived and worked. It was a huge house with seven floors and the most enormous garden I had ever seen. She explained that she had no idea what had happened to her husband only that she had received a letter saying he was "missing, presumed dead" and eventually she had to accept that must be the case. She felt she had no real roots in Holland and had therefore returned to Germany where she now worked as a housekeeper to a chief chimney sweep. Her life was hard. She got up at 5 a.m. each day and not only did all the housework, cooking and cleaning for her employer but also had to look after the garden. She had to grow all their own fruit and vegetables and she showed me the cellars where shelf after shelf was filled with bottled and preserved fruits and vegetables. It must have taken her countless hours to preserve such vast quantities. She confided that her master was often difficult to please and he frequently criticized her if he found even a speck of dust or something was not quite cooked to his satisfaction.

She told me how she fled from Holland because she feared for her safety amongst the Dutch people because she was German. She had left almost everything in her home, taking with her only a few silver spoons, which she sold to provide her with money until she found work. She said she had always been a servant and used to hard work and although her present employer was quite difficult to please at least she had a roof over her head, food in her stomach and a small income. I felt quite sorry for her. Time and time again I came across people whose lives had been totally changed by the effects of the war. We kept in touch for quite a while but gradually our letter writing became less frequent and we again lost touch with each other.

Back in Rinteln I continued working amongst the airmen in the canteen, building up relationships with the families, encouraging them, helping out in practical ways and continuing the work with the children and the church. The days were busy and there was always something new or unexpected to challenge us.

My friends with whom I had gone on holiday earlier still kept in touch and one day they suggested another trip this time a river cruise on the Rhine. I thought there was no way I would be able to afford such a trip but once again they explained there were special rates available for military personnel and the Red Shield. Who could resist? Certainly not me, so once again I packed my bags and set off for my latest adventure. I had never really seen a cruise ship before let alone travelled on one and had no idea what to expect.

We travelled by military train to Cologne then boarded the ship, which was much bigger than I expected with lovely decks, a large dining room, cinema and comfortable cabins. I was so excited I could hardly wait for the ship to begin her journey.

The next day as we cruised down the River Rhine we passed the famous Lorelei rock. Folklore said that many seafarers had seen a beautiful maiden sitting on the rock and could hear her singing. They were so entranced by her that they failed to notice how quickly their vessel had approached the rock and tragically they ran aground. Hoping our captain was not about to make the same mistake we passengers all lined the decks to see for ourselves if we could spot this legendary maiden but sadly to no avail!

We cruised at a leisurely pace past the spectacular scenery of mountains and castles and small villages. We passed the "hills of the two brothers" where legend once again told the story of two brothers each with a house perched on top of neighbouring hills. They used to look across to each other but never spoke.

We went ashore in Koblenz, through the large archway into the town bedecked with flowers. There was a large square, cafes, fountains and lovely shops. My friends were quite used to seeing such things but to me it was all new and I was fascinated by it.

We visited Strasbourg and learned how it had been constantly fought over by the Germans and the French each having periods of rule. It was currently in the hands of the French but around me I heard so many different languages being spoken. Even now, when I hear of Strasbourg in the news I think back to my visit there.

There were many beautiful buildings and large open squares and the afternoon we visited we were having a coffee in one of the open air cafes when a gentleman approached and offered to buy us all a drink. At that time I was a little less teetotal than in previous years but was by no means used to alcohol. He bought us some white wine and after a while chatting with us he suggested we try the red wine. After a pleasant couple of hours spent chatting and drinking it was time to leave and return to the ship.

I stood to get up but something was very wrong. My legs would not work properly. They kept wobbling and feeling like jelly. Surprisingly the square seemed to be going round and round too! I tried to tell my friends that my legs would not work but my words sounded funny. What was happening to me? I felt really worried but all my friends could do was laugh. Eventually I managed to ask them what was wrong with me and between giggles they explained I was drunk. Drunk? How could that be possible? They were alright, why wasn't I? They put their arms around me and supported me all the way back to the ship explaining on the way that they were used to drinking, I wasn't.

Back on board they put me to bed then went in search of several cups of strong black coffee. Gradually the room stopped spinning, my legs regained their normal control and apart from a thumping head I was not too bad. I vowed I would return to my days of teetotalism and never, ever touch alcohol again!

The following day we went to the Mosel and toured some of the many wine cellars. Not the best venue when one is still suffering the effects of a hangover. The cellars were dark but I had never seen or even realised there were so many different wines all named after a particular type of grape or the region in which it grew. There were huge basins where the grapes were pressed and we were given instruction on how to sample the wines experiencing their smell as well as their taste. I left the practical testing to my friends.

I had enjoyed my first cruise tremendously and wondered if I would ever have the chance to repeat it. It was wonderful seeing new places every day and then returning to the comfort of the ship for the evening. Everything, excluding the hangover, had been perfect and as always at the end of a holiday I felt reluctant to return to the "real world". Although we all promised to keep in touch I knew my military friends could be posted anywhere in the world with little notice and they were not always at liberty to say where they were going.

Back in Rinteln I caught up with what had been happening in the canteen and told Gladys all about my trip. The next day as I was checking the stores I was told a German postman was demanding to see me. I regularly sent money back home to Mother in Holland but the last packet had not arrived so I presumed he had come to explain what had happened to it. I should have known better.

He demanded to know my full name, address and to see my passport saying that it was illegal to send money out of Germany and I could be prosecuted for doing so. He had the last letter, which my mother had not received, as proof of my guilt. Unknown to me, during the war the Germans passed some sort of special light over the outgoing mail and any money was confiscated. Although the war was ended they were still using this practice. Trying desperately to quell my fear, I told him in what I hoped was a very authoritative tone that he was on English military property, that he had no jurisdiction there and that if he did not hand over my letter and leave immediately I would call the English police. He hesitated a moment so I stepped back and shouted "police", even though there was no one there, and the postman thrust the letter into my hand and beat a hasty retreat. Sometimes bluffing is the only way out of situations!

I reported the incident to the Major who suggested that as I was working with the RAF I should send my mail via them and that would eliminate any further problems.

One day we received news that the daughter of General Booth, the founder of the Salvation Army, would be coming to visit us and see for herself the work we were doing. Gladys got in a flap! She insisted we wore our best uniforms, shoes polished until they shone and everything be especially "spick and span". I could not understand what all the fuss was about. To me, this visitor was just another officer in the army, and no matter what our rank we were all human beings so why should one get preferential treatment over another? To this day I still have problems with such things and cannot understand why people make a big fuss over someone they consider to be more important than themselves. I expect that's just me and I know most people do not see things that way.

The visitor arrived and she was charming, friendly and interested to learn all about our work. We showed her around the canteen, the married quarters and told her about the work with the children, our Sunday services and the support we gave to military personnel and their families. She asked me about my life in Holland, about my family and about my work in the refugee camps. She seemed pleased with all she saw and heard and later we received a very good report.

One weekend I went home for Mother's birthday but as I travelled on the military train I began to feel unwell. My throat was very sore and I suspected I may have a temperature. At home I began feeling worse and Mother said I was not fit to travel back to Germany but I insisted. On the return journey I felt really ill. I could barely speak and could not manage to swallow even a cold drink. Fortunately I was met at the station and once back in Rinteln Gladys took one look at me, put me to bed and rang the military hospital requesting a doctor visit as soon as possible. When he came he took one look at my throat and arranged my admittance to hospital immediately.

They had to operate to remove my tonsils but I was so ill I don't think I cared what they did. The next day I was recovering and being given tiny sips of water and an occasional spoonful of ice cream. It was a British military hospital and of course all the staff were English. My understanding of English was by now quite good but there were medical terms that I had never come across before.

The nurses checked my blood pressure and temperature regularly but kept asking me if I had had my "bowels" open. I had no idea what they were talking about. What were "bowels"? When they asked I would look questioningly towards the door.

No, that was not it. The window? No. That was not what they were talking about. The drawer of my locker? Still not right. I understood the word "open" but could not understand what this "bowels" was that they kept asking about. I searched my mind trying to think of all the things I might open! I am not sure who was most frustrated by the lack of communication, myself or the nurses.

Eventually Gladys arrived to visit me and I told her of my dilemma. At first she found it quite embarrassing to try to explain to me but eventually she laughed and I finally understood what my bowels were! I could think of many other ways of asking the question but Gladys told me they were not very lady like or appropriate! Well, how was I to know?

The doctor was amazed when I told him I often had tonsillitis and said my tonsils should have been removed sooner. They had been so severely infected that he had to cut into my throat and stitch it up again. I told him I wondered what the little white bits of "cotton" were at the back of my throat and had tried to pull them off! He shook his head in disbelief and mumbled something about silly Dutch girls.

My annual leave was due and I was not sure if I wanted to spend it in Holland. Gladys was preparing to go home to England and suggested I join her. It was another opportunity to see a different country so I readily agreed. Two relief workers had been assigned to run the canteen whilst we were away so we packed our cases and set off for the long overland journey to England.

Firstly we took the military train to the Hook of Holland, then the boat across to Dover then a train to Liverpool and eventually a train to Southport where we would be staying with Gladys' family. I had worn a white coat for the journey and was dismayed to see that by the time I arrived in Southport it was filthy from the dust and steam of the train journeys. So much for making a good impression.

I really had no idea what England would be like. I had of course heard a lot about it and had read and seen pictures in books and magazines. The white cliffs of Dover were impressive and the countryside seemed lovely and green with lots of cows and sheep grazing in the fields.

On arrival at Southport we were met at the station by Gladys' sister and her two small children, then taken to their house. I was in for a big shock. I suppose I had become accustomed to living in fairly big houses in Germany and was unprepared for the tiny "two up two down" terraced house we were to stay in for the next couple of weeks. I wondered where on earth we would all sleep and thought fleetingly of the bedstees of my young days.

The house had a small living room and kitchen and upstairs were a couple of bedrooms. For our stay, we were to have the children's room whilst they shared with their parents. There was no front garden and only a tiny back yard with an outside toilet. It was not quite what I had expected. However, it may have been a tiny house but the warmth of their welcome was huge.

I enjoyed getting to know Southport, its lovely gardens, lake and sands where we played with the children. I loved the shops and going with the family to the local Salvation Army. We were taken out in their car and visited Blackpool. I had never seen a pier before nor a fairground and even the seaside was a new experience.

Another day we went to Blackburn where Gladys' mother still lived. There was an open air market with stalls selling anything and everything! I wondered past them all amazed to see things I had never even heard of. They were selling pig's trotters, cow heels and some horrible white stuff called tripe. I could not believe my eyes nor the fact that people actually ate those things. Then there were the cheese stalls. In Holland we prided ourselves on our cheeses - Edam, Gouda, Leerdam and Leiden but in England there seemed to be cheeses from every county and they all looked wonderfully appealing. I would have loved to taste and buy them all.

The accent of the Blackburn people was different to anything I had ever heard before and sometimes I had great difficulty understanding what they were saying. I also realised they had a completely different way of saying things for example I did not know what was expected of me when Gladys' mum told me to "put wood in th'ole". Well, how was I to know that meant shut the door? Why didn't these English people speak "proper"

English? It was all very confusing! Still we shared many a laugh as I tried to understand what they were saying.

We returned to Germany for what was to be our last year there. The church we had started had grown in numbers and strength. The children's work was as popular as ever and the families knew they could always rely on us to be there for them in any situation or trouble. Unfortunately Gladys' health was deteriorating and she was able to do less and less. Towards the end of that year more and more of the country was being handed back to the Germans and many of the British troops were being sent elsewhere. The Red Shield decided it was also time to wind up their work and so we were faced with leaving Germany.

Gladys decided to return to England and suggested I seek work there. Once again I had no idea where my path was leading but trusted God to show me the way.

CHAPTER NINE

I had spent five years in Germany and had loved my time there. Although my work in the camps had been very different to that with the RAF both had proved challenging and rewarding. Now, at the age of twenty seven I was to embark on a completely different type of work in a different country. What that work was to be I still had no idea.

Gladys and I packed up all our belongings and said farewell to the many friends we were leaving behind and then we boarded the military train which would take us to London. For a large part of the journey I was lost in thought remembering all the different aspects of my life in Germany and the countless numbers of people who had become so very special to me. I remembered especially those in the refugee camps and wondered not for the first time what had become of them. There had been so much laughter and tears.

Eventually we reached London and then began our train journey up to the North where we would again be staying with Gladys' relations in Southport only this time we would be in their new home, which I was told was much bigger than the previous one.

Once again, I was made most welcome by the family, and soon after settling in I began reading the English papers in search of employment. My attention was caught by an advertisement for Lyons coffee house in London where they required an assistant manager. I wrote to them and was advised of a date for interview and examination. They would also provide overnight accommodation in London.

The interview went well and they seemed impressed by my references, school reports and commendations from the RAF and Red Shield. The examination I was not sure about. There were questions concerning food preparation, storage and hygiene. There were menus to plan according to different specifications. All those I could cope with easily but questions regarding the preparation of jellied eels and Yarmouth bloaters left me totally at a loss. I did not even know what those things were let alone how to prepare them.

I returned to Southport to await the results, feeling sure that I would have failed. However, after about a week, much to my surprise I received a letter stating the position was mine pending receipt of my work permit from the home office. I was very pleased and eagerly awaited the required permit. However, my pleasure was short lived as not long after the authorities wrote saying a work permit could only be granted for me to do either domestic work or nursing.

I stared at the letter in disbelief. Well, one thing was certain. There was no way I was going to do domestic work. I had enough of that at home during my childhood. I would see what was involved in becoming a nurse. Suddenly I remembered at school being asked what I wanted to be when I grew up and my immediate response had been to say "a nurse". It was something I had never thought about at the time and something that I had not thought of since. Maybe God had other ideas. I would pray about it.

I went along to the local labour exchange and enquired about becoming a nurse. The lady dealing with my enquiry asked what kind of nurse I wanted to be. I looked at her as though she was talking Chinese. What did she mean "what kind of nurse?" Surely there was only one kind of nurse? She explained that I could be a children's nurse, an auxiliary nurse, a State Enrolled Nurse or a State Registered Nurse. I looked confusedly at her and said,

"I just want to be a proper nurse."

"That will be a State Registered Nurse then", she replied.

She gave me various leaflets explaining the differences and the length of training required and suggested I go to the local hospital and speak to the matron.

The next day I went along to Southport Infirmary and rang the bell on the door marked Matron. I waited but no one opened the door. I rang the bell again and suddenly a tiny woman appeared asking who had rung her bell. I thought it a stupid question as I was standing in front of the door but I replied that I had rung the bell.

"No one rings my bell. Go around to the back and I'll see

you there."

Not a good beginning. I wondered what I was letting myself in for and thought not for the first time, what a strange lot these English people were. Nevertheless when I went "around the back" she showed me into her room and told me to sit down and explain why I was there. She looked at all my references and questioned me about my family and the work in Germany and then much to my surprise said that assuming I got my work permit I could start in the next PTS (Preliminary Training School) which was due to start in six weeks time.

I was so pleased and really began to look forward to this next stage in my life. Meanwhile, I contacted my old friends Captain and Mrs Ray who were at that time living in Scotland and they kindly invited me to stay with them for a few weeks. The Lord was so good. I was living in England and now I had the chance to go to Scotland too. I was beginning to feel like quite a little globetrotter!

Since I had last seen them the Rays had adopted a lovely little girl and were thoroughly enjoying being a family. Although they were incredibly busy they welcomed me into their home. They worked for the Salvation Army running a men's hostel in Glasgow and I was happy to help them in this. Some of the men had come from good homes, held responsible jobs but then their circumstances changed and they became unable to cope and found themselves homeless and dependent on the hostel. Sometimes to give the Rays a rest I took the baby out in her pram and she was a pleasure to be with.

Despite their busy lives the Rays ensured I got out to admire the scenery of Scotland. It was beautiful. I loved the mountains, the lochs and the wonderful heather clad hills. I went by ferry along the coast and visited some of the tiny islands. It was both peaceful yet exhilarating.

There was just one slight problem being in Glasgow. I had great trouble understanding their particular form of English! The accent was so pronounced. It is perhaps not surprising that people today have trouble placing my own accent. Learning English amongst people from so many different parts of the "English" speaking world has meant I have acquired little bits of their intonations and am now probably something of a "Heinz

115

Fifty Seven Variety".

Back in Southport I was relieved to find my work permit had arrived but I was instructed to report to the police every three months, taking with me a signed letter from Matron confirming my continued employment. The police then stamped a special passport type book allowing me to stay and work in England. Today, I still have that tiny grey book with its first stamp from 1952.

The day of my impending start into the hospital world was gradually drawing closer. I had received confirmation of my place from Matron and instructions regarding where and when I was to report for training. The butterflies in my stomach became more active as the day approached. Part of me was looking forward to it but a greater part of me was terrified at the prospect. I had not felt this nervous when I had crossed the border into Germany for the first time. Perhaps then I had the confidence of youth! I prayed God would help me to do this work well and to do it for Him.

Finally on the appointed day I reported for duty at 7.30 a.m. There were twenty eight of us, many several years younger than me. We were measured and then received our uniforms of light blue dresses with white collar and white edged short sleeves, white caps and belts and white pinafore to be worn over the dress. Black stockings and black shoes completed the ensemble. No trousers or scruffy trainers in those days!

For three months we would be on trial in the PTS and if at the end of that time we proved ourselves competent, suitable and passed the final examination then we would be allowed to commence the three year course leading to the qualification of SRN.

For those first three months we had to live in the nurses quarters where regulations and rules abounded in plenty. Breakfast was at 7.30a.m. followed promptly at 8a.m. by an hours tutorial. Then it was into the hospital working on a variety of wards until the shift ended at 8 p.m. Most of us spent the evenings studying. We had fifteen minute breaks in the morning and afternoon with a further thirty minutes for lunch. The doors of the home were locked at 10 p.m.

All trainee nurses were expected to keep their rooms

spotless and tidy. The Sister Tutor checked each room whilst we ate breakfast and if she found so much as a book or item of clothing left on the floor we would be in trouble. By far the worst offence was if she considered the bed had not been made properly. In such an event she would pull off every item of bedding down to the bare mattress and in morning break we would have to go back and remake it. We dreaded that most of all.

Of course there were always those who flaunted the 10 p.m. rule and would knock on the windows of the ground floor rooms asking their fellow students to get up and open the locked door. Those caught in such behaviour were punished and threatened with expulsion from training if they did it a second time. For once, I abided by the rules and was never tempted to stay out late.

During this time I shared a room with Mary who to my amazement told me she had been a nun in a silent order. My curiosity got the better of me and I just had to ask how she came to be in PTS instead of in her convent! It seemed she had been brought up to be a good catholic and her family were pleased when she decided to become a nun. Unfortunately she chose to be part of a silent order and that was her undoing. She found it so difficult not to speak and often forgot. She was constantly chastised for this. One day she was carrying a pile of plates and somehow managed to drop the lot! Her immediate reaction was not just to speak, but to express her frustration in language not really fitting for a lady, never mind a nun! Mother Superior was not impressed. She was told she was unsuited for life in the convent and told to leave immediately. Her parents were bitterly disappointed but she felt quite relieved and decided to become a nurse where she could help others and comfort and encourage them using her voice. We became firm friends and helped each other through the course.

I found the tutorials difficult. There was so much to learn and the different language was proving troublesome too. Sometimes I could not understand the medical words used and often got them wrong. I thought leaning English was bad enough but now I was faced with so many Latin words too. Another girl, Valerie, who often sat next to me proved to be a good friend helping me with pronunciation and correcting my written English and spelling. Each week we had a test on aspects of nursing, hygiene, medication, anatomy, general health and how to care for patients and show respect to their relatives.

The tutorials on hygiene were "interesting". We talked about refuse collection and how rubbish left unattended was a health risk. Sister asked how often our rubbish was collected and I promptly raised my hand and said,

"Three times a week".

"Dutchie, you live in a different world. Here in England our refuse is collected only once a week"

We learned about "privy middens" - outside toilets where a plank of wood with a hole in it formed the toilet, the excrement going below into a hole in the ground. I never thought England would have such things. I had seen them in Holland but only on farms in the middle of the country.

One day we were taken to the local sewage treatment works. (We did all the nicest things!) I had never seen anything like it and the smell was awful. However, in a corner I spotted some tomato plants growing and asked the man if they were for sale. He laughed and told me they had come from people's stomachs! He further explained that what does not get digested completely comes out "the other end" and finished up there. It put me off tomatoes for ages!

On the wards we were given a variety of tasks but all the time we were gaining valuable experience in learning to relate to the patients and care for them. We were taught how to apply bandages and how to take them off again. We were shown the best way to lift a patient. I was later to realise to my cost that there was a lot of lifting involved in nursing.

One of the most tedious of jobs was learning how to make a bed "properly" and finish with perfect "hospital corners" to the sheets. Sister Tutor would have us doing this again and again until we could all do it to her satisfaction. Another strange thing to me was that in making the beds all the pillow openings had to be facing away from the entrance to the ward. It seemed such a triviality to me but that was the way things had to be. Later I would realise that Matron, a tiny woman but one who ruled with a rod of iron, visited every ward, every morning and checked every bed ensuring that these lessons were put into practice and woe betide any one who had made up a bed differently.

Another thing Matron checked on her daily rounds was the appearance of every nurse. She would reprimand you if your shoes had not been polished, your cap was not on straight, your hair was longer than allowed or not tied back appropriately and it went without saying that no nurse should be wearing make up or nail polish.

She would meticulously check the cleanliness of every ward running her finger around the edge of the windowsill, the curtain rail or under the rim of a locker. Her anger knew no bounds if she found even a speck of dust. Once a week all the beds were moved into the centre of the ward and the cleaners washed and disinfected the whole floor, the backs of beds and lockers. They used long dusters to clean on top of all the curtains and the light fittings and every part of the ward was left spotless.

Matron expected every nurse to know all about the patients on her ward. On her daily rounds she would suddenly ask a passing nurse the details of a certain patient. We were expected to know that patients name, how long they had been in hospital, the reason for their admittance, the doctor in charge of their care and what medication they had been prescribed. Not to know such elementary details was to Matron an admission that we had not taken the time and trouble to get to know those entrusted to our care.

Today I am really saddened as I look at the Health Service of which the British were once so justifiably proud and realise how far we have fallen from those previously high standards.

So began my introduction to nursing. After the tutorial hour we were assigned to a ward and I would like to say everything went according to plan but being me, that was not the case. We were raw recruits at that stage and really could provide the nurses with very little practical help so not surprisingly we were given the most menial and simple tasks to do. However, in my case, even these proved more complicated than I could ever have imagined.

I was sent to my first ward, which had beds for forty patients, eighteen down each side and two private rooms with two beds in each. I reported to the sister and asked what she wanted me to do. She looked at me, obviously not impressed by having a preliminary student assigned to her and curtly told me to go around with the teapot and offer a second cup of tea to the patients. This seemed simple enough. Politely I went from bed to bed asking if they would like another cup of tea and carefully pouring out the hot liquid. Returning to the sister once the job was completed I began to hear murmurings from the patients. All was not well. Being Dutch, I was used to drinking my tea black and had totally forgotten that the English put milk in their tea! I will not repeat what sister said to me.

The next day I went through the same routine on arrival, politely asking the sister what she wanted me to do. Obviously still remembering my tea making of the previous day she snapped at me,

"Oh, go round and ask them if they want cornflakes or bloody porridge".

Please bear in mind that my background in early years was very religious and since then I had been in the Salvation Army. Swearing was not something I was accustomed to especially in English. Trying to avoid any further mishaps I did exactly as told and dutifully went from bed to bed sweetly asking,

"Would you like cornflakes or bloody porridge?"

Sister raised her eyes to heaven but the patients thought it was hilarious.

Day three arrived and sister was obviously wondering what else I could do wrong so rather than let me loose on the patients once again she told me to go into the sluice room, change all the water in the flower vases and arrange any new flowers that had arrived. This was a job I was happy to do and surely being from Holland, a land of flowers, I could not go wrong. How mistaken could I be?

I carefully snipped the ends off the flower stems and rearranged them in their vases of fresh water. Some flowers had arrived from the crematorium, not an unusual occurrence but they were all wired onto an arrangement and the wires had to be painstakingly taken off before the flowers could then be put into vases. I made what I thought was a lovely new arrangement and placed it in pride of place in the centre of the ward table. All seemed well. No comments from sister.

Later in the morning Matron came on her daily ward round. She stopped by the table of flowers, and in a voice which seemed to thunder around the ward she called,

"Who has done these flowers?"

"I have Matron. Is there something wrong? They've got clean water."

"Don't you know you should never put red and white flowers in the same vase? It is a sign of death. Get them changed immediately and do not let me see such a thing ever again."

Sometimes I wondered if I would ever understand the English!

However, I took it all as part of the learning process but then later that week Sister, obviously fed up with having to find simple tasks for me to do told me she had an errand for me. I was to go to one of the other wards and tell the sister I had come for a long stand. I found my way along the maize of corridors to the appropriate ward and as instructed, told the sister I had come for a long stand.

"Stand over there where you won't be in the way"

I waited patiently, watching all the activity of the ward. Ten minutes passed and still no one had brought me the "long stand" I was waiting for. After about twenty minutes I ventured to ask a passing nurse. She smiled and went to fetch the sister.

"Excuse me sister, I've come for a long stand but no one has given it to me yet"

She began laughing and said,

"Well, have you stood long enough?"

It took a minute or two for me to realise I had been set up. Yes, I had certainly had my long stand.

Despite these minor incidents, which at least gave the staff and patients plenty to laugh about, I loved my work on the wards and after that first week began to feel that I was able to become more involved in patient care. Much of the work was of course very basic such as washing the patients, ensuring they were clean and dry and free from bedsores, making beds, serving meals and cleaning out and sterilising bedpans. Of equal importance was really getting to know the patients and taking the time to listen to them, comfort and reassure them. That is

121

something else, which often seems to be neglected in our hospitals today.

Finally my three months in PTS were ended. Our sister tutors and the sisters on the wards had all written reports on our attitudes, ability and suitability and we had one final examination. I waited anxiously to see if I had passed. When the results were announced not only had I passed with excellent marks and reports but I also received a special prize for hygiene. Some of the others wondered how I had done so well in that subject. I told them that in answer to the question about the sterilisation of milk I had written that if masks were put on the cows during milking it would make their milk sterile. There were those who believed me and rumour spread that was how I gained the prize. I had the last laugh after all!

I was now able to begin my three year training to become a qualified State Registered Nurse. I had a real sense that this was what God wanted me to do. Once again I put my future in His hands.

CHAPTER TEN

During the next year I gained experience on a variety of different wards and departments including medical, surgical, casualty and out patients. Sometimes we were on early shift, sometimes a split shift and at other times on the night shift. I soon realised that my favourite was the latter. Working from 8 p.m. to 8 a.m. for fourteen days then with three days off, was a shift that many of the other nurses dreaded, but for me it was a time when I felt especially close to the patients.

There were usually only two nurses on each ward during the night but a sister was always available to help if the need should arise. Throughout the night temperatures and blood pressures still had to be taken, medication sometimes administered, patients turned to make them more comfortable or assistance given to help them walk to the toilet.

It was during the night when patients could not always get to sleep that they would begin to worry, perhaps about an imminent operation or about a situation at home. Many would feel their pain and fears more acutely during the long quiet hours of the night and in these circumstances a friendly and caring word and a sympathetic ear could make all the difference. Knowing I was a Christian, patients would often ask me to pray with them.

One night, part way through my first year, the other nurse had gone on her meal break and I had been given the task of "laying out" an elderly lady who had just died in one of the side rooms. We had learnt how to do this in theory but I had never been in the position to do it in reality.

Gently I washed and dried her then turned her over. Suddenly the "corpse" gave a shuddering sigh. I stifled a scream, panicked and ran to the next ward for the sister.

"The lady you said was dead isn't. She's still breathing."

Sister came at once, examined the lady and said she was definitely dead.

"She can't be. I turned her over and she breathed. I heard

her."

Sister kindly explained that this was quite normal and just the final air escaping from the body. I just wished someone had thought to tell me before I started the procedure.

I was not too keen on nursing the men! Often they were difficult patients and I did not really like all their coughing and spitting nor the shaving of their private parts! Still, as they say, it was all in a days work.

Sometimes a sister's reputation would go before her and other junior nurses would say a particular sister was a real dragon. I would approach such wards in fear and trepidation but invariably found that although they were strict they respected my eagerness to learn and willingness to work hard and I got on well with them all.

I still made mistakes about the language. One day a sister was complaining about a doctor and said something about "the audacity of the man". I asked what "audacity" meant and she told me to look it up in the dictionary I always carried. I looked under "or" but of course could not find the word. Sister told me to look again under "au" and then I understood. These were not isolated events but at least I was expanding my knowledge of the English language.

One of the doctors who took us for weekly lectures would frequently say,

"And for the benefit of our foreign friend I will write the word on the blackboard".

All of this was said in good humour and although my colleagues often laughed at me when I used the wrong words or spelt things phonetically I took it all in my stride and laughed with them. Even today I can still sometimes use the wrong word and set people laughing.

The weeks turned into months and I loved the new challenges and experiences. Twice a week we had lectures each lasting an hour but the rest of the time was spent on the wards. We learned most by actually doing things whether it be lifting patients, assessing and meeting their needs, administering medication or applying dressings. Nothing was considered too menial and all nurses were expected to be very involved in the real care of the patients. To me, this is what nursing is all about.

In the evenings, back in the house I still shared with Gladys and her family, I spent hours reading and learning from my study books. At the weekends I attended the local Salvation Army with the rest of the family and although I gave myself very little free time I was content.

About that time I had got to know one gentleman quite well whilst he had been a patient and after he was discharged he asked if I would accompany him to a Masonic dinner. His wife had recently died and he did not want to go alone. Not really knowing anything about the Masons I agreed to go. We spent a pleasant evening although he was a little surprised I drank only orange juice. After the meal people began to dance. I was happy to watch but my friend had other ideas. Despite my protestations that I had never danced in my life he persuaded me on to the dance floor. I had no idea what I was supposed to do and we probably made a peculiar sight but I gave it a go. Another time he took me to a licensee's dinner and amongst all those publicans I caused a real stir when I asked for a glass of orange juice!

I felt that nursing was my real vocation and loved every aspect of it. In our weekly tutorials I was always pleased to learn new things, how the blood vessels and different organs worked, the effects of different illnesses and accidents and the treatment of a multitude of different problems. We were constantly assessed and had to pass different tests during our training. The results were always posted on the notice board in the staff dining room and thankfully my name was always in the top group.

Results were not the only thing we watched out for in the dining room. There were also the cockroaches! I was horrified to see them. The other nurses took great delight in standing on them and listening to them crack. How could a place that was kept so spotlessly clean be home to cockroaches? I was told it had nothing to do with cleanliness and everything to do with the age of the building and the fact that it was always nice and warm. Years later when I travelled to hot countries I would frequently see cockroaches and often think back to my hospital days.

Every day a report from each ward had to be in Matron's office by 6 p.m. It detailed new admittances, discharges and a note of any particular problems. One day it had been really busy and the Irish Sister in charge had been late sending in the report.

The ward telephone rang and I answered it. It was Matron wanting to know where our daily report was. I said I would ask Sister. The reply was that she had sent "one of the youngsters with it". I duly repeated the reply but was unprepared for the outburst that followed.

"Don't call them that. There is no such thing. They are junior nurses. You had better pull your socks up Nurse Hanenburg."

I looked down just to check I was definitely wearing my black stockings and replied,

"But I don't wear socks on duty Matron."

"Report to my office immediately Nurse."

Mortified and wondering what would happen next I went to her office.

"Are you trying to make fun of me Nurse? I will not tolerate impertinence."

"No Matron. It's just that when you told me to pull my socks up I checked but as you can see I am not wearing socks."

Thankfully she at last understood that this Dutch nurse had not understood the simple English expression and had taken it quite literally. She admonished me to give staff their appropriate title in future.

Despite her insistence on correct protocol and that everything be done to her high standards Matron was a very compassionate woman, something that I was soon to learn at first hand.

I was working a few weeks on one of the women's wards and one of the patients was a lovely farmer's wife. She told me all about the chickens they kept and suggested I come and visit and perhaps help them when I had a free afternoon. I had no idea how I could possibly help but agreed to go and see them.

My new friend explained how they reared the chickens, the types of food they used and the different breeds of chicken. She also explained how they hand washed every egg so it fetched a higher market price. At the end of my visit she gave me a basketful of cracked eggs to take home with me and suggested I come whenever I wanted to and help with egg washing. She said she would be happy to repay me with fresh eggs.

This arrangement worked well and sometimes on my

free afternoon I would cycle over to the farm. We enjoyed chatting together as we washed the eggs and our friendship grew. The following year on a visit back to Holland I took her with me. Mother thought she was great but Father gave her disapproving looks because she wore makeup! Soon after that the farm was struck with fowl pest and they lost their livelihood, had to give up the farm and move away. I missed my visits out to the countryside.

I had now completed my first year as a student nurse and was thrilled to have passed my end of year examinations. Sadly, not all those who began the course with me were successful and some had to leave because they were considered unsuitable or because they themselves had decided nursing was not for them.

I now faced a further two years of study and practical nursing before my final exams but I loved my work so much I was determined to do my very best and gain my qualification. We continued to have just two hours each week in the classroom and we were expected to continue our studies in our own time. The main part of our learning was as always practical and "hands on" as we worked in the different wards and departments. Once again I see the difference in the way training is done today - so much theory but very little actual nursing experience!

I found it easy to get along with most people and although some of the junior nurses were a little in awe of the doctors I found it easy to talk with them. I soon discovered that some of the final year doctors had young families and were often desperate for someone to baby sit and allow them a much deserved and needed night out with their wives. We came to an agreement. I would baby sit for them during the evenings when I was not on duty and in exchange they would allow me to use their study books. This arrangement worked really well and I had access to their medical books, which often gave more detailed information than the ones we nurses used. I promised myself that no matter which shift I was on I would study for at least three hours each day.

Despite this I still managed to have a social life and enjoyed being part of the fellowship in the local Salvation Army where I was a member of their "songsters". Whenever I could I would go out into the country lanes riding my bike and

127

appreciating the fresh air and countryside. I wrote home regularly, kept in touch with various pen friends around the world and enjoyed living and working in the seaside resort of Southport with its lovely promenade and gardens.

In 1953, just after I had finished my first year training Matron called me to her office. I immediately wondered what I had done wrong this time! Instead of her stern voice she kindly told me to sit down and asked if I had heard the news that day. When I told her I had not she told me that one of the dykes had broken in Holland and parts of the country were flooded and many people had drowned. She told me the floods were in the south of the country but if there was any possibility of my family being in trouble she was happy for me to return home immediately. I told her we lived in the north but thanked her for her kindness. She reiterated that if I was worried at any time I should come back and see her and she would help me all she could. I was so touched by her concern.

Some months later I received a call from my father saying Mother had fallen down the stairs and broken her neck. He said I should come home immediately. I went to Matron and explained the situation. Once again she showed me such kindness and told me to go straight home. She promised to keep my position open and help me as much as she could but warned that if I was away a long time my training period may have to be extended.

Some years earlier I had returned home for a visit and wanted to take my mother out and treat her to a nice meal. I was going to draw some money from my post office account to pay for it but Mother told me there was no money left in it. I could not believe it. I had regularly sent money to the account all the time I had been in Germany but it seemed my father had needed money for the shop and had somehow managed to withdraw all the money from my account. I had been furious but his reply had been that as he had paid to bring me up all those years he had a right to my money. Since that time I had never used an account in Holland but now I was thankful that I had a little money saved to pay for this unexpected trip home. I knew that whilst I was away I would not receive any wages and hoped I would have sufficient to meet my needs.

The journey back home was awful. It seemed to take

forever. I kept thinking of my mother and wondering how critical her situation was. Knowing she had broken her neck I felt sure she would be paralysed but to what extent I could only speculate. I wondered if the damage would be permanent or if she would she be left an invalid. I had so many unanswered questions and anxieties but could only pray that God would be with her.

I took the train to Liverpool, then to London and Dover and eventually I was on the ship crossing to the Hook of Holland. After another long train journey I eventually arrived in Amsterdam and went straight to the hospital.

My mother was paralysed all down one side of her body. It seemed she had fallen down the stairs and had called to Jan who was still in the house. He in turn had called for a neighbour and together, they had managed to lift Mother on to the bed. Her legs had felt cold and the neighbour had filled a hot water bottle and placed it along side her leg. The doctor was called and when he examined Mother they discovered the hot water bottle had badly burnt her leg because being paralysed, she had been unable to feel the heat. The doctor called for an ambulance and Mother was taken to the spinal unit of the local hospital.

I stayed with her for a while and tried my best to comfort and encourage her, then eventually made my way home. At that point I had not seen any of my family as none of them had been at the hospital.

I called into Father's shop where he was busy with his customers and apart from acknowledging my presence he continued with his work saying he would see me later. I let myself into the house, tired from my long journey and emotionally drained by the circumstances of my visit. The normally tidy house looked like a bomb had hit it. There were dirty dishes stacked up in the sink and piles and piles of dirty washing. I stood dazed. Why had none of the others kept the place tidy?

I set to work clearing up the mess and waited for the rest of the family to come home. Henk was the first to arrive as he was still at school. Ellie, Leni and Jan arrived home from work and eventually Father returned. Esther was no longer living at home as she was married.

Having given Father some dinner I sat down to talk to

him about Mother and how best we could all help. That however, was apparently not an option. Father said in no uncertain terms that as he was busy in the shop, Henk was still a school boy, Esther was married, Jan, Leni and Ellie all had jobs then it was my duty as the eldest to put the family first, give up my training and stay at home to look after them all.

To this day I am still not sure why I did not just refuse. I suppose all those years as a child when the family needs had always come before my own were hard to shrug off. I remembered only too clearly the arguments when I had wanted to go to the better school and when the elders of the church had wanted me to give up my schooling before I had the chance to take my final exams. In many ways I had been rebellious and yet Father had always had the final word and what he said was the way it was.

Reluctantly I took up the reins of running the household. I kept telling myself it would not be for long. Matron had promised to keep my place open for me and I was determined I would return, take up my training again and qualify as a nurse.

The days turned into weeks, the weeks into months. My life seemed to be an endless round of chores - cooking, cleaning, washing, visiting Mother and being at the "beck and call" of the whole family. When I went shopping for food I had to ask Father for money and he gave me the smallest amount then insisted I show him the receipts for everything I purchased and give back to him any money left over.

I had left England in the late summer and now it was winter. I had no warm clothes with me and no money to buy new ones. I explained the situation to Father and asked him for some money to buy a pair of trousers and a warm jumper. His answer was to slap me across the face!

"You expect money for doing your duty in this house? I kept you until you left school. Paid for your food and clothes. It's your duty to look after this family, that's what you're here for. I'll give you no money for clothes or anything else."

I was heartbroken. Luckily I had a very good friend with whom I had worked in previous years and when I went to see her she helped me out. Her family were very supportive towards me and I do not know how I would have endured that time without them.

Against all the odds Mother was slowly recovering. She came out of hospital but had to return three times a week for physiotherapy. It was quite a distance to the hospital but my friend kindly offered to come with me to help getting Mother on and off the trams.

At home Mother had limited use of her hands and her walking was still very slow and unsteady. She had exercises to do each day to strengthen her limbs and hands and I spent hours doing these with her, encouraging her when she wanted to give up. I had to sleep with her as she needed assistance during the night when she had to go to the bathroom or when she wanted to turn over in bed.

Father still used me as unpaid servant and although Matron was true to her word and kept writing telling me news of the hospital and how my fellow students were getting on I was beginning to wonder how long she would be able to keep my position open for me.

My good friend, Ellie, who had helped take Mother to hospital left to work in Germany and I missed her greatly. Her family were still supportive of me and I spent several evenings at their house playing cards and enjoying their conversation. One evening her brother said he and a couple of friends were going on their motorbikes to visit Ellie in Germany and suggested I go with them.

I told my parents I would be away for the weekend and predictably Father was furious. However, by this time I was so fed up I took no notice of him and went anyway. I had never been on the back of a motorbike and was quite looking forward to it. My anticipation soon turned to fear. We had a tremendous thunderstorm and the rain came down in torrents. The lightning flashed and the thunder roared. We were soaked to the skin and I was terrified!

Amazingly we eventually arrived safely and Ellie welcomed us into her home. The next day a cold wintry sun awakened us and we were able to go out on the bikes and see something of the surroundings. It was good to be back in Germany again. It was a short but fun filled weekend and thankfully the weather was kinder to us as we made our way back to Holland.

The situation at home had not improved. Father was still objectionable and the rest of the family "did their own thing" leaving me to look after the home and Mother. Now, even more than in my childhood I felt totally taken for granted.

Things came to a head one day when Father, in a particularly ugly mood announced that he wanted Mother back in his bed where she belonged. It was the final straw and I snapped.

"Fine. You take her back in your bed. You get up with her in the night. You help her dress and do her exercises. I've put my life on hold for over three months. Now it's your turn. You look after her. I'm going back to England."

There was a stunned silence, unusual for Father, but I think at last he realised how selfish he had been to expect me to give up my life when none of the others had even offered to help. I packed my small suitcase and left the following day.

When I finally arrived back in England it felt good to be back. I was still worried about Mother but knew that as long as I had stayed the family would have continued letting me do everything. I reported to Matron's office hoping against hope that she would still have a position for me. She welcomed me back, asking after my family with genuine concern and confirming that I still had my place on the course. Unfortunately because I had been away for so long, she had no option but to insist I do an extra six months to catch up with all I had missed. It would mean I would not qualify at the same time as the girls I had started out with. I was bitterly disappointed but then told myself I was lucky to still be on the course and I would work even harder to make up for lost time.

Ironically at that time I received a letter from the Home Office saying that I now had permission to stay and work in England indefinitely and I was free to pursue any employment I wished. I thought of all the other jobs that would now be available to me but there was nothing that matched nursing. For me, it was the best job in the world.

I returned to full duties the following week and soon it was as though I had never been away. I caught up with all my old friends and discovered the things they had been learning and which wards they had been on. I resumed my private studies in the evenings and my baby-sitting for the doctors, which enabled me to use their medical books for further knowledge. I was determined to learn as much as possible and be the best nurse I could possibly be.

The three year course involved us nursing on all the different types of wards. Casualty on a Saturday night was an experience never to be forgotten. There would be a steady procession of drunks many of whom had been involved in fights or had just fallen over!

There were also tramps who sought the warmth and compassion of the hospital. These men always had to be given a bath before they were admitted and mostly I was the nurse called upon to administer such a treat. Many of the men had not had a bath or maybe not even a wash for a year. Their nails were as tough as old boots and their hair was usually a tangled mess. I won't even attempt to describe their body odour!

Getting them to take off their clothes was always a challenge. It amazed me how suddenly shy and vulnerable they became at this point. Then they had to be persuaded into the hot water, liberally laced with Dettol. The next procedure was for me to give them a good scrub! Finally they emerged fresh, clean, hair shining and nails cut. Dressed in hospital pyjamas they looked like different people to the bedraggled ones they were before. Many of them had appallingly sore feet, bad chests and awful coughs but it was our job to care for them and provide them with a little love, dignity, comfort and support before they eventually had to return to their often desperate way of life.

In addition to medical, surgical and children's wards we also had to spend time at New Hall Hospital for infectious diseases. Many of the patients had tuberculosis and at that time an important part of their treatment involved getting plenty of fresh air, even if it was cold outside. They would sit out on the balconies for most of the day but if it was raining they would be allowed to stay inside with all the windows wide open. It was so different from the main hospital where it was always nice and warm.

Whilst I was at New Hall there was an outbreak of polio and we had many patients arriving and being put into iron lungs, the only way to enable them to breath. It was heartbreaking to see them, many only young children, paralysed by this cruel disease. I felt being with them and caring for them was a real privilege and felt that was what nursing was all about. It is amazing to think that today polio is virtually unknown in our western society.

I also spent time at the Promenade Hospital, which specialised in orthopaedic and spinal injuries. This was heavy work with the patients requiring a lot of traction and lifting. This was not good for nurses backs and of course in those days there were no hoists to assist us.

Perhaps my least favourite department was theatre. I preferred my patients to be awake and then I felt I could really care for them. I confess also that I did not really like the sight of so much blood. I used to keep telling myself it was just red lemonade! The mind over matter did not quite succeed but it worked well enough for me not to pass out. I hated the sound of cracking bones, the drilling and sawing of joints and the rhythmic sound of the breathing apparatus. It all seemed so sterile, detached and impersonal. I felt it all to be a little robotic and longed for my time in theatre to be over so I could speak with my patients and ask how they were feeling.

Back on one of the wards I was in the kitchen washing dishes. At weekends the maids did not work and so dishes were washed by the nurses. Myself and another nurse were happily chattering whilst working and when one of us began to sing, the other readily joined in. We were having a great time when suddenly Matron's dulcet tones rang out.

"Nurses. What do you think you are doing?"

We nearly dropped the plates in fright.

"I don't mind you being happy in your work and singing but I do not want to hear it in my room and I'm sure the patients would like a quiet rest after their lunch."

I could hardly believe that the three years plus the extra six months had now almost come to an end. I was about to sit my final examinations. These would be taken in several sections. At Southport I would take written and oral exams for qualification by the hospital. To gain the State Registered Nurse Qualification I had to take a further written examination at the Royal Hospital in

Liverpool and then a practical assessment at the Women's Hospital in Liverpool. I had studied long and hard and had worked as best I could. Now I was to see if that diligence had paid off.

The examination days arrived and I faced them with a mixture of trepidation and hope. I knew I could only do my best. The written exams were not too bad, covering subjects such as the liver and spine, which I felt I knew well. The oral exam was more nerve wracking but I felt I coped reasonably well. The practical exam involved a great variety of tasks, some easier than others such as taking blood, making up beds for different types of patient needs, assessing diabetic insulin levels and applying dressings. When they were all finished all I could do was wait patiently during the next few weeks.

Finally, the results were posted up in the canteen. I had passed all of my exams with flying colours. A date was set for the presentation of awards and certificates. A large hall in the hospital building was set aside for the evening and the mayor, local dignitaries and prominent medical personnel were present along with many of our colleagues, fellow nurses and doctors.

Each nurse was called by name and had to climb the steps to the platform where she received her coveted SRN medal and certificate. It was a proud moment in all our lives. There were then special commendations and prizes and I was overcome to learn I had been awarded the special Matron's prize for the best overall nurse and the much sought after gold medal awarded to the nurse with the highest marks.

Amidst great cheering from all my friends I went up on to the stage once again to receive these honours. For perhaps the first time in my life I was speechless. I had battled with a foreign language and in some ways a different culture but my hard work had indeed paid off. It was the proudest moment of my life.

The following day the Sister Tutor came and hugged me. She said she was so proud of everything I had achieved. I was grateful to her but a little part of me wished my family felt the same way and that they too could be sharing in this special time, but that was not to be.

Now I was a fully qualified State Registered Nurse and at the end of the month I had to advise Matron if I wanted to stay in the same hospital as a staff nurse or go elsewhere. I chose to stay and became the staff nurse on the women's surgical ward. Another new era was about to begin.

With my sister
Esther (I'm the
one in the dark
dress)

The Hanenburg Family (about 1942)
Jan, Johanna, Esther, Ellie, Father, Henk, Mother, Leni

Pictured during my time with
the Salvation Army

With refugee children dressed in
their national costumes

With refugee children in their ordinary clothes

Proudly wearing
my nurses
uniform

With John on
our wedding
day - 1962

Admiring the flowers

John with his favourite pipe

Lifeboat drill on my first cruise - 2003

On holiday with Irene - 2005

With my sister Ellie - 2002

Nephew Kees and wife Annelies with
daughters Mirjam and Marjolein

With my brother Henk - 2005

With my brother
Jan - 2003

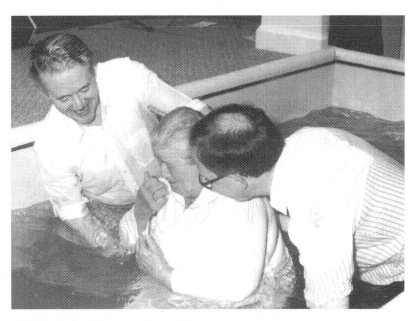

Being baptised by immersion - 1994

Muti Kuzzidem -
February 2001
aged 95

Pictured with
my scooter

Alan and Irene
- 2003

CHAPTER ELEVEN

I soon realised that working as a staff nurse was very different to working as a junior nurse. It was much more a partnership with the sister in the running and organising of the ward and when the sister was off duty or taking her meal break the responsibility for the ward was in my hands.

There was a great deal more paper work and reporting to be done together with the supervising and teaching of the junior nurses. Often there seemed to be a hundred and one things requiring attention at the same time but gradually I became used to the new routines and duties.

Each day I would have a list of those patients going into theatre and I had to ensure they were both mentally and physically prepared. Many needed reassurance both before and after their operations.

The doctors would do their ward round often accompanied by their students and again I had to be available to assist in any examination of the patient and to answer any questions relating to the patient care, how they were coping with their medication, pain levels and what progress they were making.

When test results came back on to the ward they had to be checked and placed in the patient's file but also if there was anything unexpected or if a result had been required urgently I had to ensure the relevant consultant was notified immediately.

I remember one lady in particular who had several lumps on her head, which had been bleeding. The surgeon had removed them but sent samples to the laboratory for further examination. The results came back showing secondary cancer. I telephoned the surgeon who asked if she had complained of pain anywhere else and when I questioned her she said she had suffered "indigestion" from eating irregularly. The surgeon arranged an x-ray, which showed she had stomach cancer not indigestion!

Of course there was also Matron's daily ward round

which often entailed a frantic dash to ensure that everything was as it should be. Between all of these things there were reports to write up, practical instruction and supervision of the junior nurses and cleaning staff, advising the kitchens of special dietary needs, the telephone to answer, the drugs cabinet, sterilisation room and linen cupboards to be checked and restocked as necessary, dressings to change and the general care and observation of the forty patients on the ward.

When patients returned from theatre their progress had to be carefully monitored, as it was in those first few hours after surgery that their condition could suddenly deteriorate. They were often on drips or oxygen and their blood pressure and level of pain medication had to be checked frequently.

Visiting times sometimes meant extra work in arranging flowers or talking to the relatives, explaining procedures and giving reassurance and advice when they were worried about their loved ones.

Many times the shift was technically over but there were still things needed doing or a patient or relative just wanted to ask something or maybe the result of an urgent test was not back and so I stayed later. When I eventually returned home to my room in Gladys' house I was often exhausted but usually felt satisfied with my day and still loved being a nurse and caring for my patients.

I continued to be staff nurse on the women's surgical ward for a year when I knew I could then apply for promotion to sister. However, I had another idea. I felt it was the right thing for me to broaden my training and qualify as a midwife. I went to discuss this with Matron who was not happy for me to leave. She raised many reasons as to why I should not go but eventually realised that I had my heart set on a different path. She said I was a good nurse and she would be sorry to see me leave. She also said she did not think I would enjoy midwifery and told me she would hold open my position for a few days in case I changed my mind.

I scanned the local newspapers and medical journals and saw a vacancy for a trainee midwife at Mill Road hospital in Liverpool. I applied and was accepted for a training programme. I looked forward to learning the skills required in midwifery.

CHAPTER TWELVE

I had two important arrangements to make - somewhere to live and a convenient way to travel to Liverpool. The first problem was easily solved. I agreed to share a flat with two other nurses, one of whom I already knew. The second was not quite so easy. The journey to the hospital was not straightforward and involved taking the train, and two buses. Not the simplest of journeys during daytime but when I was on night duty it would be virtually impossible. In Holland most people ride bicycles or scooters and so I went in search of a reliable scooter. It would be economical to run, required little maintenance and could easily be parked. I loved that first scooter and in fact still owned a similar one until very recently!

I was not familiar with the route into Liverpool and enquired of friends the best way to go. They kept mentioning street names, none of which I knew, so finally, in desperation they wrote out an itinerary which marked all the local public houses and I could easily see them and follow the route. It became quite a joke that I knew all the pubs from Southport to Liverpool!

I loved being at Mill Road. I loved the hospital, the staff and the work. After just a couple of days I telephoned the matron at Southport and told her I would not be returning. In my typical way I wanted to know everything there was to know about delivering babies and I wanted to know it as soon as possible and as thoroughly as possible.

There were tutorials of course, but like my nurse training at Southport, most of the learning was by experience. Both junior doctors and pupil midwives had to watch a certain number of deliveries before they were allowed to be in charge of a patient, firstly under supervision, and then by themselves. When a delivery was imminent a bell would ring and those students available would endeavour to be present at the birth.

I watched in awe the very first delivery I had ever seen. I thought it was the most wonderful moment of my life. To be present when a new life came into the world, to hear its first cry, to watch in fascination as the midwife cut the umbilical cord making that tiny infant a complete and whole new person was to me a tremendous privilege and I was just so thankful to God for allowing me to be a part of that miracle. The wonder of that first delivery never left me throughout all my years as a midwife and each birth filled me anew with the wonder of God's creation and each baby was to me equally precious and special.

At Mill Road all the delivery rooms had the name of the patient on a card outside. All the women were treated as individuals and given equal care, support and understanding. It made no difference what their particular circumstances were, whether they were rich or poor, married or unmarried. Sadly, this was not always the case in every hospital at that time.

My training involved being with a qualified midwife who would take me into a patient's room, go through her medical history and talk me through the developing birth stages.

The first time mums were always more anxious, not knowing what lay ahead of them and it was our job to offer them support and encouragement. At that time it was the rule that all first babies had to be delivered in a hospital but subsequent births could be at home provided the mother's health was good and there were unlikely to be any complications during the birth.

Most of the junior doctors disliked midwifery and only did it because it was part of their course but for me I could not get enough of it. I enjoyed talking to the mums-to-be and sharing their excitement, their hopes and dreams. I listened as they told me what preparations they had made at home, the type of pram they had bought, the names they had chosen and in such a way the bond of trust between patient and midwife became stronger. After all, they were about to entrust to their midwife not only their own life, but also the life and safe delivery of their precious child. I always felt a pang of sorrow for those who for a variety of reasons felt the child they were about to deliver was unwanted but I still gave them all the care and support I could.

In the final minutes before a birth a midwife has to have all her wits about her checking that the baby is facing the right way, in the correct birthing position and the cord is not around its neck. Sometimes at the last minute some of these things have to be rectified. Finally the baby would emerge and I would rub its back. My heart would be beating frantically until I heard that first cry, then I would relax and breathe more easily. Having cut the umbilical cord I would wrap the baby in a towel and place it into its mother's arms. The look on her face was all part of the miracle and another very special moment.

Of course not every story had a happy ending. Sadly there were the tiny premature babies who were whisked away to intensive care with little opportunity for the mother to share those first precious moments. Other babies were born handicapped and for some the birth process proved too much. When these things happened the mothers would rely on their midwife, family and friends to give them all the love, care and support which they so desperately needed at such times.

Our sister tutor was a wonderful Irish lady with a great sense of humour and a real love for her work. She never tired of explaining things to us passing on not just her knowledge but also her considerable amount of practical experience. One such thing I recall was her telling us that if a baby did not cry immediately, do not accept defeat but continue trying to get it to breathe. To this end she suggested a rather unorthodox method, which involved placing the baby in alternate baths of cold then hot water and repeating this process for up to half an hour. We took note but I think many of us were a little sceptical. However, in years to come I would remember her words and when involved in a home delivery with a baby who had not taken its first breath I applied this "technique" for a full twenty minutes and was eventually rewarded with a gusty cry from a then very healthy baby.

During my training I had got to know one of the gynaecologists quite well. He was writing a medical article about the blood supply to the placenta and was hoping that when finished it would help him gain promotion. He often discussed his research with me, knowing how interested I was especially in learning about the causes of premature babies or abnormalities.

One day he told me he had an article in German and another in Dutch, which he believed could be helpful to him, but was unable to translate them into English. I offered to try to translate them for him and spent hours in the central reference library looking up the medical words with which I was unaccustomed and then typing out both documents in English. He was thrilled with my work and even paid me for doing it. He suggested I use his money to buy myself a good set of suitcases, as he knew I always liked visiting other places! To this end he also gave me an introductory letter to take to the largest maternity hospital in Amsterdam where a quite famous Dutch professor would be delighted to show me around. I could hardly believe my good fortune. When I had a weeks leave I went to Holland and spent a wonderful day being taken through the whole hospital, delivery rooms, research laboratories and learning all the different things this eminent professor believed in and was working towards.

Back at Mill Road some weeks later I was approached by another doctor who came from the Baltics. He had an article about facial abnormalities, which he was interested in, but unfortunately he could not read it as it was written in Dutch. I translated that for him and he rewarded me with a medical book which I still have.

I had a very brief "romance" whilst at Mill Road. His name was Noel and I'm not sure why I agreed to go out with him, as he was rather dull. He had a car and we went for drives or walks. I asked him to come to the Salvation Army with me but he said he did not believe in God so I knew there was no future in the relationship. As the weeks went by I was getting more and more bored with his company. He had no life in him, no sense of fun or adventure, no ambition. I told him I did not want to go out with him anymore and thankfully returned to my work and my studies. Who needed boys anyway?

After six months training I was about to sit Part A of the midwifery examinations. As usual, these involved three aspects, written, practical and oral. I passed all three with high grades. Another career decision now needed to be made. With Part A I could either return to general nursing or stay at Mill Road and work on the mother and baby or premature baby wards. Alternatively I could continue training and gain Part B of the qualification, which would enable me to work as a fully qualified, unassisted midwife both in hospitals and on the district. I prayed for God's guidance and spoke to my sister tutor before deciding the next step.

I would continue training. I loved midwifery and wanted the full qualification.

I applied to Ormskirk hospital, which was nearer to Southport, enabling me to live with Gladys and her family once again. I was accepted and told I could begin the following week. With great reluctance and sadness I said farewell to friends and colleagues in Liverpool. It had been a wonderful six months spent there and I had loved every minute of it.

The contrast between the two hospitals could not have been greater. I had loved Mill Road and now I hated Ormskirk. There were only a few delivery rooms and the patients were treated impersonally with just numbers on their doors. When someone needed attention Sister would say,

"Go and see to number three".

It felt like a production line and that the nurses were just expected to get the baby out with no real empathy for the mother. It was a rude awakening.

The journey to the hospital was not ideal either. Although in miles it was probably a little less than going into Liverpool the route consisted mainly of going across country on unlit lanes. Often at night I was afraid and had to constantly remind myself to keep trusting in God. I learned to always carry a spare plug and tools for my scooter as if the plugs got dirty the engine would not start.

I was gaining more experience in the delivery room and got used to checking for problems such as cleft palate, jaundice or unresponsive reactions. However, nothing could have prepared me for one awful delivery.

The sister sent me into one of the delivery rooms telling me the mother would soon be ready for delivery. She told me nothing else. The woman was ready to begin pushing her baby out but seemed very disinterested and unenthusiastic. I tried my best to encourage her, chattering about how soon she would be holding her baby in her arms and all the pain would be over. Still there was no response. I got on with helping her to deliver, still encouraging her as much as I could, asking if she was hoping for a boy or a girl. Eventually, with one final push the "baby" emerged. I stood horrified. I had never seen anything like it before. I looked at the mother and instantly knew she had known all along what the end result would be. The "baby" had died within her womb three months earlier and she had been made to continue the pregnancy and deliver what was then left of her child.

I comforted the mother as best I could and apologised profusely for all my previous insensitive remarks. She was amazed and initially found it hard to believe I had not been told the reality of the situation. I felt so sorry for her. It appeared that she was a staunch Roman Catholic and when she had told the priest the baby had died he had told her a termination even in such circumstances was against the ruling of the church and that she must continue the pregnancy and give birth in the normal way. I could not believe such cruelty was possible.

Next, I went to see the sister and forgetting all my nurse training about respect for seniors I let rip all my fury. How dare she send me into a delivery like that totally unprepared when she had known the circumstances of the case? Why had she not informed me? Why had she let me encourage the poor woman when she knew all along that her baby would not just be still born, always difficult for mothers, but that this particular baby had died three months earlier and now bore little resemblance to what a full term baby should have looked like? My anger knew no bounds. Eventually the sister had the good grace to apologise but it was too little too late. The whole incident served only to confirm my initial feelings towards the hospital. I truly hated the place.

On a lighter note, one of my duties on the wards was to help mothers "express" their milk if they had more than their own babies required. This was then used to bottle feed the babies in the premature unit or to help with feeding other babies in need. I became quite adept at this procedure and gained the nickname of "milk maid".

I began my night duty shifts with the other nurses telling me that the doctors often came in during the shift asking for cups of tea although they had their own staff room just down the corridor. Kitchen supplies were carefully monitored and there was never any surplus so supplying the doctors with drinks meant we were often left short for our own patients. After several nights of making tea for the doctors I thought I would teach them a lesson. Instead of pouring ordinary milk into their cups I used some of the "expressed" baby milk. I had no idea how it would taste in tea but was soon to find out.

The doctors gathered round and took up their cups to drink. Almost simultaneously they spat out their first mouthfuls with various unrepeatable comments. When they asked what on earth I had done with the tea I sweetly told them that as they were using up the patients tea they might as well have the patients milk too! They used their own supplies after that.

Finally and thankfully my three months at Ormskirk came to an end and I was to spend the next three months accompanying a district midwife. I had been warned that some of these midwives had been doing the job for decades and could be a little old fashioned in their views and methods. One such problem was that, at that time, after the delivery of the afterbirth mothers were given an injection to prevent further bleeding. Some of the older midwives had not accepted this procedure, feeling it unnecessary and frequently refused to give the injections. I was given a supply of the syringes and told to keep them in my own bag in case I needed to use them. I wondered with some trepidation where I would be sent to and what the midwife would be like. In some ways my fears were justified.

I was sent to a small place called Penwortham, which is about fifteen miles outside Southport. I went on my scooter but I had to live in the house with the midwife I had been assigned to assist. She was a lot older than me, had been a spinster all her life, was very old fashioned, a staunch Roman Catholic and to me, very nun like! She did not approve of the injection following birth. It looked like being another interesting three months ahead. She had an old Ford car which I felt sure must be the same age as her and was as unreliable as a car can be. It seldom started first time. I wondered on numerous occasions how her patients coped when she repeatedly arrived ages after they had called her. Perhaps the "grapevine" had told them about her car and they rang for her assistance with plenty of time to spare!

However, she was a kindly soul and happily showed me around her area and encouraged me to learn where the various streets were. Our days were filled with antenatal clinics, home visits to new and expectant mums and of course home deliveries, which could occur at any time, day or night. Unlike working in the hospitals where you had a particular shift and worked within those times, on the district you were never really off duty except for one day each week when a midwife from a neighbouring area would cover for you. Many a time during those three months and in the years ahead I would be awakened from sleep, hastily dress, grab my bag and head out into the night to welcome the arrival of another new baby into the world.

One night we received a call to come quickly as the wife was ready to start pushing. Not for the first time I wondered why some women left it so late before calling for us. My colleague told me to go on my scooter and she would follow in her car. I was scared. If she did not arrive in time this would be my first delivery without a more experienced midwife in attendance. I grabbed my bag and headed for the door hoping I would find the appropriate street and everything would go according to plan.

I found the house and ran up the stairs to the bedroom. The mother had everything ready but was about to deliver. I had no time to prepare things or to sterilise instruments in advance I just hoped the boiling water would have done its work by the time I needed them.

Taking a deep breath and encouraging the mother to do the same I set about safely delivering her baby. Everything went smoothly, a healthy baby was soon crying gustily, the cord was clamped and cut, the afterbirth delivered and I administered the anti bleeding injection. I just had time to whisper to the mum not to tell the older midwife about the injection when she came huffing her way upstairs apologising for her lateness because her car had not wanted to start. She questioned me about the delivery and I told her everything had been straightforward with no complications and omitted to mention the injection.

I had done it. My very first unsupervised delivery with no senior midwife in attendance. I was ecstatic and gently gave the baby a cuddle before I left. It was a fantastic moment knowing I had brought him into the world.

Back at the house I wrote up my report and proudly put my name in the space for attending midwife. During the next few weeks I gained more and more experience and learnt to be extra careful that my patients did not require any stitches because only the doctors were allowed to stitch and often they were not very pleased to be called out for this.

On my day off I looked forward to returning to Southport, spending time with my friends in the Salvation Army and generally enjoying being in the town again.

Towards the end of my three months working in Penwortham my senior had arranged to have two weeks holiday and as I was not qualified to work the area unsupervised I was sent to a tiny place called Darwen. It was a little village on the edge of the moors not too far from Blackburn. I enjoyed the views whilst riding my scooter through the countryside but as it was so isolated I speculated that attending night deliveries must be a bit scary.

I was welcomed by the two midwives in charge of the area and showed to my room in their house. They were much younger than I had expected and soon we were laughing and talking like old friends. They told me about their work and the type of people living in the rural area. They warned me not to expect much in the standard of housing as most of the people were quite poor and their accommodation reflected that. After a while they took me out to show me around.

Despite their warnings I was unprepared to find that many of the villages consisted of just a row of perhaps eight or ten terraced cottages with a shed set across the road. Inside this shed was the only toilet that was shared by the whole village and it consisted basically of a wooden bench with a hole cut in it. Below was a septic tank, which was emptied at not too frequent intervals. Many of the cottages had no running water or electricity. Water was collected from a standpipe in the centre of the "village" and light was supplied by gas lamps. All the cooking and heating of water was done in the big old-fashioned black fireplaces, which had ovens set to one side and a place to put a huge kettle. I felt I had stepped back into the middle ages.

Back in the midwife's house they told me a little more of their routine and explained some of the problems associated with living in such an isolated area. Firstly, it would take an ambulance about fifty minutes to reach a patient so if one was needed we had to ensure we allowed for the time both of its

155

arrival and then for them to take the patient back to a hospital. Making that judgement came with experience.

Another consideration was that as the patients were divided over a very large area it was imperative that all our instruments were kept ready at all times. It was no use going to a delivery miles away and part way through realising a piece of equipment had been left behind. There would be no time to return home for it.

They told me about their routine anti natal clinics and the pre and post birth home visits. Finally, after another cup of tea and the assurance that they would knock on my door to wake me if there was a call during the night I went up to bed. My mind was filled with all this new information and I wondered if I would ever have the confidence they appeared to have.

My first delivery was at an isolated house in the middle of nowhere. We were shown inside and told that everything was ready, including water boiling in the kettle on the big black grate. This was used to sterilise our instruments. The only heating was from the fire. Some houses had an additional fire in the bedroom upstairs but those without could be very cold.

Often midwives assess their patients then leave them for an hour, check on other patients then return. In the Darwen area the patients were so isolated and widespread this was not an option. We assessed the progress of the birth and my colleague said there was plenty of time so she would go for a walk for half an hour and left me in charge. I was very aware of how isolated the place was. Most of the "villages" had a public telephone box but of course at that time there were no such things as mobile phones or pagers. I was on my own and hoped my colleagues assessment of timing was correct.

Thankfully the other midwife returned in plenty of time and she allowed me to complete the delivery. Mother and baby were both well.

In the hospital there had been certain procedures undertaken with the afterbirth but out in the district it was a different story. My colleague told me that there was a superstition in the Darwen area that if the afterbirth was put on the fire to burn, the number of times it made a "popping" sound denoted the number of babies the mother would give birth to in the future!

I soon got used to living in the country and visiting the patients in their own homes. Before the birth it was very important to get a detailed medical history of the patient including how many previous pregnancies they may have had, whether there had been any problems or complications in those, and how their general state of health was at the present time. If there had been problems in the past we would not allow them to have a home delivery this time. Some patients objected to this and then I was told that some preferred home delivery because the state paid them £32 whereas the state paid them only £3 for a hospital delivery!

For a home delivery the patient's own doctor had to sign a form stating he was willing to be present at the birth. In reality very few ever actually came. Sometimes a husband would call for an ambulance and the ambulance would in turn call us and even sometimes collect us en route. Generally both doctors and ambulance staff preferred midwives to do the deliveries rather than themselves. That suited us. We felt we had the better training and certainly far more experience.

Some days we might have four or five deliveries and other days there would be none. On such days we would leave a note on the door of the house and tell the local police and ambulance stations that we were going into town for a couple of hours. All the patients knew that this was the system and would contact us accordingly. Life would certainly have been easier if mobile phones had been available.

If we had delivered a baby in the morning we would check on the mother and child again in the evening. If a baby was born during the night we would check on its progress   the following day. We were always available for visits or just advice over the phone should any mother have any worries or concerns.

Unfortunately my two weeks at Darwen soon ended. I had really enjoyed my time in the country and had gained a lot of useful knowledge and valuable experience, which had boosted my confidence. I returned to Penwortham for my remaining few weeks working out on the district, and then went back to Ormskirk for my final examinations, which I again passed with good results. I had now gained both parts of the midwifery qualification and was able to deliver babies either in a hospital or district situation without supervision.

I had loved my three months working out on the district. I felt it provided a real chance to get to know patients right through their pregnancies and to be personally involved in their care and eventual delivery. I felt it provided an opportunity for the building up of trust between patient and midwife in a way that was impossible in the hospital situation, and so I knew with absolute certainty that this was what I wanted to do more than anything else.

I saw an advertisement for a fully qualified midwife for the Litherland area of Liverpool. It sounded ideal so I applied and was called for an interview. I was a little overawed to find the designated place was a huge building in the centre of Liverpool but that feeling was nothing compared to how I felt when I was eventually called into the interview room.

Ahead of me thirteen men sat around a huge big table and they told me to sit at a smaller table placed in front of them. I had expected perhaps three or four people but was totally unprepared for so many. They must have sensed my apprehension and told me to relax and not to look so alarmed!

They asked me about my whole life, not just my nursing career. They wanted to know about my family, life in Holland, what it had been like during the occupation. Why had I gone to work in Germany and what had that work involved? Then I had to explain why I had come to England and what had made me decide to enter nursing. They wanted to know why I had chosen to leave general nursing and specialise in midwifery. They wanted to know if I would be worried living and working on my own and being in charge of a district. I told them I had not been afraid to cross the border into Germany without a permit and not really knowing what lay ahead so I would certainly not be afraid of living and working on my own in England. Finally they questioned me on a whole spectrum of medical issues and suggested various complications I may encounter in being a district midwife, asking how I would deal with such problems.

I answered all their questions as best I could but felt quite exhausted when it was finally over. It was by far the most difficult interview I had ever attended.

I was asked to wait outside the room whilst they discussed my application.

Eventually after what seemed like hours I was called back into the room and to my astonishment and absolute delight I was offered the position of District Midwife in Litherland. I was told my salary, more than I had previously earned, and was informed that a three bedroom house went with the job. I could hardly believe it. They asked if I had any furniture and I told them I had only a single bed and a small chest of drawers but I was sure I would be able to get some second hand furniture from somewhere and friends would help me move. The only stipulation they made was that I was to have some type of desk or bureau that could be locked, so that confidential patient details could be kept secure. They asked what transport I had and laughed when I told them I had a scooter!

I went back to Southport and told Gladys and the family the good news. I had three weeks to get myself sorted out with furniture, curtains, crockery and saucepans before I took up my position but I was so excited I think I would have started right away even without those things.

Everyone in the Salvation Army rallied round to help and many gave me furniture and other necessities. The house itself was part of a terrace designated for the use of police and midwives. There was one other midwife in the house next to mine and the others were occupied by police officers and their families. It was a lovely little house with three bedrooms, a living room, front room, bathroom and kitchen. There was also a long back garden, a garage and a shed. Best of all, it was mine for as long as I worked for Litherland. I had never had a house to myself before and took great delight whenever I put my key in the lock and opened the front door and closed it behind me again. I felt as though I was entering my own private world. It was wonderful.

With the help of friends I made curtains, moved in my newly acquired furniture and began to settle in. I wished I had more of my own personal things like ornaments, pictures and books but most of these I had packed into a large box and left in Holland when I first went to Germany. On my next visit home I went in search of that box only to be told that Father had got rid of it. I was horrified. He told me the church had been collecting paper and ornaments and without even asking me he had given them all my books, personal papers and even worse, the certificates I had gained throughout school, night school and during my time in training with the Salvation Army. I had treasured those so much. They represented all my hard work when I had struggled to study and achieve despite the lack of parental support. I felt everything I had ever worked for had been taken away. I was devastated that he had thought so little of their significance to me that he threw them away. All my photographs had also gone plus a couple of paintings and a small wooden cross I had bought as a child during that wonderful time in Austria. These things had all been so special to me and a reminder of happy times with friends and colleagues. They could never be replaced. I am unsure which emotion was the strongest, anger or loss.

CHAPTER THIRTEEN

I soon settled into my new job and began to familiarise myself with the neighbourhood. The other midwife living next door told me she was a Roman Catholic and suggested that she take the RC's and leave me with the "rest". Amazingly this worked well and we both had a similar number of cases. We had a supervisor based in Preston and she visited periodically to check our work and records but apart from that we were left to manage our district between us. I had one day a week off duty and once a month a free weekend. I also had four weeks holiday each year. On our days off the midwives in the neighbouring area would cover for us and we in turn covered their off duty times.

The people of Liverpool were mainly warm hearted and generous. Many were quite poor but they would share with you what little they had and were always ready to help any one in need. Soon I was getting to know my mums-to-be quite well. The thrill of delivering babies never left me and each time it felt special. I thanked God for the opportunities in life He had given to me.

I was getting to know my way around the area and one day I had been booked to deliver a baby to a mother living in what I thought was just an ordinary terraced house. The delivery went well, mother and baby were fine, I completed the necessary forms and handed them in to the Town Hall. I thought everything was as it should be. A telephone call from a very irate Lord Mayor was soon to shatter that illusion.

"Is that Nurse Hanenburg?"

"Yes. Who's speaking?"

"This is the Lord Mayor of Bootle. What do you think you're doing delivering babies outside your area?"

"I'm sorry, I've no idea what you're talking about."

"You are only supposed to deliver in Litherland not in Bootle."

"I haven't made any deliveries in Bootle."

"Yes you have. I have your report here. You delivered

Mrs. Jones this morning."

"I delivered a Mrs. Jones in Litherland this morning."

There then ensued a long conversation between us with the mayor becoming more and more angry. He was adamant Mrs. Jones lived in Bootle. I was equally adamant she lived in Litherland. He told me she paid her rates to Bootle. I told him I hadn't asked her where she paid her rates! He wanted to know in which room the delivery had taken place and where that bedroom was in relation to the bathroom. I could not believe the absurdity of the man's questions. He went on and on with more seemingly stupid questions and then asked,

"Which council empties her dustbin, Litherland or Bootle?"

I had had enough and answered in no uncertain terms that I was employed to empty wombs not dustbins! I then put down the phone without waiting for his answer.

Not long afterwards the telephone rang again and this time it was from the Medical Officer saying he had received a complaint from the Lord Mayor about my work and asking what it was all about. I told him the saga and he laughed then promised to sort it out for me.

The situation was unbelievable. It seems the particular road where Mrs. Jones lived was divided between the two councils, with the district boundary line running through the centre of the houses on one side of the road. According to some ruling the front half of their houses belonged to Bootle and the back half belonged to Litherland and they paid half their rates to each council. That was why the pompous Lord Mayor had demanded to know in which room the baby had been born. If it had been a room at the back of the house it was considered to be in Bootle but a room in the front of the house was deemed to be in Litherland. I had never heard such a load of rubbish and could not believe such a stupid situation existed. The Medical Officer smoothed things over but I was very wary the next time I delivered a child in that road.

My area was quite large stretching from the well known Johnson's Dye Works right across to Linacre Lane. It included twenty military houses and a newly built estate where the houses all had bathrooms and gardens. These were considered very "posh". There were also a few farms just before the canal that marked the boundary of my area, and visiting those reminded me of my time in Darwen. They were quite isolated.

I clearly remember my first delivery as a newly qualified district midwife. My patient knew I had only just arrived in the area but she had no idea she was to be my first delivery. I had found the house straight away, had checked her notes which showed everything had progressed well throughout the pregnancy and then I carried the bowl of boiling water upstairs ready to sterilise my instruments. The lady already had five boys and they kept coming up the stairs to see if the new baby had arrived. Finally they were rewarded by hearing their baby brother give his first cry. The mother had no idea what to call the child and asked me to suggest a name. I said the first one that came into my head, which was Jan, pronounced in Holland as "Yan". She seemed to like the idea and Jan he became. I finished all the clearing up, checked again that mother and baby were fine then returned home to complete the paper work. I was so proud and if I am honest, a little relieved that all had gone well.

The state provided each mother expecting a home delivery with a sealed box containing essential items such as protective sheeting, towels and cotton wool. These boxes had to be delivered by the attending midwife well in advance of the birth. They were quite sizeable boxes and I could only carry two on my scooter so sometimes the other midwife would take mine in her car if she was going to a house nearby.

Although scooters were more popular in England at that time than perhaps they are today the sight of a midwife arriving on one often caused laughter especially in the children. Sometimes they would play a joke on me and hide my scooter around the corner. They took great delight in seeing me emerge from a house wondering where on earth my scooter had disappeared to. It was all only harmless fun though and there would always be one of the kids around to show me where they had put it - after a suitable period of consternation on my part of course!

Many of the people in Liverpool were quite poor and their houses reflected that. However, what they lacked in material wealth they more than made up for in their generosity of spirit. Most of them were kindly and caring, looking out for each other and helping whenever there was a need. Their sense of humour is legendary and although at first I did not always understand it I soon came to appreciate their quick wittedness and sense of fun even though it was often directed at themselves or even at me! There was a real sense of community, especially amongst those living in the terraced houses and they gladly shared in the ups and downs of each others lives celebrating births and marriages and consoling one another in bereavement. Throughout all my years working amongst them I was to be shown their simple care time and time again.

On many of my visits to homes I would be offered cups of tea, "bacon sarnies", "Connyonny sarnies" chip "butties" and even bowls of "scouse". I needed an interpreter to explain to me what these "foreign" foods were! I knew people from Liverpool were often referred to as "scousers" but I had no idea why. I was soon introduced to the delights of scouse. For those who have no idea - it is made with cheap cuts of lamb, potatoes and lots of root vegetables and onions all cut into small pieces. These ingredients are then put into a large pan together with a small amount of water and seasoning then left to cook slowly and gently on the stove. For families with less money, a cheaper version, minus the meat, was known as "blind scouse".

Some of the houses still had no hot running water or electricity and the toilet was in an outbuilding at the bottom of the yard. To the people living in such places a bathroom was a luxury they could only dream about and yet so often it was these people who had so little who shared what they had with me.

Once, filling in the time awaiting a delivery a mother was telling me about the clothes and bedding for the baby's cot and then for some reason we began discussing sheets. I told her I had only one set, which I washed, ironed and put back on my bed the same day. We continued to chat and I thought no more of the conversation until a couple of days later a parcel was left on my doorstep. Inside was a note saying thanks for a safe delivery and would I please accept these two sets of sheets, which had been made from parachute silk. I never asked where the parachute material came from but was touched by the woman's thoughtfulness.

On another occasion a patient could see that my back was very painful - the result of too many hours leaning over low beds in patient's houses. She asked about it and I told her the doctor had suggested I put a hard piece of wood beneath my mattress but commented that I didn't have anything suitable. Later that day, when I had safely delivered her new daughter, her husband appeared at my house with a wooden door that he had taken off his shed.

"Here, nurse, let me put this under your mattress for you."

I was so grateful. He had not only thought of me but had been prepared to take off one of his own doors just to help me. Their kindness was amazing. I thanked God for sending such people to meet my needs.

In hindsight I think my years spent on the district in Litherland were probably some of the happiest and certainly the most fulfilling of my life. No two days or for that matter, any two nights, were ever the same. Each home and family circumstance was different. Each woman responded to the birth process in different ways. There was always a sense of challenge and unpredictability for no matter how smoothly everything appeared to be going there was always the possibility that something may go wrong at the last minute and I had to be prepared for that. Of course, most deliveries were routine and yet never boring. There was always the thrill of the new arrival, the satisfaction of a job well done and the joy of seeing a tiny baby in its mother's arms for the first time.

Often the unpredictable happened not in medical terms but in other ways. One day I was with a patient in the final stage of labour when she suddenly called out to me,

"Quick nurse. Go downstairs and turn the picture around before my hubby comes home."

I had no idea what she meant. In between gasps and groans she explained that at the foot of the stairs was a picture of King Billy, a symbol of her Protestant belief. Unfortunately her husband was a devout Roman Catholic and in the same frame, but on the other side, was a picture of the Pope. As far as the husband knew the picture had only one side, showing the Pope. It appeared that every day after the husband left for work the

165

wife turned the picture over to show King Billy then turned it around again to show the Pope before the husband returned! The mind boggles at the duplicity of it all. Now, about to give birth, her urgent request was not for pain relief or a hand to clutch, but for the Pope to be facing the right way when her husband came home. I did as requested.

It was not unusual to be made aware of the very strong feelings between the Protestants and Roman Catholics and mainly they all got along well together. At first, I was surprised by the number of times I was asked whether I was a "Proddy" or a Catholic before a woman booked me for her delivery but then I was informed that if a woman or unborn child were at risk during delivery the R.C. ruling was to save the child as a new member of the church, even if it meant allowing the mother to die. I had many R.C. women book me because of this ruling, knowing that in such dire circumstances I would fight to keep the mother alive. She could always have another child. This often caused my R.C. colleague next door to become very annoyed.

Many of the couples had large families, especially those who were Catholic. In one street there was a family with eleven boys. Living opposite was a family with eleven girls. Both mothers longed to have a child of the opposite sex to those she already had and they asked if I had any suggestions to make this happen. I had no idea but joked that perhaps they should swap husbands or beds. Time went by and unbelievably both women were again pregnant, and both expecting around the same time. The woman with boys gave birth to a little girl and the one with all the girls gave birth to a boy. Both families were thrilled. I was pleased for them too, but did not dare to ask if they had followed my advice!

Superstition was a part of life for many of my patients. They would not walk under a ladder, threw salt over their shoulder if they had spilt any, said "red and green should never be seen" and that if you wore green you would then wear black, meaning a funeral! I could not understand it. There was yet another that I often came across. Many would not part with the baby's pram or cot even when they had decided there would be no more children. They said as long as they kept those items in the loft they would not have another baby but if they got rid of them they were sure they would fall pregnant again. I reckoned it took all sorts!

Money was short for many of my patients. I remember one woman telling me her husband earned just six pounds a week working on the docks and out of that they had to pay for rent, fuel, food and clothes for six children.

In one home I visited the seven children looked shabbily dressed and in need of a good meal. The children kept pestering their mother saying that they were hungry and could they have some money but the mother said that until their father came home with his wages she had no money. I noticed a half crown (equivalent to about 12 pence) on the mantelshelf and asked why that could not be used. I was told that was for the priest who came every Friday night to collect money. My sense of injustice welled up and I grabbed the money and told the eldest child to go and buy some fish and chips for them all, including his mother. The poor woman was worried sick and asked what she was going to tell the priest when he came. I told her to tell him what I had done and to add that the midwife thought food in her children's stomachs was more important than money in his church. I also told her to send him to me if he thought differently! Not surprisingly I never heard from him.

Most of the babies I delivered were in their own homes but there were always the odd cases where for one reason or another the baby arrived more quickly than expected and the mum-to-be was caught out. One evening I received a phone call from one of the local publicans saying he had a pregnant woman in the bar standing in a pool of water, shouting out in pain and please would I come quickly. I grabbed my bag, climbed on my scooter and headed off towards the pub.

When I got there it was obvious the woman had been drinking heavily and when she was not yelling with the pain of her contractions she was giggling. No one was sure where she lived and she was too drunk to tell me. I rang for an ambulance but it soon became obvious the baby was not going to wait for that. I managed to move her to a less crowded part of the bar and begged the onlookers to give us some space and privacy whilst telling the landlord to hurry up with the boiling water! The baby was born just as the ambulance arrived. Not the best entry into

167

the world but no doubt a talking point for the future.

Some mothers had made no practical arrangements, either because of financial limitations or because the baby arrived prematurely. Some had no cot so they used a drawer and lined it with a towel. Others had no baby bath so they used the washing up bowl from the kitchen sink. Others had no clothes in which to dress their new arrival.

I had other patients, usually those living in the better areas who had more than enough for their babies and if they were not planning on having other children I would ask them for outgrown baby clothes which I then gave to the poorer mothers. They were always happy to help in this way and so I became a sort of Robin Hood figure - taking from the rich and giving to the poor. It was a system that worked well and really benefited many of the poorer families.

Life on the district was often full of surprises and it never ceased to amaze me the different ways in which people lived their lives but it was not my job to pass judgement, just to support the mothers and deliver their babies.

One such family I remember all too well. The lady was married to a local rag and bone man - for those unfamiliar with the term these men went around the area with their horses   and carts collecting and buying any unwanted items. In exchange for very small amounts of money they would take away anything from clothing to furniture. They would then try to sell these goods in a variety of ways but mainly to the local scrap dealers. The rag and bone man was quite a colourful part of Liverpool life and children would often run out into the streets to see him when they heard his call and the clatter of his horses hooves.

Mary already had six children and was nearing the end of her seventh pregnancy. Her blood pressure was seriously raised and I was concerned about her. I really felt she should be in hospital but she adamantly refused. Constantly I told her to rest more but her answer was always the same. How could she rest with six small children and a husband to care for?

One day I went around to her house to check on her, knowing that the baby was due any time. I knocked on the door but got no answer. I knocked more loudly. Still no answer. I went around to the back but still got no response. I was getting quite worried. Back at the front I banged hard on the door and pushed against it. It began to move slightly. It was unlocked but something was behind it. Fearing the worst, that Mary was perhaps slumped unconscious behind the door I pushed it with all my might. Suddenly there was a loud noise but the door opened enough for me to squeeze through.

Inside the hall I could hardly believe my eyes. Staring at me with doleful eyes was a donkey. He began to bray loudly and I felt like turning and running back out. You do not expect to see a real live donkey in someone's hallway! Keeping my eye on the donkey and on his stamping feet I tried to keep calm and called out for Mary. Her voiced answered that she was on the sofa in the living room. The hall was only narrow and I knew to get to Mary I would have to get past the donkey. If I opened the front door wide he would run off but if I pushed past him in such a confined space he might kick me. Oh the joys of district midwifery!

Breathing a quick prayer I slowly eased my way past uttering, what I hoped were soothing and calming words. I reached Mary and asked what on earth a donkey was doing in her hall.

"Oh, that's Barney. He pulls my husbands cart."

"Yes, but why is he in the hall?"

"Well, you see nurse, the wheel on the cart wasn't right so my hubbys gone to get it fixed. He couldn't leave poor Barney out in the cold so he left him in the hall."

Obvious really!

I examined Mary and knew she ought to be in bed. Her blood pressure was higher than ever and the birth imminent. Her husband had bought a second hand bed and put it in the front room, which Mary now proudly showed to me. The room was empty apart from a single bed in the centre and that had to be seen to be believed. In an endeavour to raise the bed higher from the floor to make it easier for Mary to get on it the enterprising husband had all the corners raised up with a miscellany of items. One corner had several books, another a couple of old tins, the third a pile of wood and the fourth some house bricks.

I got Mary settled into bed and began preparations for the birth hoping the donkey would stay in the hall out of the way. Soon her labour was progressing well but the baby was in distress. Mary still refused to go to hospital or to have a doctor and so I had the oxygen ready for the baby and gas and air ready for mum.

Finally I told Mary to give one last push to deliver her baby and just at that moment the tins holding up one end of the bed collapsed, the books moved and everything including Mary tilted towards the floor. Just to add a little extra excitement there was suddenly the sound of mewing and scurrying from under the half collapsed bed and out from beneath it came a litter of kittens running in every direction!

Shaken, I tried to ignore fallen beds and scurrying kittens and attend to the newly born infant who was not breathing. I gave him oxygen, massaged his chest, rubbed his back and tickled his toes. Nothing seemed to be working. Suddenly there was the sound of loud braying outside the door. I felt I was in the middle of a zoo. The braying became even louder and suddenly the infant took a big breath and let out a loud yell as though he was not about to be outdone by the braying of a mere donkey.

Later, when my work was completed and I had made Mary a cup of tea I left them. They were as comfortable as possible in the circumstances, with the baby in a towel lined drawer, mum in a tilted bed, kittens running everywhere and a donkey in the hall but the new mum was as pleased and proud as any mother I had ever seen.

Occasionally I was called to houses where cleanliness was not a priority. Dirty plates would be piled high in the kitchen or left lying on the floor where dogs and cats would lick the remnants of food from them. The people were still generous of spirit but when offered a cup of tea in such houses I usually managed a reason to decline. If this failed and I was given a drink, I looked around for a pot plant that needed a cup of tea to revive it!

Once, when my supervisor from Preston accompanied me on a delivery that happened to be in such a house, she was appalled. She told me that in future I was to ensure patients houses were clean and that they themselves had clean nightdresses, bedding and clothes for the baby. It was difficult to explain to her that this was the way these people lived and it was not for us to be judgemental and superior. All we could do was offer a safe delivery and encourage them for the sake of their baby to endeavour to make changes in their lifestyles. It was not something we could enforce.

At the other end of the scale were patients living in the "posh" houses. One day I received a call from a very well spoken gentleman requesting I call at his house to speak with him and his wife. The house was privately owned, had a lovely well-kept garden and inside everything was spotlessly clean with decorations and furnishings of a high standard.

The husband told me he had heard I had an excellent reputation as a midwife and therefore he wanted to book me for his wife's delivery but to pay me and accept her as a private patient. I explained to him that I was employed by the N.H.S. and if he wanted private care he should take his wife to one of the private clinics. He told me they already had an eleven year old daughter and as his wife was over forty years of age this pregnancy was unplanned and had come as rather a shock. For these reasons he wanted extra care taken of both his wife and the unborn infant. Part of me could understand what he was saying but a greater part of me was indignant. I told him that to me all my patients were equal. It did not matter what their background, age or economic status was they all received the very best care I could possibly give to them. I outlined how I would be involved in her anti natal, birth and postnatal care and managed to convince them that they had no need to pay for private services. They must have been convinced because they booked me as their midwife.

During the coming months as I kept a check on her progress we became firm friends. I was also able to help their daughter come to terms with the idea she was about to have someone else share her parents affections. Finally I delivered their healthy baby son. The following day I found a note behind my front door saying a parcel had been left for me in the garden shed. It was a thank you from this couple and contained a paraffin heater. It proved to be a very useful and much appreciated present as often when returning from a delivery in the middle of the night the house would be cold but this gave me virtually instant heat.

We continued to be firm friends and I would often call in

for a cup of tea and a chat. She kindly gave me all her outgrown baby clothes to pass onto other mums and we kept in touch for many years. The wife moved back down South following her husbands death and just a few years ago the daughter wrote to me saying she would always remember me. Both she and her brother were married but sadly her mother had recently died. Such friendships with patients have been very special to me.

On Thursday afternoons we held maternity and baby clinics. The gynaecologist on duty with us was well liked by both staff and patients and she always called me "Dutchie." One day Mrs. Dunn came to the clinic. She lived in two houses that had been made into one large one, as she already had twenty two children! Now she was pregnant again. The gynaecologist told me to have a word with her and explain that her health was at risk from repeated pregnancies and that after this latest birth her husband should come to the clinic where he could obtain free contraception. I did as requested but Mrs. Dunn said it was nothing to do with her and I should come to the house and tell her husband. It was not a visit I relished but duty called.

I went to see Mr. Dunn one evening and tried to explain that his wife's health was really at risk by all these pregnancies. He was not impressed. I tried another angle, suggesting that if she should die in childbirth he would be left to look after all these children on his own. That did not seem to bother him either as he said it was no problem - the older ones would look after the younger ones. I explained about the free contraception but his reply was,

"Have you ever been in the bath with your socks on?"

I looked at him blankly wondering what that had to do with anything.

My response that I did not wear socks in the bath only made him fall about in laughter. I had no idea what he was talking about.

Leaving the subject of socks aside I tried to suggest that if they kept producing children they would soon run out of space for them all but he had an answer for that as well. The older ones would leave home and then there would be room for more babies. Nothing I could say seemed to make him realise how unreasonable he was being to his wife and in the end, in absolute frustration I said,

"Mr. Dunn. Don't you think you've done enough?"

He laughed at me and told me to tell the gynaecologist that he would decide when he'd done enough. He failed to attend his wife's confinement and did not even bother to ask the sex of the new child or enquire as to the well being of his wife. He never came for contraception either.

I retold these events to the gynaecologist who was furious but laughed when I told her about his question regarding socks in the bath. This English saying had to be explained to me. It was the first time but not the last that I came across such sayings.

One day I was called to a nearby house where the mother was booked for a hospital delivery. She had left it too late in calling the ambulance and the baby was about to put in an appearance. I grabbed my bag and dashed across the road. The mother looked very weak and on examination the baby felt very small. I listened for the heartbeat and was sure I could hear two. The mother said she had visited the hospital and her doctor for regular checkups and they had never mentioned the possibility of twins. I rang her doctor and asked him to come as doctors were always supposed to be in attendance for multiple births. He said I was wrong, there was only one baby and he was too busy to come!

Back with the mother I was certain she was having twins and yelled for her oldest child to bring extra towels and call the ambulance again telling them to hurry and to bring two incubators with them. The baby arrived, a tiny girl weighing just under two pounds. I could tell there was definitely a second child lying transversely but I succeeded in turning and safely delivering it. Another tiny girl, this one weighing just two pounds six ounces. Their chances of survival were slim but I wrapped them in towels and gave them to the mother to hold. Where was that ambulance? Eventually it arrived and thankfully it carried two incubators as requested. The ambulance men wanted to know why I had delivered twins at home without a doctor being present and I explained the circumstances. They too were angry with the doctor.

The mother did not want to go into hospital but I made her realise that her children needed hospital attention and it was best if she went as well. I waited with her other children until the father returned home and gave him the news that he had not one but two more children. Many months later I saw the mother pushing her babies in their pram. One of them was handicapped. I could not help wondering whether the outcome may have been different if a doctor had realised earlier in her pregnancy that she was carrying twins. I will never know that answer.

Another delivery had a happier ending although it could have been very different. The baby had been born in a lovely home where everything had been carefully prepared for its arrival and the parents were thrilled with the arrival of their third child. There had been no complications and mother and baby were well. However, when I visited again the following day the baby was not feeding properly. He would begin to suck and then would suddenly begin gasping for air. I checked him over but could find nothing physically wrong and so gave him back to his mother to try again. The same thing happened.

I called the doctor and told him to come straight away. He did and we demonstrated what happened when the baby tried to feed but the doctor insisted there was nothing wrong. I insisted there was and said I wanted a specialist from the children's hospital to see the baby immediately. The doctor was not pleased but reluctantly said he would call out a specialist but that it was on my head and my responsibility if there was nothing wrong and I had wasted the consultants time.

The consultant soon arrived, saw how the baby struggled to breathe and feed at the same time and immediately called out an ambulance saying the baby needed an emergency operation to save his life. The ambulance came, complete with incubator and hospital nurse and the baby was whisked away.

Hours later the consultant called me at home to tell me the baby was fine. He had a very rare type of hernia where the bowels and stomach had gone into the lung space. Usually such babies died before there was the chance to operate to save their lives and this was the first time in many years he had been able to show students the problem and how to fix it. He thanked me and said it was because of my insistence that there was a problem that the baby was still alive. Later a huge bunch of flowers and note arrived as a thank you from the parents. A week later their baby returned home and remained fit and healthy. I also received a thank you letter from the Medical Officer who had received a report from the consultant saying my observation and insistence had saved the baby's life. Whilst it was good to receive such notes of appreciation I was just thankful to God that every day He helped and guided me in my work.

I continued to love my work even though it often meant disturbed nights and long hours. I loved the joy of new birth and the adrenalin rush of ensuring nothing went wrong. I thanked God each time a perfectly formed baby arrived well and healthy but prayed also for those who presented with problems, perhaps with misshapen heads, deformed limbs, Spina Bifida or Downs Syndrome. Such children would need all the love they could get and I often prayed with and encouraged mothers who initially found the birth of such babies difficult to accept.

The years passed. It was 1959 and one night, about nine o'clock, I was returning from a delivery when a neighbour came out of her house. She had been waiting and watching for me to come home. She said she had an urgent message for me. It was not about a patient. It was about my mother. She was in hospital and not expected to live long. I was stunned. I had only received a letter from her the previous day.

The neighbour, wife of one of the police officers, had made all the necessary travel arrangements, booking tickets for the trains and ferries. She had even told the other midwife to cover for me. I quickly went into the house, packed a few things and began my journey to Holland wondering what could have possibly happened to my mother.

Once I got on the boat taking me across to Holland tiredness overcame me. It seemed a very long time since I had been asleep and I must have looked as exhausted as I felt because one of the stewards asked if I was alright. I thanked him for his concern and we began chatting and soon I was telling him all about my sudden departure from England. He told me there was an empty cabin I could use and I was so grateful to be able to lie down in privacy and catch a little sleep. Sometimes it is in moments of need that God shows His love through the kindness of others.

The boat arrived at the Hook of Holland and I made my

weary way from Rotterdam to Amsterdam where my brother Henk had arranged to meet me. He took me straight to the hospital explaining on the way that Mother had been in considerable pain for a couple of days and had been diagnosed with kidney stones. At the same time the doctors discovered she had only one kidney, which was malformed. Despite this they operated to remove the stones and she appeared to make a good recovery but the following day she had developed a pulmonary embolism in her lungs. I knew that at that time such a complication could indeed prove fatal.

When we arrived at the hospital all the family were gathered around Mother's bed and she was mumbling about going to Heaven. I crossed the room to her; she raised her head to see me better, said my name and then passed peacefully away. It was as though she had been waiting for my arrival and having seen me for one last time she was ready to leave. I was so shocked.

Many of my patients in Liverpool had a saying "when one leaves another arrives" and in the few days before Mother's funeral those words would come to my mind. One afternoon someone came banging on our door asking for me to go to a friends house further up the street as she was about to give birth and the midwife had not arrived. I ran down the street and found my friend on her bed crying out in pain and begging me to help her. I had no instruments with me but obviously she needed help right away and the baby was not going to wait. I called for boiling water, string and scissors. Thankfully there were no complications and five minutes later I delivered a beautiful baby girl. Using the scissors and string which I had sterilised in the boiling water, I cut and tied the cord and had just finished clearing up when the official midwife arrived. I never cease to be amazed by how "God moves in mysterious ways His wonders to perform". I was once again in the right place at the right time.

Back once again in Liverpool my work kept me as busy as always. Today we often read of babies born with drug problems as their mothers have been drug addicts during their pregnancy. Life has not changed so much since my midwifery days only then alcohol was the problem.

I was booked to attend a Spanish lady who lived in a

particularly poor part of the city amidst some gipsies. My colleague had told me that this woman always got drunk prior to her deliveries and so I had repeatedly asked her not to drink when she suspected she might be going into labour but her response was that she needed plenty of brandy to dull the pain. I told her I could give her something to lessen the pain and she agreed to try this time.

When the call came to attend her delivery I was half expecting to find her a little "merry" but instead she was "blind" drunk. She could barely hold a conversation and trying to make her understand when to push and when to wait was virtually impossible. Despite her lack of effort I somehow managed to get the baby delivered but there was no response from her. She was alive and breathing normally but no matter what I did she would not cry. I tried every trick I knew but the baby lay motionless. Eventually I told the mother how concerned I was but she just giggled and said all her babies were like that for the first couple of days.

Over the next couple of days whenever I visited I tried in vain to rouse the baby and get her to feed but she was completely "dopey" and unresponsive. There was nothing obviously wrong with her and I had discussed the case with my colleague who said it was normal for this woman's children. It seems the poor baby was just very drunk. Completely hung over! I had never seen anything like it before. Sure enough, after three days the baby opened her eyes, began crying and took to her feed with enthusiasm. I tried to make the mother realise this was not a good start to her baby's life but she was adamant that a couple of bottles of brandy was the best painkiller in the world and it did the babies no harm. In fact, she thought it was great as it kept them quiet for a few days, which in turn gave her time to sober up!

I tried to encourage her to use contraception and so avoid further drunken babies making an appearance into the world and she agreed that if I gave her free condoms she would get her "fella" to use them. All seemed to be going well until about two years later when she came to the clinic asking me to be her midwife once again. I asked how she had become pregnant when she was supposed to be using contraception.

177

"Oh, well, you see nurse, it wasn't his fault. The condom burst."

"Stupid man. He must have used the wrong size."

She looked at me strangely and the gynaecologist smiled and said she would speak with me after the clinic was finished.

I wondered what I had said or done wrong and later when the gynaecologist explained that condoms were all the same size I felt quite embarrassed. Well, how was I to know?

Word spread and for months afterwards if condoms were ever mentioned someone would say,

"Ask Dutchie - she knows all about them."

CHAPTER FOURTEEN

One day The Medical Officer telephoned me and said he thought I should consider buying a car. It was a fact that occasionally the children would steal things from the carriers on my scooter but his main concern was for my safety especially in the winter and during night deliveries. I explained that I never felt at risk but he was adamant that for safety and security I should use a car.

I began looking around the garages and eventually found a second hand Ford Popular. All I had to do was take some driving lessons and pass my test! At first I did not like driving a car. It seemed so big and wide compared to my scooter and I soon found I was not as good as I thought I was at judging spaces. The first time I drove it through my garden gates to put it in the garage I managed to knock the gatepost down!

However, my driving did improve and I passed my test. I never felt completely confident or comfortable in the Ford and as soon as I could afford it I changed it for a new Austin A40, which I loved. That little car was to serve me well and not long after I passed my test I took it abroad. Friends thought I was mad to attempt such a long journey when I had so little experience but I have never been one to be thwarted by a challenge.

Gladys and I set off on our journey driving first through Holland, then along the Rhine in Germany and eventually into Austria where I had spent that wonderful childhood holiday during the war. I managed to locate the hotel I had stayed at and unbelievably the same lady still lived there. Of course she had retired by that time but her nephew, the one who had showed me my first cinema film, was now in charge. I went inside, looking all around me. Very little had changed. The same beautiful marble staircase was before me and I just had to ask if I could go into room fourteen, "my bedroom." I went to the window and looked out towards the mountains and a host of memories came flooding back. I think it will forever be a very special place to me.

We continued our journey and headed up on to the

mountain passes. The scenery was spectacular. I felt quite confident with the steep inclines and the hairpin bends but admit to feeling a little anxious when we were driving on the outside edge of the road with sheer ravines just feet away. Soon the light began to fade and evening was approaching. I felt sure I was on the wrong road but there no sign posts to show us the way. It became darker and as we headed down yet another mountain road I was beginning to become a little scared and told Gladys we would stop at the first hotel or guest house we came to.

Thankfully we did not have long to wait and pulled into a small Bed and Breakfast establishment where we were made most welcome. Over a light meal I explained our travel plans and was told that instead of still being in Austria we had somehow managed to cross the border and we were in fact in Italy! I had not seen a border crossing and was somewhat perplexed to know how I had managed to cross into another country totally unawares.

The next day we retraced our route. We had travelled over one more mountain than we should have done. We crossed back into Austria and resumed our travels. Partly to save time and partly to give me a rest from driving we decided to put the car on a train and go to Bologne. Unfortunately about one hundred kilometres from our destination the train stopped and everyone was ordered to get off. The train had developed a fault and so we had to get back in the car and drive the rest of the way. From Bologne we took the boat across to England and then faced the long journey back up to the North. When we finally arrived back in Southport I felt very, very tired but it had been a wonderful experience and we had seen some spectacular scenery.

Time passed and I was still enjoying my midwifery but had noticed a strain on my back from lifting patients and bending over their low beds. One day my local doctor saw me and commented on the fact that she did not think I was walking properly. She told me to go to the hospital for a check up and x-ray. I was unprepared for the hospital results, which showed I had a slipped disc. The doctor wanted to admit me immediately but when I explained that I had women booked for deliveries he told me to go home, make arrangements with the Medical Officer and return the following day.

I was admitted and put on traction with the hope that my back would stretch and the disc would repair itself. It was not a pleasant experience. After a while the doctors considered the treatment was not working and increased the weights from twenty pounds to forty! Lying immobile in a hospital bed for three months was not my idea of living. I missed my work terribly. I was lonely and very, very bored. Listening to the radio or reading a book are not so bad for a short time but day after day for three months became unbearable.

During my stay in hospital my brother, Jan and sister Leni arrived unexpectedly. They had been surprised to learn that their elder sister was in hospital for such a long time, and had come to see for themselves what the problem was. They were unimpressed with the treatment but at least their daily visits for the next couple of weeks cheered me up.

After three months I was allowed to go home but had to have regular physiotherapy. Although I think my walking had improved I generally felt worse than when I had first gone into hospital. After a while longer I was at last deemed fit to return to work. I could hardly wait. Little did I know at that time that this problem with my back would be recurring and would eventually lead to me having to give up the job which meant the world to me.

Time sped by and once again I became immersed in my work, loving the challenges and unexpected events that made each day interesting. Some days were quieter than others but there is one night that I will never forget. I began to think at one point that someone above was either testing me to my limits or having a jolly good laugh at my expense.

It was customary for midwives to leave a note on the outside of our doors saying where we could be reached in case of emergency. About 2 a.m. one morning I was attending a delivery when an anxious husband came knocking on the door saying his wife needed me immediately. Fortunately I had just completed the delivery, so telling the mother I would be back soon I hurried across the road to mother number two.

It was just as well I had been nearby for ten minutes later her baby arrived. I was just washing him when there was a loud knocking on the door. I was worried that something had gone wrong in the first house, but no, this was yet another husband living in the same street whose wife was again about to deliver. I could hardly believe it but had no time to ponder the odds of this happening again, and placing the newly washed baby in a clean towel, I gave him to the mother saying I would return as soon as possible.

I dashed into house number three and within a short time I was again bringing a new baby into the world. Having completed my work there and ensured mother and baby were well and settled I raced back to houses number one and two to check on them.

It had been quite a night. I had never delivered three babies in such quick succession and all in the same road. I wondered what they had all been up to nine months before and if perhaps they had all been to a party and got drunk! I sterilised my instruments, repacked my bag, made a cup of tea and went to bed. I felt so tired. I must have been asleep for perhaps fifteen or twenty minutes when the phone wakened me. Surely this could not be another delivery. It must be one of the three mothers wanting some reassurance. I picked up the phone to hear a frantic husband saying his wife was in labour and could not stand the pain any longer. Please would I come? I told him I would be there in a few minutes.

Once again, I grabbed my bag, started up the car and went to my fourth delivery of the night, which was in the street next to the other three. A baby girl soon announced her arrival. Not surprisingly, it was daytime when I returned home but at least all four babies and their mothers were healthy. I'm not sure the same could be said for their midwife who was totally exhausted.

The remainder of that week was also hectic as each new mother was visited twice a day for the first few days to advise and help with feeding, bathing and general care. Of course all the mothers knew the events of that night and they all laughed about how I had dashed backwards and forwards between them all. One nice outcome was that all four mothers and their children became good friends. I dearly loved my work but one thing was certain - I never wanted to have another night like that one, ever again!

That year I took Gladys and another family with me on holiday to Holland and Germany. The six of us travelled in two cars and we became quite adept at following closely behind each other. At first, we stayed at the home of Leni in Holland and then we travelled to Germany where my sister Esther had invited us to use her house whilst she herself was away on holiday. The house in Germany was lovely and everywhere we looked we saw expensive furniture, pictures and ornaments. In the kitchen her crockery also looked to be expensive and I was afraid to use it in case one of us broke something. I suggested that we bring in our picnic cloth and the beakers and plates we used when travelling and my friends agreed this was a good idea.

We spent a lovely holiday in the area discovering new and interesting places to visit. We were very impressed with the autobahn. At the beginning were signs that stated that if you drove at the recommended fifty kilometres per hour, all the traffic lights would be on green and you would not have to stop. We put it to the test and it worked perfectly. What a good idea! One night towards the end of the holiday I heard a noise downstairs and went down to investigate. My sister Esther and her husband had returned early from their holiday. I was obviously surprised to see them but even more surprised by the angry words she hurled at me for using our picnic things. I tried to explain that we had been afraid of breaking her beautiful crockery but she took no notice and told me how insulted she felt! Sometimes in life it feels you just cannot do right for doing wrong!

Despite this, my sister welcomed us all properly the following morning, entertained us during the day and made us a lovely meal that evening, using all her best crockery of course. The next day she insisted she take us all out to the American Club for a meal. I had no idea what such a place would be like but Esther explained that you paid one fixed price on entry and then you could eat as much as you wanted. I had never seen so much different food displayed at any one time. There was everything you could possibly imagine, from salads, soups, hot and cold main courses to mouth-watering desserts. Many of the things I had never seen before, one of which was caviar. I had heard of this and knew it was very expensive but I never for one moment thought I would ever have the opportunity to taste it. I was spoilt for choice but determined to try as much as I could, especially those things that were new to me. I have to say, I enjoyed the taste of the caviar but did not think it was worth the money!

The following day we set off on our return journey to England. We had enjoyed another wonderful holiday, seen many different places and I had been able to spend a brief time with two of my sisters and their families. The Lord was good and I thanked Him for these opportunities.

Back home I was booked to care for a lady during her second pregnancy. Two years earlier I had delivered her daughter and she also cared for the daughter of her brother whose own wife had died in childbirth some years earlier. I now went on a routine visit to this mother and on examining her I felt certain she was expecting twins. Once again her doctor thought it would be only a single birth. Sometimes I despaired of those doctors! I tried to persuade the mother to have a hospital delivery but she still believed the doctor was right and was adamant that she wanted to stay at home but said her sisters would be around to help. I had met both her brother and sisters on my visits to the house and they assured me they would all rally round.

The first baby was delivered but was having trouble breathing. The second kept changing position and was proving difficult to deliver. I needed to be giving the first twin oxygen whilst attending to the mother and trying to deliver the second twin. What I really needed was at least another pair of hands! I told the brother to call for the doctor and tell him to come immediately.

The doctor arrived and I asked him to deliver the second twin but he could not get it in the right position. Handing him the oxygen and the first baby and praying for God's help I managed with great difficulty to turn the baby and deliver him safely. He too needed oxygen. We spent a tense half hour but eventually the babies stabilised and I told the doctor the mother needed stitches. He looked at me and asked if that was necessary. I think the glare I gave him said it was! I was furious with him! When were doctors going to realise that in matters of childbirth midwives had far more knowledge and experience than they did even though the rules still said doctors must be in attendance for multiple births or complications. If he had believed me when I said she was having twins and had been there from the onset of labour much of the stress caused to both mother and babies could have been avoided.

I continued my visits to the mother and often her brother, John, was there visiting his little girl. He had thanked me for taking such good care of his sister and explained how anxious he had been. Apparently, his wife had been born with a heart problem and was advised against having children. However, once she was married she really began to long for a child and had visited her doctor to ask his opinion. The doctor told her that as long as she took plenty of rest he thought it would be safe to go ahead with a pregnancy. Sadly, during the hospital delivery the strain on her heart had been too much and although John's daughter had been born safely his wife had died the same day.

Unable to care for the child on his own his sister had decided it would be best if she cared for her and brought her up as one of her own children, with John visiting regularly. He was not particularly happy with the idea but felt at the time it was the only solution. We then chatted about things in general and suddenly he asked if he could take me out. He said he was so grateful that his sister and the twins were alive and taking me out was his way of saying thank you.

I thought for a moment and told him that if he would come to the Salvation Army on Sunday I would go to the pictures with him on my free night the following week. I never expected him to agree but much to my surprise he did and he actually enjoyed the service! I didn't know then that this man would eventually become my husband!

We began seeing each other quite often. He came with me each week to church and if I went to Southport to see Gladys and the family on my day off he would travel to Southport in the evening and we would go for a walk or drive the car on to the beach and sit talking. I remember the first time we went on the beach I had made up my mind that if he "made a pass at me" I would give him a kick but he behaved like a perfect gentleman.

I had heard quite a lot of stories from my patients about the way their men treated them and there was no way I was going to be like them. Some were used just as glorified servants with the men expecting meals on the table when it suited them but equally they may just not bother turning up for a prepared meal and go to the pub with their friends instead. Others were frequently used as a punch bag when their husbands returned home drunk. I had also heard "bedroom" stories, which quite frankly scared me rigid. I vowed if any man tried to do some of those things to me his "manly equipment" would be out of action for quite a long time.

I think the two best things about my relationship with John was the way we could talk and laugh about everything. He worked on the docks taking goods in small boats from the main ships to smaller piers and docks within the huge dockland complex. He worked hard and had never had a day off sick. He often told me about the day to day happenings and the different cargoes they had been unloading. He was popular with the other men and shared that very special and unique brand of Liverpool humour. Often he would have me laughing until my sides were fit to burst as he recounted events of the day and the things people had said.

We shared a love of quiz programmes and crosswords and in the years to come spent many contented evenings discovering which of us could answer the most questions or finish a crossword first.

There was one big difference between us. I loved to travel and explore. At that time John had seldom been out of Liverpool and then not much further than thirty miles away. I began telling him about the places I had visited and the other countries I had been privileged to see and I promised that one day we would see those places together.

Soon he began coming around to my house on the strict understanding that if I was called out he would have to leave and there was definitely to be no staying overnight! One day we were discussing our lives in general and I knew things were getting serious between us so there was one thing he had to know. I told him I would not give up the job I loved and become a stay at home housewife. John understood completely how much my work meant to me and agreed without hesitation.

I suppose it was inevitable that some of my patients would get to know that I was seeing John and it was not long before people began telling me to be careful and not get too involved. Others were more specific and said that he had already buried two wives and being the superstitious kind, they were afraid I was about to become the third.

I asked John about it and he explained that he had married early and his first wife had been just eighteen. Sadly she contracted tuberculosis and died. He was alone for ten years before his second marriage to his daughter's mother who I knew had suffered with a heart complaint and had died giving birth to Carol. I felt he had suffered enough and deserved another chance at happiness.

We continued to see more of each other. Gladys and her family thought John was a good man and that we were well suited. He had been prepared to come regularly to church and because he knew I did not drink he had even stopped going to the pub at Sunday lunchtime with his brothers-in-law and friends.

Eventually John asked me to marry him and I agreed. We went out and bought a ring and became engaged in November 1961. I can't in all honesty say I felt madly excited and "in love". I thought kissing and cuddling were a bit of a waste of time and preferred talking! I was thirty five years of age and I don't think romance was something I had ever really known. We had a good, solid relationship, enjoyed each other's company, loved and cared for each other and that was enough for us both.

John was a good father to Carol, going every night after work and spending time with her. I too had grown to love her and we discussed and agreed that we both wanted Carol to live with us when we were married. That however, was to prove more difficult than we could ever have imagined.

People soon began asking when the wedding was going to be. I hadn't really given it much thought as I was still engrossed in my work but gradually we began making plans. My friend Gladys was still a Salvation Army Officer and so I asked her to conduct the wedding. It was to be a quiet affair. It was too expensive for my family in Holland to come over and stay so there would just be John's family and a few friends. We would have a meal in a small hotel and as I had only the weekend off duty it would have to be a very short honeymoon - just one night - in Blackpool!

I had never been to a wedding in England and was unprepared for some of the customs. My friends asked who was giving me away? I didn't know what they were talking about but I told them I was quite capable of giving myself away. That obviously was not the "done" thing. Gladys' brother stepped in to fill the role. Then apparently there had to be a best man. Why? What was so special about some man that he was called "best"? Stag and Hen nights were also beyond my comprehension. What strange ways the English had!

It seems tradition also said that I should wear a long white dress and a veil. By then I had given up trying to understand and just went along with what everyone told me. Trying to find a dress to fit my short, round figure proved impossible and I had to have one specially made. The cost appalled me and I thought it was a waste of money. What did it matter what I wore? Nevertheless I got the dress and must admit I felt good in it.

The third of March 1962 - the day of my wedding - soon arrived and I left Gladys' house with Carol as my bridesmaid. One of my patients said I was always smiling but on my wedding day I should try to look more serious. I could not understand why I should look serious when I was about to marry the man I loved so I smiled as usual.

When we got to the church I was amazed. Many of my patients from Litherland had come to see their midwife married. There was a huge line of prams and more children than you could possibly imagine. It was not so much a guard of honour as a whole platoon! I was deeply touched by their kindness and affection. They had made quite a long journey by bus and train to offer their best wishes and I was so pleased to see them.

The service was simple and sincere with two of my Salvation Army friends singing a beautiful hymn. Many of the people there were surprised to see a woman minister but they enjoyed her message. A brother-in-law of John was his best man and had been entrusted with the ring. Unfortunately he missed the train and did not arrive in time for the wedding. I had planned to use my mother's wedding ring as my own and as the appropriate time in the service drew near the best man had still not arrived. Turning to a friend behind us I whispered my dilemma. Without hesitation he took off his own ring and passed it to John. Not the best start to married life!

When the service was over and we had signed the register we made our way outside where all the mothers and children were cheering loudly. One little boy whom I had delivered, shyly came forward with a little basket of flowers and said,

"That's for you 'cos you got married".

It didn't happen often, but for a moment, I was speechless!

We arrived at the hotel for the reception; just a small number of family and close friends and some of them were not impressed by the fact that there was to be no alcohol or smoking. John and I sat at the head of the table and we had soup to start followed by roast chicken. I looked down at my plate then at John's. He had been given a big chicken leg and I had been given the chicken breast. To this day I prefer the leg and so without hesitation I swapped plates. A moment later a waiter profusely apologised and began changing them back again. I explained I had changed them because of my preference and he looked at me as though I were completely mad. English etiquette has never been one of my strong points!

We left our friends on the Saturday night and went to Blackpool. We were booked into a small hotel just for one night. The following morning at breakfast other guests began wishing us well and telling us to enjoy our honeymoon. We had no idea how they knew until one of them said we had left confetti in the bathroom! We were both red with embarrassment. We spent most of that day looking around Blackpool and walking along the sea front then we made our way to Preston where the friends who had sung at the wedding had invited us for a meal prior to the evening service. After that we made our way back to Litherland ready for work the following day.

When we had told John's sister that we wanted Carol to live with us there had been a lot of family opposition. Carol was happy to move but his sister was reluctant to let her go. This was understandable as she had cared for her since the day she was born and Carol was now seven. Eventually, but not without ill feeling, she came to us. The day after the wedding we went to collect her and I asked her what she had done with my bouquet, which I had given to her. She told me her aunt had taken her to a place with big stones and told her to leave it there. This proved to be her mother's grave, a place she had never been taken to before. I felt hurt that the aunt had chosen to take her there at that point and to put my wedding bouquet there.

The midwives house had been made ready for John and Carol to join me. We had moved the single bed into a freshly decorated room for Carol and bought a new double bed for John and I. Carol brought bits and pieces, which were important to her, and John just brought a clock, which was special to him. I had made arrangements for Carol to attend the local school, which was just across the road, and for a friend to collect her from school if I should be out on a delivery. That first evening when we were all together I thanked God for the new life about to start. John was happy to pray with me if I said the words and this proved the pattern for a long time.

I bought new clothes for both Carol and John and when we visited his sister, Carol proudly twirled around showing off her new dress. She had settled in well at the new school, made lots of friends and got on really well with the friend and her children who looked after her if John and I were out at work.

John and I enjoyed being married. He was good company, caring and kind. We laughed a lot and talked together for hours. We enjoyed reading and often discussed different books as well as the news of the day. We enjoyed going out into the countryside for a drive and gradually John began to see new places. As both of us were working we shared the household jobs especially meal preparation and cooking. If I was out on a delivery he would always have the meal ready or a cup of tea to welcome me back depending on the time.

John was a hard worker and would never stay off sick. Once he had the flu but was adamant he was still going to work. He was really weak and on the way to work he collapsed and fell off his bike. Fortunately he was not badly hurt but it taught him to take a little more care of himself. Soon after that incident I began to teach him to drive the car and when he passed his test first time Carol and I were so proud of him.

A few months after the wedding we agreed to let Carol stay at her aunts for a few days. It seemed an ideal time to take a "proper" honeymoon and so we went to Holland. We stayed with my sister Leni and all the family visited us, including my father, with his new lady friend! The family all liked John and wished us every happiness. For all the years I had lived in Holland I had never once been to see the famous tulip fields or to Keukenhof Gardens where the spring bulbs were displayed in all their glory. Now John and I were able to go and we had a wonderful day there. The mass of colours was truly spectacular. John loved being in Holland. It was a whole new world to him. Little did we know at that time that one day we would be forced to leave Liverpool where we were so happy and return to Holland to live.

CHAPTER FIFTEEN

We were happy in our life together and Carol proved to be a bright and intelligent child doing well in her school lessons and enjoying going out with us in the car to different places when I had a weekend off duty. Once we took her and a cousin to Butlins in Pwhelli, North Wales and although it was not really my choice for a holiday the girls thoroughly enjoyed all the activities and entertainment on offer.

I still had periods when my back became unbearably painful and once I had to spend two weeks lying flat in bed. Not the prescribed treatment these days but quite normal at that time. During those weeks the kind-hearted Liverpool people rallied around and visited me. Although John was a good cook they often brought meals for us to save him cooking when he came home. Many of these people had been my patients and once again I thanked God for placing me amongst them.

Having more or less recovered I returned to work and one night received a phone call from a distraught mother whose sixteen year old daughter was about to give birth and she hadn't even known she was pregnant. I told the mother to ring for the doctor asking him to attend, as the girl was so young. The doctor was flabbergasted. The girl had been going to see him regularly because she was concerned she was gaining weight and in all that time he had never considered the possibility that she may be pregnant. When I heard that, it was my turn to be flabbergasted! I'm not sure who was in the greater state - mother, child or doctor.

The baby arrived without too much difficulty but of course nothing was prepared for his arrival. There were no nappies, sheets, baby clothes, cot or pram. I once again used a drawer as a cot, this time lined with some old curtains and a towel, tore up an old shirt and used it as a makeshift nappy and wrapped the poor baby in a cardigan. I promised to find them some essential items the next day.

The whole family were in a state of shock and the girl's

mother kept repeating that when her daughter was complaining of stomach pains she thought she was just constipated. Life as a district midwife was certainly never dull!

Today, teenage pregnancies are not uncommon but back in the early sixties they were fairly rare and certainly caused a great deal of distress to the families concerned. Unfortunately, this particular girl was not my youngest patient.

Some time later I had to call in the police and social services when a fourteen year old was pregnant. This poor girl was adamant she had done nothing more than "cuddling" with her boyfriend who was then aged sixteen. The baby was delivered in hospital, the boys father gave him a good thrashing, both parents forbade them to see each other again, but two years later when she was pregnant with another child by him they got married and raised their two children together!

One day I received a letter from my father in Holland saying he was going to re-marry. I thought it somewhat ironic that his future wife had been a Salvation Army Officer. In marrying Father she would, of course, have to give up her commission. I thought of all the arguments at home during my childhood and how he had initially forbidden me to go to the Army meetings. Perhaps he had mellowed as he grew older or maybe he just needed a woman around the house to look after him? I had no holiday entitlement left and so was unable to attend the wedding but I wrote and wished them every blessing and happiness in their new life together.

A new estate had been built in my area. The houses were considered to be "posh" and indeed they were a vast improvement on the many terraced houses most of my patients lived in. These new houses had bathrooms, nice kitchens and running hot water. Outside there were small gardens. These features were indeed a luxury few had experienced before.

I was called to a delivery at one of these houses. The mother-to-be looked tired and I knew her baby would not arrive for another few hours so suggested she go and have a nice warm bath to help her relax.

"Oh, I can't do that, nurse. The bath's full of coal".

I could scarcely believe my ears.

"Why is the bath full of coal?"

"Well, you see, if we put it in the coal shed out the back it gets nicked. So we keep it in the bath instead".

I suggested it might be a better idea for the husband to put a lock on the coal shed but she answered,

"Oh, that won't work either, nurse. They'd only break the b...... lock"

I kept visualising this lovely new bathroom with its lovely new bath scratched, dirty and filled with coal. Sometimes, to use a Liverpool expression "the mind just boggles". I thought I had seen and heard it all but then along came something else to surprise me.

Another delivery took me to a poorer part of the area but the family were doing their best to improve their living conditions. Everything was ready for the baby and the mother proudly invited me to sit on her new couch whilst we had a cup of tea. Later, when the baby had been born she instructed me to get the nappies and baby clothes from a cupboard in the sideboard. I opened the door and tins of salmon came tumbling out.

"Oh, that's the wrong door. They're tins of salmon me hubby got on special offer at the docks. Try the door the other side".

I'd often heard the phrase "fell off the back of a lorry" but "special offer at the docks" was a new one!

Later that day I began to itch. Then I began to itch even more and noticed red marks beginning to appear all over my body. By the end of the day I could not stop scratching and went to see my doctor who said it must be an allergic reaction to something and he gave me some tablets.

The following day I went again to visit my lady with the new couch and cupboard full of salmon. Whilst examining her I noticed some insects crawling on the bed. Horrified, I asked her what they were.

"Oh, don't worry 'bout them, nurse. They're only bugs".

I rang the health authorities and instructed them to fumigate the house where they found a nest of bugs in the "new" couch.

I returned to the doctor who then decided my red patches and itching were the results of bug bites and not an allergy. He gave me some ointment, instructed me to go home and put all my clothes in a bath filled with strong disinfectant and to check there were no insects crawling up the walls during the night. I even had to steam my shoes! Thankfully I got rid of them all and it was the one and only time I had such an experience. I felt sorry for the poor woman who had been so proud of her "new" furniture and had only wanted to make her home look nice but it made me very careful where I sat in future.

At the back of our house we had quite a long garden and I had made a vegetable patch and took great delight in growing our own vegetables and some soft fruits. It was quite an unusual thing to do back then but I loved the sense of achievement when I picked freshly grown food. Often there was too much for us to eat ourselves and I was more than happy to share the surplus with friends and patients.

I had acquired a small second hand organ and taught myself to play it. I spent many happy hours playing hymns and singing along to them. It was something I loved doing and at the end of a busy day it helped me unwind and relax.

Whilst waiting for a birth I would often keep myself busy either with my knitting or crocheting and made myself, John and Carol sweaters and cardigans. This time of waiting was also a time when mothers-to-be often unburdened themselves of their anxieties, not always just about the imminent birth. All my patients knew I was a Christian and sometimes they would ask me to pray with them about their problems and concerns. Occasionally if I thought a new born baby may not live I would "baptise" it and pray for it, telling the parents what I had done and encouraging them to get their priest or vicar to perform an official baptism. No matter how sickly a newborn might be I always felt it right to thank God for its life and ask His blessing on it.

John and I still exchanged amusing incidents from our work lives but one day he complained that his supply of tea kept disappearing faster that it should. All the men on the boats took their own supply of tea, sugar and sandwiches each day. John now suspected one of his work mates was helping himself to his tea. He devised a plan whereby he mixed a large amount of Epsom Salts (used to cure constipation) in with some of his tea and left it in the usual place. Sure enough, during the day, one of his "mates" began having griping pains in his stomach and kept dashing to the toilet. He said he must have eaten something which disagreed with him. John told him it was not what he'd eaten, but what he'd drunk and told him that in future he should use his own tea and keep his hands off John's. It was a lesson learned the hard way.

John had given up smoking cigarettes and now smoked only a pipe. This seemed much more healthy. Little did we know at that time that it was just as dangerous and would eventually cost him his life.

Meanwhile my back was causing increasing concern, and despite numerous different tablets and injections the pain was getting no better. Then, towards the end of 1964 I received news from Holland that my father had suffered a serious stroke, was in hospital and not expected to recover. Once again I made the journey across the sea.

The pain in my back was incredible. The only relief I could get was by raising my leg and supporting it against a wall - not an ideal way to travel by train and boat. After almost twenty four hours I at last arrived in Amsterdam. The hospital had a small flight of stairs at the entrance and this proved an almost insurmountable obstacle. However, I eventually arrived at the ward only to find my family just leaving. My father had passed away just a few minutes earlier. Despite all the hurts of childhood he was still my father and I was so sorry I had not been in time to say goodbye.

Whilst waiting for the funeral I stayed with my sister Leni and during that time my brother Jan insisted I pay privately and go to see a specialist about my back. After examination and x-rays he told me I had a severely slipped disc, which needed surgery to correct it. He suggested that as soon as I returned to England I get it seen to.

Once I was back home I went again to see the doctor and was eventually seen by a specialist who informed me that my back was too severely damaged, an operation was out of the question and there was nothing they could do for me except to try to provide a reasonable level of pain relief. I was devastated.

I contacted the Medical Officer and discussed it with him.

I was seen by the medical examining board who declared me medically unfit to continue working as a district midwife. They accepted that my work had contributed to the problem and paid me £325 as compensation! It seemed as though my world was falling apart.

Consequently, as I was now not employed as a midwife I was no longer allowed to live in the midwife's house. I felt I had lost everything. John and I discussed the situation and knowing that doctors in England would do nothing for my back, but that surgeons in Holland were prepared to try, we felt we had no alternative but to leave England and go to Holland.

I knew that if the surgeons in Holland were able to operate my recovery would take some time. We considered the possibility of putting our furniture into storage but as we had no idea when, if ever, we would return to England it seemed best if we disposed of it. Consequently, we sold or gave away our furniture, including my much loved organ and most of our possessions. John resigned his job at the docks and we packed up the rest of our personal keepsakes and clothes. I was dreading another long journey by train and boat. Fortunately, Stan, Gladys' brother had a good idea. He offered to put a mattress in the back of his van so I could lie down during the journey and he would then drive to Holland with John and Carol in front with him, and our cases in the back with me.

It was an undignified way to be leaving the country that had given me so much, and I was heartbroken. I had been married for just three years and was only thirty eight years old. I had envisaged being a midwife for perhaps another twenty years but obviously that was not to be. I felt utterly devastated at leaving behind such good friends and above all, a job that had meant the world to me. The Lord certainly moves in mysterious ways but at that point I could see no purpose to His plans.

CHAPTER SIXTEEN

The journey took two days but at least I was reasonably comfortable in the back of the van. We stayed with my sister Leni and Stan returned to England the following day. Not for the first time I wondered why God had allowed this to happen. I knew that being a Christian was definitely not a guarantee that our lives would be without problems but it was still hard to accept. I kept reminding myself of Bible verses telling me that God had a plan and a purpose for my life but at times it was difficult to accept these latest events were part of that. I continued to pray and knew that others were praying for us too. Gradually my faith increased again and even though I did not know what the future held for me or even for us as a family I learned again to trust in Him.

I went to see the specialist again for further tests. They drew fluid from my spine, which was excruciatingly painful, and finally they agreed to operate to remove one of my lumbar discs and fuse together part of my spine. The operation was considered successful and after two weeks I was discharged but months of physiotherapy lay ahead of me.

I returned to Leni's house for a few days but then the widow of my father, whom we called Tante Miep, suggested we go and live with her. She had more room than Leni and her house was nearer to the physiotherapist. This seemed a sensible arrangement and so we moved in with her.

Whilst I was undergoing daily physiotherapy, we enrolled Carol in the local school where Leni's children attended and John managed to secure a job on the docks. We settled into this new phase of our lives and within six months Carol was speaking Dutch fluently. John did not find it quite so easy, not having the advantage of youth but he began to understand more and more of the conversations around him. One of the Dutch customs he really enjoyed was each day at 11 a.m. a man came around the docks selling raw herring. He soon enjoyed letting them slide down his throat in true Dutch style!

My physiotherapy and the operation had enabled me to walk again without too much pain but I knew I would not be physically able to take up a nursing position again. Whilst we all got along well at Tante Miep's it was not an ideal situation and John and I were missing being in our own home together. My brother Jan told us of some new houses being built in a different part of Holland near to my sister Ellie and having visited the estate we decided to put down a deposit and wait for them to be ready. Unfortunately the months passed, the house was nowhere near completion and both Tante Miep and ourselves were getting more and more discontented with living together. We prayed and talked about our options. Both Carol and John were happy to live either in England or Holland but John was concerned that from the new house he would have a long journey to work each day. Finally, we made our decision to return to England.

My family thought we were mad. They all arrived to try to persuade us to change our minds and could not understand why we wanted to go back. Only one family member seemed to see the difficulties from our point of view. He understood that if Tante Miep died we had no claim on the house and would be without a home. He also understood our longing to be back amongst our own friends.

Meanwhile I had written to Gladys asking if she and Stan could look for some suitable rented accommodation for us. Her reply brought the assurance that we had made the right decision.

At that time Stan worked as a self-employed distributor. He bought goods from wholesalers, had them delivered to his house, then taking them out in his van he sold them to retail shops. Now he felt it was the right time to open a shop of his own and he had found just the right premises with a small flat above. He proposed that we live in the flat, rent free, and that I work in the shop for a small wage of £3 per week. It seemed an ideal solution to our problems and a real answer to prayer.

We returned to England just less than a year after we had left. Our only possessions were those in our suitcases but when Gladys and Stan met us in Liverpool we were all so glad to be back.

We stayed that night with Gladys and the following day went to see the shop and flat. To say the flat was basic is to put it mildly. I clearly remember thinking that it was not much but it was something, and for that I was grateful. There was no heating, kitchen or bathroom   just a small sink and a toilet. On the positive side there was a big living room and two smaller rooms, which would become bedrooms. We could add a bath and knock through into the adjoining property to provide a kitchen. It needed a lot of work doing on it but I was determined to make it "home" and knew that little by little I would get there.

Once again my friends at the Salvation Army rallied round and promised items of furniture and curtains. We set to with builders knocking through the wall, then cleaning and decorating and within a couple of weeks we were able to move in. Life was not easy. Money was tight but we managed. We had a little money saved from John's work in Holland and we found someone prepared to install a bathroom and basic kitchen at a reasonable cost and to save money I decided to have a go at tiling the walls in these rooms myself. I had never tiled anything in my life but reckoned there had to be a first time for everything!

I measured the walls, none of which were straight, I bought the cheapest tiles I could find plus the required amount of cement and set to. I worked from early morning until late at night but after a few days the job was completed and I was completely exhausted! The results were really quite acceptable, even though I say so myself!

John was desperate for work and prepared to take anything offered. He accepted a job as a bin man. He was concerned that I would not approve but I told him if he was happy with it then it was alright by me. Secretly I was so proud of him for his willingness to find work and not take the easy option of going on unemployment benefit.

During the following week we got Carol settled into school, John started his job and I was busily stacking shelves in the new shop which was to sell haberdashery, underwear and clothing. Eventually we were fully stocked and ready to open. Running a shop was a totally new experience for me and so very, very different from my nursing profession but as time went by I was to discover that God could use me to care for people in more ways than nursing.

The shop was in a busy street in Southport and our

customers were women from the nearby houses and workers from the local factories, bakery and other shops. At first, sales were slow and in between customers I was able to go back up stairs and do some more work on the flat, coming back down when I heard the ring of the shop door bell. Gradually trade increased and it became quite a busy shop.

Originally we had little in the way of shop fittings and only an old cash register for the money. All the sales had to be written down by hand and at the end of the day this written account had to be added up and correspond with the money in the till. Gradually Stan got some extra shelving and drawers for the stock and our reputation for selling good quality but reasonably priced goods began to spread through the area.

Soon I began to get to know the regular customers, those who came in for nylons, baby clothes and school wear for their children. It surprised me how often these people would talk to me about their problems and providing a sympathetic and listening ear became as much a part of my job as finding the right shade of knitting wool or nylons. I remembered how kind people had been to me in the past and whenever I had the opportunity I would pass on a kindness to someone else. Of course, when I saw expectant mothers and later their new born babies I still had occasional pangs of regret at having to leave midwifery but God had given me different opportunities now to encourage others and I felt quite contented and happy with this new phase in my life.

I worked long hours in the shop and did all the book keeping in the evenings. I had only Sunday and one other day off in the week and often that day would be spent accompanying Stan to the wholesalers to buy stock for the shop. I enjoyed helping to choose what we would sell and as some of the wholesalers also had food departments it meant that whilst I was there I could do some of my own grocery shopping and buy boxes of tinned or packet goods at reduced prices so saving me time and money at the local shops.

John had settled in well at his new job and seemed happy enough. Carol however, was proving more difficult. She was an intelligent girl but her stories about the behaviour of the other children in her class gave me cause for concern, as did the fact

201

that she didn't appear to be learning anything new. I went to see her teacher.

It appears she had pretended she knew very little English and had therefore been placed in the lowest class with those who because of learning or behavioural difficulties actually learnt very little. I was appalled. Her teacher said Carol had made her believe that she had forgotten how to speak English and that her reading, arithmetic and writing were also poor. I told the teacher she had been born in England, spoke English all the time at home, was an intelligent girl, good at reading and all her other lessons and had in fact managed to learn Dutch in less that twelve months! Not the profile of someone who should be in a remedial class!

The teacher was amazed. Carol was furious that her plan had been discovered and that she was then moved into a higher class where she was expected to work hard, achieve good results and actually do homework. She had been very successful in manipulating the teacher and getting her to believe her lies. It was a side to Carol that we had not seen before, but with which we were to become only too familiar in the coming years.

After a while I began to feel the need to learn something new myself and so once again I enrolled at Southport College for night school classes, this time in Italian. The teacher was excellent and really encouraged us. I had always loved learning languages and now as my Italian progressed I just had to remember which language I was supposed to be speaking!

As a family we all attended the Salvation Army and Carol was involved in the Girl Guides, which she seemed to enjoy. Some Sundays we would go to Litherland to visit John's sister and the rest of his family and sometimes I think Carol missed having her cousins nearby.

John successfully applied for a job as a local bus driver and having passed the required test began familiarising himself with the various routes. His hours were irregular, depending on which shift he was on but he never complained and quite liked the changes. He loved the feeling of being virtually the only one about when he left home at 3.15 a.m. for the long walk to the depot to start his 4 a.m. shift and he often volunteered to be the driver who took the first bus out collecting the other drivers en route. When he was on "earlies" he would be home again at 2.30 p.m. and loved that afternoon time when he could do whatever he wanted.

The drivers took the fares as passengers entered the bus and on one of his first days he took the fare of two elderly ladies who then sat behind him. At the end of their journey one of them commented at how unusual it was to see such a smartly dressed driver with nice short hair. Without thinking, he told them it was because he had just been released from prison. Later, when he returned to the depot the supervisor called him into the office. The two old ladies had complained that ex-prisoners should not be allowed to drive buses when elderly people were passengers! Fortunately, knowing John's sense of humour the boss had guessed which of his drivers was responsible and had assured the ladies it had only been a joke and that John was a very upright citizen.

Despite such rare "complaints" he loved his work and used to tell me about some of his regular travellers often joking about being on the "bun run" when the bus was filled with expectant mothers making their way to the hospital for their anti-natal classes. He was known to be a caring driver always ready to help anyone, especially the elderly and infirm. He also had a special sensitivity to those who were blind and explained that in his youth he had known someone who was blind and knew how much they struggled with so many every day things the rest of us take for granted. His caring attitude and his great sense of fun combined with the indomitable Liverpool humour made him popular with passengers and colleagues alike.

We were happy together and on the odd times we had an argument it was always John who remained quiet and calm (which infuriated me) whilst I was the one (not surprisingly) who did the ranting and raving. I suppose I have always been a rather vocal person!

The shop was doing well and although I no longer went up stairs between customers my knees and back were again beginning to feel the strain. One day as I was coming down the stairs my knees gave way and I fell headlong to the bottom where I lay unconscious for some time. When I came to I tried to move or shout but somehow nothing seemed to respond. John eventually came home, found me and called an ambulance.

The next thing I remember is saying to a doctor bending over me,

"Why have you got two noses and two mouths?"

He explained I had been very lucky to have survived such a fall and to have no broken bones but added that I did have very severe concussion. I was kept in hospital for a few days and then discharged into the care of the specialist eye hospital in Liverpool. My vision was still not right but they were hopeful it would eventually return to normal. I was unable to work for a further two weeks and during that time the shop had to close, as there was no one else to take my place. When I did open it again I was amazed at the concern of so many customers. Yet again God had brought me through and I was assured of His love and care.

One day a gentleman came into the shop and began talking in very broken English. He explained that he had a wife and six daughters living in Poland and he wanted to send them a parcel containing clothes. He was unsure which styles and sizes to choose and asked for my advice. He told me that in Poland his family had so very little and I sympathised, telling him of my own experiences in Holland and the German refugee camps.

As we began choosing items we talked some more and discovered we both spoke German and could converse much easier in that language. He told me his name was Joseph and that during the war he had been captured and eventually sent to England and placed in a prisoner of war camp. When the war ended he was given his freedom but discovered his hometown was no longer part of Poland but had become part of Germany. He had only a Polish passport, which was then unacceptable for his return.

His wife applied many times for permission to leave and come to England but each time the authorities refused. It was a desperately sad situation. Joseph had already been separated from his wife and family since the beginning of the war and although he kept applying for permission to go home or for his wife to come here, time and again permission had been refused.

We finished choosing all the clothes and he was so grateful for my help. During the coming months he became a frequent customer to the shop but at the time I had no idea how involved with his family I would later become.

All was not going well with Carol. She was difficult at home and neglecting her work at school. She had got in with bad company and despite serious talks from her father began staying out later and later and some nights not coming home at all. There were constant arguments. One day after she had been out all night John confronted her and she literally went berserk. We called the doctor to try to calm her down and he said she needed professional help and he would try to arrange something. It was not soon enough.

That night she ran away. She took some clothes and the savings book in which I had saved money for her every week. We contacted the police and eventually they found her. She was sixteen and the law could not force her to return home. The police were not allowed to divulge where she was without her permission, which of course, she would not give. All they could tell us was that she was living with some drug addicts. It broke her father's heart.

After some time we did manage to find out where she was living and went to see her. The house was filthy; she was sleeping in a bed with dirty, urine soaked sheets and despite our pleadings she refused to return home. Some years later we heard she was getting married and although uninvited we went to the town hall to see the ceremony. She would not speak with us and when she moved house again we sadly lost contact with her.

Since I first became a Christian and gave my life to the Lord I have always believed that if you look for it you can always see God's love and provision in every circumstance. Both John and I were deeply affected by these events with Carol but we continued to pray for her and entrusted her to His care.

Some months later I was to receive another knock to test my faith. I had been a member of the Salvation Army for many years when an incident occurred within the fellowship and I strongly felt that the decision taken by one of the Officers was totally out of keeping with all that the Army stood for. I was not personally involved but thought his actions were unreasonably harsh and unjust.

It may seem strange and difficult to understand to some people reading this that Christians who are supposed to "love their neighbour as themselves" could behave in such a way. God forgives and asks us to forgive each other but sometimes we are not always very good at that. Churches are made up of ordinary people who have been saved by God's love and grace, but they are still ordinary people. We are not suddenly made perfect, far from it! We continue to have different personalities, views and opinions. Sometimes, despite our best intentions it is these aspects of our natures which can be the cause of disagreements and hurt, but that is not God's fault, it's ours!

Now I had to realise this again but as someone who has always struggled with injustice I wondered how I would cope at the Sunday service the following week. I prayed about it. Once again God was to show me how He moves in ways we could never anticipate.

In addition to my Italian classes I had also enrolled at a German class. Although my German was quite fluent I had never studied the grammar of the language but merely learnt to speak it. My teacher understood perfectly and brought me some of her own books to study. Her name was Lotte and over the months we had become good friends. That week, quite unexpectedly she invited me to join her at the German church she attended in Liverpool. It seemed as though God had prompted her invitation just at the right time.

I went that Sunday and immediately felt at home. The people were very friendly and welcoming and there were not just Germans but several other nationalities some of whom were students studying at the nearby university. The service was conducted in German but when it came to singing the hymns many people sang in their native tongue. For someone who loved languages I thought it was great but rather than sing in Dutch I was happy to sing in German. It was in this church that for the first time I heard the Ten Commandments and the Lords Prayer spoken in German, and suddenly they took on fresh meaning.

Of course some of the ways of doing things were very different to the Salvation Army but surprisingly that did not seem to matter. I felt that I was amongst people worshipping God, listening to His word and that other differences were unimportant.

The pastor had several different churches to look after in

different towns and cities throughout the northwest and so the service in Liverpool was only held on alternate Sundays. I went home that day looking forward to going again in two weeks time. It was the beginning of a new fellowship for me, which has continued to the present day although in the past few years I have been able to attend only occasionally. Despite this I still have contact with many friends in the church and always receive cards at appropriate times of the year.

As I began attending the German church regularly my connections with the Salvation Army lessened and many of the people, Gladys and Stan included, were unhappy with the change.

Although the years had passed since taking up work in the shop my wages had remained the same and sometimes we struggled financially. John took overtime whenever he could and often this entailed Sunday work. To further supplement our income I became a "home worker" and spent several evenings a week packing false nails, eyelashes and cosmetics for the princely sum of five pounds but as they say, "every little helps". I also knitted and crocheted and sometimes I was able to sell these items.

On rare Sundays when John was not working and there was no German church we would take off in the car for the day. We loved being out in the countryside and the fresh air. I would make up some sandwiches and we had a tiny gas stove which boiled a kettle of water for a pot of tea. On odd occasions we would treat ourselves in a cosy café for afternoon tea and cakes but mostly we were content with our picnics. There were so many places within just a short drive that neither of us had been to. We loved the Trough of Bowland with its rolling hills and meandering streams. We enjoyed the Lake District with its mountains and vast, peaceful stretches of water. We explored the Wirral and the Yorkshire Dales and with our maps we would find the smallest roads winding through picturesque villages where we would stop and enter quiet country churches. We never tired of these special days out together.

By contrast John took me down to the docks and I was amazed at the sheer size and variety of vessels and the different cargoes being unloaded. He took me on a boat past the different buildings pointing out their interesting features or the goods being manufactured there. He told me of past times when the Port of Liverpool had been in high demand and when the dockers had arrived for work on the "dockers umbrella", a long overhead railway. Listening to him talking he made it all sound so interesting.

We also had a lot of visitors from Holland. My sisters came and stayed with us and many of my nieces and nephews also came for holidays, often bringing college friends with them. We had only one spare room but undeterred I borrowed mattresses and put them down in the living room and the young people were happy to sleep there. Often it felt like a youth hostel but on the whole they were no trouble, always ready to do some shopping for groceries and help with the cooking. However, they did require an awful lot of feeding and sometimes it felt as though I was feeding an army. Young people in those days seemed to have insatiable appetites. They seemed to enjoy their stay with us and we enjoyed their company, sitting chatting or playing games long into the night. It was just a shame John and I were both working full time for we often felt exhausted when our visitors had left. We were neither of us getting any younger and sometimes it showed!

One day a regular customer to the shop said she had heard that I used to be a nurse and wondered if I could help her. I told her I would do my best and asked what it was she wanted. This lady had an elderly mother living close to the shop and each day she visited the old lady and helped her in various ways. However, the mother needed to take certain tablets at eight thirty each morning and the daughter was finding it difficult getting there so early as she had a young family to get ready for school. She wanted me to go in each morning during the week, ensure the old lady was alright and that she took her tablets. I said I would be happy to help. The shop did not open until 9 a.m. so I could easily be back in time.

This early morning visit soon blossomed into another friendship and we found we had many things to talk about. Often I would call in during the day and spend some time with her, which she appreciated for she was unable to get out much and was often quite lonely. We found we often discussed the Bible and the way God guided our lives and one day she said she had told her daughter that she wanted me to have a special book. It was a Bible concordance, used to look up any verse in the Bible by using just one word as a point of reference. The difference about this particular book was that it was dated 1880 and had been in her family all those years. I was overwhelmed that she should want me to have it and it is something that I still have and treasure to this day.

As a midwife I had loved holding all the newborn babies and then watching them grow and develop their own personalities. John and I had hoped to have children of our own but as the years passed it became more and more unlikely. However, soon after my fortieth birthday I suffered a miscarriage. It was a shock and a great disappointment to us both. After waiting for so long it had never occurred to me that I might have become pregnant. Gradually we came to terms with the loss and accepted that we were not meant to have children.

Some years later when I was almost forty five I began to bleed severely. John called an ambulance and I was admitted to hospital. The doctor examined me and did various tests then delivered the seemingly impossible news. He thought I was pregnant again. I could not take it in. He ordered me to have complete bed rest until further blood tests were completed. His diagnosis was correct but sadly I had miscarried once again. We went through a dozen different emotions and questions. I tortured myself with a host of "if only's" - if only I had realised I was pregnant; if only I had not been working so hard; if only I had not been constantly going up and down stairs; if only I had taken more care - then perhaps our baby would have lived.

It was harder to accept this second time. It was strange because I thought I had begun the menopause, was too old to conceive and yet I felt I had accepted that fact. Now events had proven that to be untrue and I wanted so much to hold a child of my own in my arms. I wondered why life could be so cruel.

Gradually we took up the threads of life once again but we were careful not to let such a thing happen a third time.

CHAPTER SEVENTEEN

One day, Joseph, the Polish man came into the shop bursting with excitement.

"She's coming, she's coming!" he shouted and coming around the counter he gave me a huge bear-like hug.

Stumbling over his words in his rush to tell me he explained that at long last his dear wife was being allowed to come and live in England. It had been almost thirty years since he had seen her! He had left behind a young wife and mother and that wife was now aged seventy two years. I marvelled at the love that had sustained them through all that time apart.

The arrangements had been made and she was to arrive in London at the end of the week. He wanted to make his house perfect, buy her new clothes, give her all that she had been deprived of, hold her, look into her eyes, see her smile and a thousand other things and he didn't know which he wanted most or which to do first. Before he left the shop that day he made me promise to come and meet her in his home.

The next week he was in the shop again asking me to come and visit. He told me there had been a very anxious time in London when he feared at the last moment that permission had been denied for her to come. The train had arrived on time but there had been no sign of Muti. He was unfamiliar with London's main station and of course everything was strange to Muti, travelling alone and arriving in a country where she spoke none of the language and knew only one person.

There had been a mix up over the platforms. Somehow Muti had been standing on one platform whilst Joseph had been waiting on another! They didn't find each other. Totally alone and bewildered Muti did the only thing possible. In her purse she had a little English money and the address of a distant relative living in London, which Joseph had sent to her in case of emergency. She bravely showed the paper to a taxi driver and went to the address where she stood outside not knowing what else to do. After waiting for an hour at the station and imagining all sorts of problems from missed boats and trains to awkward officials, Joseph also went to that address and found his dear, brave wife. It had been a wonderful reunion.

A few days later, keeping my promise, I went to meet Muti. She was a tiny lady with the most beautiful smile you could ever imagine. She spoke not one word of English but her laughter and smiles spoke volumes. Joseph translated for me but after a while she became more confident to speak her broken German to me and so we were able to communicate fairly well. It was the beginning of a very special friendship that was to last for more than twenty years. During that time both John, my friends Lotte and husband Alan and later my friend Irene would all come to know and love her as I did. She was one very special lady.

Gradually over time I learnt more about her life in Poland. She had lived on a farm in her younger days and married Joseph who worked as a coal miner. Life was not easy and there was never much money except for the basic essentials of life but they had considered themselves rich in love for each other and their three children. When war began Joseph joined the Polish army and went away. That was the last time they saw each other for almost thirty years.

Left alone with the three children Muti coped as best she could. Life in Poland had always been fairly harsh with few affordable comforts and bitterly cold winter months. News of the impending arrival of the Russian troops brought added fear. The Russians wanted to control Poland and rumours were rife that any pretty women and young girls were often brutally assaulted and raped by their soldiers. Sometimes when the Russians were in the vicinity she would hide herself and her children in sacks amidst the piles of potatoes or grain. At other times with hostile aircraft overhead and fearing for their lives she would run to the fields, push her children to the ground and lay on top of them trying to shield them with her own body.

Now, she was in England and she could scarcely believe all that she was seeing. Joseph had taken her to the shops and she was amazed at all the goods on the shelves. I don't think she had ever imagined there could be such a variety and vast amount of food and clothes. She kept telling me that in England you could just go and buy butter, matches and biros. Such little things to us but to her it was a whole new way of life. In many ways it brought back to me memories of my war years in Holland but for Muti the deprivation had never really ended.

Slowly she began to get used to life in England and she was so happy. Many couples may have felt that after so long apart they had little in common but that was never the case for Joseph and Muti. Every day together was a bonus and they revelled in it. However, I suppose it was inevitable that at seventy two she was going to hold on to old ways. She never considered our weather to be cold. Often, especially in later years when Irene and I visited we would ask why she had no fire switched on even though it was the middle of winter. The flat would seem freezing to us but she would reply,

"It's not cold until your hands stick to the frost on the doorknob!"

Muti never learned more than a few words of English. She could manage "hello", "good" and "O.K." but that was about the sum total. She watched the pictures on the television and knew if there was fire, earthquake or famine and she laughingly explained that she knew what was happening in the "soaps" because she could see who was kissing each other!

She was the most contented person I think I have ever met. Her faith in God was strong, she accepted all that life gave her, both good and bad and she never complained. She always gave a warm welcome to everyone and her wonderful smile and laughter was always evident. In coming to England she had only one regret. She had to leave behind her three children and her grandchildren and she missed them greatly. Yet again, I could only be amazed at the strength of love for her husband, which even after thirty years apart had given her the courage to leave those precious children to once again be beside the man she loved. I visited Muti at least once every week and I never tired of her company.

Life continued without any major events. I still worshiped at the German church; worked long hours in the shop and in the evenings did the books; John drove his bus and we enjoyed our free time either visiting different places or contentedly watching television and amiably competing against each other in the various quiz programmes. John was beginning to cough and become breathless and my back and knees were again causing problems but apart from these signs of our increasing age we were reasonably well and very happy together.

Muti had been in England for about two or three years when one day a stranger came into the shop and asked, in broken English, if I was the Dutch lady who spoke German to Muti. When I said, "yes" the man said,

"Please come, help. My father dead."

I was stunned. After all those years apart Muti was now alone again, but this time in a foreign country. Joseph had died suddenly from a heart attack.

I went to the house and helped as best I could. Poor Muti was distraught. Sometimes I wondered why life had to be so unfair. None of the family spoke much English and they had no idea what to do about arranging a funeral, sorting out his affairs and the numerous other things that have to be done at such a time. In all these things they not only needed direction but also an interpreter. I was just so thankful that between us we could manage to communicate the basics in German and I could then instruct English undertakers, registrars and solicitors. This was all new to me too. I was used to bringing life into the world and not arranging its departure. Also, I was unfamiliar with Roman Catholic and Polish traditions but somehow I managed to sort things out.

During the next weeks and months I visited Muti frequently. She seemed to get smaller before my very eyes and yet her indomitable spirit which had seen her rise to countless challenges and hardships throughout her seventy five years now helped to ease her pain. However, I could only guess at the depth of her loss and grief. She remained as openly cheerful as ever and I tried my best to bring whatever help and comfort I could.

In practical terms I managed to get her some extra money and arranged for a priest to call regularly to give her Holy Communion, which was important to her. She could not understand the words he said but she knew the significance of the bread and wine and she appreciated his coming.

I also got her a telephone and showed her how to use it, giving her my number which I told her she could call at any time.

In addition to the television and small radio she also had

a tape recorder and her family would send her tapes they had made themselves, with the grandchildren singing or talking and also music tapes in her own language which she loved to listen to. Her children visited a couple of times each year, taking her out and generally looking after her and these times became like holidays to her which she loved. Sometimes John and I took her out for a drive and one Christmas I took her to the German church with me and she really enjoyed the candlelight service.

Muti was to live to a ripe old age, but more of that later!

CHAPTER EIGHTEEN

One day a letter arrived from the town hall asking me to contact someone who worked there. When I rang I was asked if I still spoke Dutch and would be prepared to act as interpreter when a team from Holland came to take part in the forthcoming It's A Knockout competition. I was thrilled to be asked and excited at the prospect of being part of this popular event, which was watched on television by millions of people throughout Europe. I arranged with Stan that I would take a weeks holiday and soon received detailed instructions of what my duties would entail.

The team would arrive and I would meet them and help them settle in their hotel. Each day I would accompany them either to the Y.M.C.A. hall or the local swimming pool where they would be practising various skills and on the days they were involved in actually competing I would be there to translate and ensure they fully understood all the rules and results.

It was lovely to meet the fifteen young people aged between eighteen and thirty and to share their enthusiasm. We laughed so much during that week but although when people see the programme it is easy to think it is all just a lot of fun, the amount of serious training which goes on behind the scenes is amazing. The team would practise climbing on ropes, walk along parallel bars to improve their balance and throw and catch all sorts of odd shapes and sizes in the gymnasium. In the pool they would practise swimming and diving wearing a variety of clothes, dive into hoops and collect any number of items scattered around the water. They endeavoured to be in peak physical condition but not knowing what their particular games would involve meant they just had to increase their agility and fitness in as many ways as possible.

They had a little free time and enjoyed walking along the sea front. They were surprised that the sea was such a long way out. I explained that it seldom came in. The next day was unbelievable. The sea not only came right up the shore, but it crashed over the promenade and into the road. That in itself must have been a day for the history books! Of course the team thought it was really funny and teased me about it all day. They also wondered why there was no bridge linking Southport to Blackpool as it seemed such a short distance between the two and I explained that it was a question many people had been asking for more years than they could imagine.

Each day the competitors were given their assigned challenges. Some days the Dutch team did well other days they lost. After three days the German interpreter became ill and I was asked to interpret for that team also. It certainly kept me busy. The excitement of the crowds cheering on the teams was tremendous. I shouted just as loud if not louder than anyone else although there was a slight conflict of interest when the Germans, Dutch and English were competing at the same time and I'll not divulge for which team I shouted loudest.

On the final day the scoreboard showed Holland to be the winners. We shouted, cheered and hugged each other in triumph. That evening there was a big celebration dinner in the Floral Hall and afterwards the awards were presented. I felt so proud to have been part of it all.

The day arrived for the team to set off back to Holland and surprisingly they were flying from Blackpool. I went with them to see them off and just before they left the coach they gave me a beautiful silver bracelet and a Dutch doll dressed in national costume, complete with wooden clogs. Even as a little girl I had never had a doll of my own and had not expected to receive one at that stage in life! Both presents are treasured to this day.

The team left and I returned from my brief moment of fame to the more mundane business of running the shop but soon I had a greater concern.

John's coughing was getting worse but a visit to the doctor said it was just bronchitis due to his many years as a smoker. He smoked his first cigarette when he was just eight years old and had been puffing away ever since. He had managed to change to a pipe which at the time we thought was better and he did try to cut down even further by just sucking the end of the pipe even though it was empty of tobacco. Old habits die hard! I was concerned at how breathless he was becoming but again the doctor said it was "only" bronchitis.

I decided we both needed a holiday so we went to Spain where we stayed in Benidorm. It was the first time John had ever been in an aeroplane and he enjoyed the flight. The holiday was perfect. The hotel and food were good, we loved the long promenade, the lovely sandy beach, the many cafes and entertainment and above all, the sunshine. John's breathing became much less laboured in the warmth and we were able to go for long, slow walks (interspersed with frequent sit downs), and even swam in the sea. Sometimes we would just lie and relax on the sand or by the pool. We took a few trips out into the mountains and small villages where time appeared to have stood still and together we fell in love with the country. It was to be the first of many visits.

Towards the end of 1981 I began experiencing severe stomach pains and a specialist said it was due to gallstones. I agreed with him but told him I thought I also had stomach problems. He replied,

"You nurses think you know everything, but there's nothing wrong with your stomach."

On January 1st 1982 I was admitted to the Southport hospital where I had trained as a nurse and the following day taken to the theatre to remove several gall stones. I still thought I had something else wrong but the surgeon would have none of it. I awoke from the anaesthetic to find myself swathed in bandages from my waist to my groin and I knew I should have only had a small incision to my right side. I shouted for a nurse to come and said,

"What has he done to me?"

The poor nurse was nearly as distressed as myself and said she would get the doctor right away. The surgeon who had operated had not the courage to come himself but sent his assistant. The young man was most apologetic. He explained that they had removed several gallstones but unfortunately my own diagnosis had proved to be correct. There had indeed been something else wrong. I had many perforations in my duodenum, too many to repair and so the surgeon had performed a gastro-ileostomy. Basically this now meant I no longer had a valve on my stomach and my stomach had been

217

stitched to my bowel. I was told I would just have to learn to live with the consequences. I did not fully understand at that stage what those consequences would entail.

Back home the huge wound with almost sixty stitches in. It was slow to heal, causing concern both to myself and the district nurse, and I was beginning to realise the implications and results of the operation. Little of my food was being absorbed and I had constant diarrhoea. I went back to the hospital and a doctor who was an even greater idiot than the one who performed the original operation then performed an anal stretch and sent me back home. An hour later my insides literally fell out!

I called an ambulance and was rushed back to the hospital. A different doctor said the previous two operations should never have been performed. He "patched me up" as best he could and apologised for the mess his colleagues had made. His apology was of little consolation and their ineptitude meant I would have to live with the consequences for the rest of my life. I have tried many and various medications some of which help slightly but nothing works fully or consistently. The era for pursuing medical negligence claims had not yet arrived. It would be different today.

I had been trying for many years, without success, to get a council property for us. John was nearing retirement and I was finding it harder to cope with the work in the shop and the steep stairs up to the flat. One day a letter arrived telling us that a property had become available in Ainsdale, just a few miles away from Southport. We arranged to go and see it. The complex consisted of bungalows and two storey flats, purpose built for elderly and retired people. The flat shown to us was quite small but enough for our requirements and outside there were communal gardens, a community centre and health clinic. We met some of the neighbours who seemed very friendly and after giving it some consideration we accepted the offer.

I told Stan that we would be leaving the flat and I would be giving up work in the shop. He was not pleased! He suggested I continue to travel in each day and he would still pay me my £3 a week! I told him I would do that only for a few weeks until he had found someone to take my place.

Friends who had helped with the original alterations to

the flat in Southport agreed to use their van and move us. We did not have a lot of furniture but we had plenty of books. (Some things never change!) I began packing the smaller items, pictures, ornaments, crockery and books. We were fortunate to have plenty of empty boxes in the shop and soon we were ready to move.

In Ainsdale the German pastor came and put up bookshelves and curtains. I asked how he came to be such a good preacher and so practical at the same time. He told me he often worked with refugees arriving in Liverpool who were placed into the most basic accommodation and he did what was necessary to make them more comfortable.

After a few weeks I gave up going back to the Southport shop and began to enjoy, for the first time in my life, the luxury of not having to work. Now, I was able to spend time in my own home and it felt wonderful. When John was not working we enjoyed going out into the neighbourhood and walking the country lanes nearby. I bought an annual car-parking pass for the beach at Southport and we would often go and sit in the car, have a picnic or a walk along the sands.

Occasionally I would dig for cockles and muscles in the sand and then take them home, soak them in a bucket overnight and boil them for John to eat the following day. He thought they tasted better than the ones you could buy!

One day I was walking along the edge of the sea, my favourite place as I loved to hear the swish of the waves, when without warning, one of my feet started to sink into the sand. I tried to pull it out but the other foot began sinking too. I panicked but then I remembered reading somewhere that if you get into sinking sand you should lay your body as flat as possible, feel with your hands for any firmness and gradually ease the length of your body in that direction. I had no way of knowing if it would work but it had to be worth a try. Tentatively I lay on the sand and then began shouting for help! Fortunately, people not too far away realised what was happening and came to my rescue, succeeding in pulling me out whilst staying safe themselves. I was so grateful. I returned to John who was blissfully sitting in the car, reading his newspaper and unaware of the drama. After that, he took a pair of binoculars with him each time we went to the beach and kept a watchful eye on me!

In what seemed a life time ago I had been aware of God telling me that there were more ways of caring for people than just nursing them and delivering their babies. Over the years he had shown me the truth of that and now, living in Ainsdale, he was to show me once again. My neighbours were all elderly and often they were grateful for someone to chat to, fetch some items of shopping, the daily paper or a prescription from the doctor. Sometimes when they were feeling unwell, lonely or perhaps that life had become too much of a burden I found myself in their homes, making cups of tea and encouraging them.

John and I settled well in Ainsdale and enjoyed having a place we felt we could really call our own. However, when a niece wrote from Holland asking if she and a friend could come and stay for two weeks we looked at our small living room and equally small bedroom and wondered where we could put them. Undaunted, we went out and bought a sofa bed for the living room. The girls came, both students, hoping to become teachers and we took them to different places. I even arranged for them to spend a couple of days at the local school seeing how the English education system worked, and it was considered a great success by them and the headmaster.

We were approaching our first Christmas in Ainsdale. John had a few extra days off work and we were really looking forward to enjoying a peaceful time on our own. We had planned everything, including where we would put a small Christmas tree. Then a letter arrived from Holland asking if my nephew and his girlfriend could spend Christmas with us. What could we say? They arrived and thoroughly enjoyed a traditional English Christmas complete with turkey and all the trimmings. They had never tasted turkey before and thought it was great - so great that the bird I thought would last a couple of days had disappeared by the end of Christmas Day. The huge trifle I made went the same way and the catering tin of peaches, something else they didn't have in Holland, was enjoyed for supper! Still, what is Christmas without family?

The following year John and I went on holiday to Ibiza and whilst there we became friendly with a nun. The weather was hot and sunny and every day this nun looked longingly at the cool water of the hotel pool but explained that she had never been swimming in her life, in fact, had never even worn a bathing suit. I decided that could soon be remedied. I took her to a local shop that sold inexpensive swimwear and managed to persuade her to try some. She was very self-conscious but only fractionally so compared to how she felt when some time later she appeared by the pool in her new outfit. She kept looking at her very white bare arms and legs and trying to cover them with her hands! They had never seen daylight and sunshine before. Gradually we coaxed her into the swimming pool. At first she gasped and then began to laugh as I gently splashed her. Soon she was ducking her shoulders into the cooling water and holding on to my hands she allowed me to pull her around the pool whilst she splashed her legs with gusto.

Another day John and I took her out on the sea in a pedalo. By the expression on her face you would have thought all her birthdays and Christmas had come at once. She was so excited. How she explained it all to her Mother Superior when she returned I never asked but we stayed in contact for many years until she passed away.

Whilst in Ibiza we went to see for ourselves the famous "hippy market". I was astounded. Never before had I seen so many young people dressed in long, flowing, colourful clothes, flowers and jewellery. Many of them had been students at university and had "dropped out" for a variety of reasons including drugs, debts and unwanted pregnancies. Some were homeless and slept on the beach at night. What they did in the cooler winter months I shuddered to imagine.

One girl caught my attention. She was painfully thin and was carrying a young child with very sticky eyes. It was obvious the child had a severe eye infection. I began talking to the mother and mentioned the child's eyes. The mother said she couldn't go to a doctor as she was not registered and she had no money for medication. I was concerned that if left untreated the child's sight could be severely and permanently affected.

I went to the local pharmacy, explained the situation and bought some ointment. I prayed I would be able to find the mother again amongst the crowds of people. God answered that prayer and I was able to show the young mother how to administer the ointment. She promised me she would apply it three times a day until the course of treatment was finished and the child's eyes were better.

Another incident from that holiday stays in my memory. John began having "holiday tummy" but no matter what I gave him he continued to be sick and had to rush to the toilet. He looked awful and obviously felt the same. One night one of the waiters asked where he was and I explained. He went up to the bar, reached down a bottle from the top shelf and poured out a measure of some black liquid. He told me to give it to John and come back for another glass just before bedtime. He promised me it would work wonders. It certainly did. I do not know what the "magic potion" was but by the following day John was feeling fine.

In 1983 John retired from his work as a bus driver. To mark the occasion my brother Jan suggested we join him and his wife on a three month touring caravan holiday. We jumped at the chance! It was to be one of the most memorable experiences of our lives. My sister Leni and her husband joined us with their caravan for the first three weeks and we carefully planned our route spending ages pouring over maps and each contributing to the places we would like to see.

Our chosen route took us from Holland, through Germany, France, Spain, Portugal, Switzerland, Belgium, Luxembourg and finally back to Holland. We visited so many fabulous places, some we stayed for a few days but at others we stayed several weeks. We enjoyed Grenada with its beautiful gardens and snow capped mountains glistening in warm sunshine. We drove precariously in first gear over the Pyrenees, admired the scenery from the foot of Mont Blanc and basked in the sunshine almost every day for three whole months. It was wonderful.

Jan drove the car, I navigated and we all helped with the shopping and cooking. In Portugal Jan and I swam out to some rocks and scraped fresh muscles from them which we then soaked overnight and fried in butter the following day. They were delicious.

We seldom stayed on official caravan parks, preferring to find local farmers willing to let us camp in their fields. Sometimes they allowed us to stay free of charge if I agreed to teach their children some English. If we ever found ourselves looking for somewhere to stay at night and there was nowhere obvious we simply parked up near a local cemetery where the land was flat and water was always available.

We passed tiny villages where there appeared to be no shops but when we asked we were told that they were in the front rooms of the local houses, hidden behind curtains. You just knocked at the front door and asked for whatever it was you wanted to buy. English cigarettes were always popular and sometimes the locals preferred payment with these rather than their own currency.

Our caravan often drew the attention of the local children who found the "foreigners" quite entertaining. Many times they would gather around us in the evenings trying to pick up odd words of either Dutch or English and sometimes they would sing their local folk songs to us. Everyone we met was friendly and helpful, advising us where to buy petrol and fresh food and where the nearest springs or water fountains were.

One night we found ourselves at the end of an unmarked narrow road with only a deep ravine ahead. The road was too narrow to turn the caravan around and so we had to try to push it back up the hill. Soon some of the local men appeared to help and we then spent a pleasant evening in their company.

One place that I will never forget is Fatima in Portugal. Many Roman Catholics make a pilgrimage there as it is considered to be a place of miracles and healing, not dissimilar to Lourdes. Here I witnessed people crawling up the hill to the "holy statue" on their bare hands and feet. Many were already elderly or infirm and their journey was tortuous. Some had hands, feet and knees bleeding with the effort of hauling themselves up the rough and stony ground. I felt sickened. I could not believe our God required such self-harm to gain His favour.

Apart from that one place, everywhere else was wonderful. We walked in the Black Forest in Germany, enjoyed Grenada and Valencia. We frequently swam in the sea, often just diving in when we came to an isolated beach. We explored narrow country lanes, picking blackberries as we went; walked around cool, dimly lit churches and enjoyed learning all about the local history and culture of the places we stayed.

Our hundred days passed with remarkable speed and not once did we feel we had become bored with life on the road. Perhaps there is a little bit of the gypsy in us all. Finally we arrived back in Holland after what had undoubtedly been a holiday of a lifetime and a superb beginning to John's retirement.

The months continued to pass and John and I really enjoyed being at home together. We would go for short walks or into Southport and sometimes he would meet with his bus driver colleagues and catch up with their news. Neither of us missed working and we were contented in our life together.

It was several years since Muti's husband Joseph had died and we had continued to visit her regularly. She was now about seventy nine years old and had a real desire to visit two of her children who were living in Germany. John and I agreed to take her but first I had to get the required permissions. The polish embassy had to issue a permit for her to leave England and the German embassy had to issue her with papers permitting her to enter their country. The train was to pass through Holland, making a brief stop there and I was informed Muti would also require a permit from the Dutch. I could scarcely believe the red tape involved to take an old woman to visit her children for a week! Eventually everything was ready and I helped her to pack a small suitcase despite the fact that she said for a week she could just take a few things in a paper bag!

The journey by coach to London, then boat and train took almost twenty four hours and we were exhausted. So much was new to her. She seldom went out and now she was afraid of the crowds and the noise all around her. She was frightened to eat in case the food upset her stomach and she could not find a toilet, but eventually we arrived in Cologne and the joy on her face when she saw her children made all the effort pale into insignificance.

She loved being with her children and meeting some of her grandchildren. They showed her the sights of Cologne and made her welcome in their homes where she slept three to a bed, partly because of lack of room and partly to make her feel more secure! It was also quite normal practice in Poland where they had often slept several to a bed in an effort to keep warm during the long, harsh winters.

The following year when she was eighty years old she again asked if we would take her to Germany. We readily agreed, but on one condition. This time we would drastically reduce the travelling time by taking an aeroplane. It would be her first flight. Reluctantly Muti agreed. To say she was terrified is somewhat of an understatement. She prayed so many "Hail Mary's" I lost count, and keeping her eyes tightly closed for the duration of the flight she held onto my arm for dear life. Despite this she was made of stern stuff and not about to let a great chunk of metal get the better of her!

Once again she thoroughly enjoyed her visit and we succeeded in bringing her safely back to England.

One day I noticed in the local newspaper an advertisement saying there would be a live satellite link to Dr. Billy Graham preaching. The Southport Theatre was to be the venue. Like most people, I knew of the famous preacher but had never actually heard him preach. One of the Southport churches was arranging transport for any one unable to get to the meetings on their own and with John's encouragement I went along.

It was marvellous. He preached the Gospel so clearly and many people responded and gave their lives to the Lord. The couple who had taken me asked if I attended church and I told them a little of my background adding that although I enjoyed being part of the German church it was only every other week and I missed the fellowship of a local church. They suggested they call and take me with them on weeks I didn't go to Liverpool and so it was that I began attending Elim Pentecostal church. It was again very different from anything I had ever known before and some of their ways and practices I was not too sure about but the people were friendly, the preaching was good and the singing and fellowship were great. Soon I was attending regularly, even going on Sunday evenings the week I went to the German church. The services lifted my spirits and I felt that God had drawn me to their fellowship for a purpose.

The people got to know about John who by that time had become weaker. He was coughing more and everything he tried to do left him gasping for breath. Antibiotics did not help and the doctors had finally diagnosed emphysema. Some of the people from the church visited him and they offered prayer, help and practical support to us both.

John's health was deteriorating rapidly but he encouraged me to go out whenever possible. I began to attend Bible studies held in the homes of some of the church members and some Mondays I went to the luncheon club and listened to the speaker after the meal. John was always interested in hearing all the news and what the sermons had been about and it was good that I had something different to tell him.

The weeks turned into months and John's condition worsened. He had little breath for anything and I had to wash, dress and help him in almost every way. He never complained and caring for him was an act of love on my part although it worsened my own back problems. Finally, one day he was coughing so much we knew the time had come for him to go into hospital. Unfortunately the ambulance men were on strike! A neighbour offered to take us and wait to bring me home again.

After a long wait in casualty John was eventually admitted to a ward where he was diagnosed with broncho-pneumonia. His conditioned further deteriorated over night and by the following day he was suffering kidney failure. I stayed in the hospital with him and friends from the church, including the pastor came to support us. They sat with John, prayed and talked with him whilst I went for a welcome cup of tea. I stayed another night and the following day the sister said he was reasonably comfortable and stable and that I should go home and rest for a couple of hours. She promised to call me if his condition changed.

I took the bus home, made a pot of tea and some toast but was unable to settle. I rang the hospital. The sister said,

"You've only just left. I'm sure he's fine but I'll go and check just to put your mind at rest."

She went away and returned to the telephone a moment later with the news that John had just passed away. It was March 6th 1990.

A neighbour took me back to the hospital. I felt numb. I had not even had the chance to say goodbye. I sat with him for a little while then reluctantly left him in his hospital bed. The numbness was slowly turning to anger. Why had the nurse told me to go home? Why had she not called me back in time to speak with him one last time and tell him how much I loved him? Why did he have to die in a strange hospital bed when I had nursed him all those months in the comfort and familiarity of his own home?

Back at home, time spent with tears, anger, regrets and now a deep emptiness, I rang some of my church friends and told them that John had died. They came immediately. I was too shocked to know what or how to do anything. They rang my family in Holland, took me to the registrar, contacted funeral directors and organised the dozens of other things that have to be done at such times.

I went where they said, did what they told me to do, but in reality I felt as though I was walking in a bad dream, hoping and praying for it to end and life to return to the way it was. I felt as though half of my life had been taken from me and there was just a great big hole where it had been.

Several family members from Holland came over. They brought their cars on the ferry and stayed in hotels in Southport. The date for the funeral could not be arranged immediately as there was to be an inquest and so the family used the intervening days to see something of the surrounding areas. They took me out with them but everything felt strangely surreal. At night they returned to their hotels and I was left alone in Ainsdale. I felt more desolate than ever wishing that just one of them had suggested staying with me.

Finally the day of the funeral arrived. I had received so many sympathy cards, many from church friends but also many from John's friends on the buses and I was overwhelmed to see how many of them had taken the time to attend his funeral. The service was taken jointly by the German pastor and the one from Elim, and the hymns were sung in a mixture of English, Dutch and German. John would have liked that.

Before they returned to Holland my brothers washed down the walls and ceilings in the flat before repainting them. I had not realised John's tobacco smoke had caused so much discolouration - proof if any was needed of the damage nicotine does to lungs and surroundings!

Finally, everyone returned to Holland and I was left

alone. I kept looking at John's empty chair and pillows. I had spent all my energy and love caring for him and now he was gone. Now, it seemed I had nothing. No more holidays together, no more long talks and laughter. No more comparing answers to the quiz programmes. Just a great big emptiness. Gradually I took up the reins of life again. I talked to God and Christian friends who continued to be a great support to me.

Several months later the Elim church decided to start a new church in Formby and asked for some members of the Southport congregation to consider committing themselves to the new venture. About fifteen of us agreed and with a new, young pastor we began services in a community hall in Formby, about five miles away from where I lived. It was very different from meeting in the big church in Southport and I missed some of my friends there, but gradually I got used to it and it was good to be able to welcome new people as they came to join us.

One such couple were Alan and Irene and their eldest son, Graham. Soon they were attending regularly and I often talked with them. I had no idea at that time that meeting them would eventually change my life.

I often had to attend hospital for different reasons and one Sunday I happened to mention an appointment I had that week and Irene offered to take me. Another week when I was feeling rather low she invited me home for Sunday lunch. Her three sons were all at home at that time but they welcomed this strange Dutch lady and asked me lots of questions about life in Holland, especially how they made the dykes and kept the water from the land.

Not long after John died I had to go into hospital for what was supposed to be a simple exploratory bladder investigation under general anaesthetic. I was told the procedure would last only about five minutes and I could return home the same day. I woke up in intensive care! Had the anaesthetist read my notes he would have realised that after the big stomach operation performed earlier he should have put a riles tube down my throat. He had not done this and consequently I had suffered a cardiac arrest whilst on the operating table. With hindsight I should have made an official complaint but I didn't. Instead, I spent a week in hospital and then when I was told I could not go home if there was no one to care for me some friends from the church took me to stay with them for the next couple of weeks.

Some months later I had to have a similar procedure for my stomach and rather than risk general anaesthetic again I told the doctor I would endure the discomfort and stay awake! It was awful but at least I did not have another cardiac arrest.

Sometimes it seemed as though the different parts of my body were fighting to see which could give me the greatest trouble! Now my back was getting worse again. I had great difficulty climbing stairs and one of my legs was gradually becoming paralysed. Walking was becoming increasingly painful and difficult and often I had to use a wheelchair. My family, aware of these things, suggested I return to Holland permanently.

They reasoned that as John had died there was nothing to keep me in England any more and if I returned to Holland my spine may still be able to be fixed and the family could keep an eye on me. I was still desperately missing John and knew that it was only a matter of time before I would become housebound and unable to use the stairs. Reluctantly, feeling almost as though there was no alternative I agreed to return to Holland. It was a decision made when I was still mourning and one that I would live to deeply regret.

My sisters Ellie and Leni came to help pack up my things. Sometimes I thought I had spent half my life packing, giving things away and starting all over again. Once again, to make the move simpler, I was forced to part with many of my precious books and furniture. In church that week I went around everyone begging them to write to me in Holland. Irene, along with others, promised that she would. With a heavy heart I said my final farewells.

Meanwhile my family had been busy. They had found me a lovely bungalow in a place called Lelystad, which was about an hour by train from Amsterdam. I would have preferred to be in Amsterdam itself but that had not been possible.

The bungalow was perfect. It was built on reclaimed land that had previously been part of the sea. The Dutch have tremendous expertise in this field. There was a reasonably big bedroom and shower room and an open plan kitchen, living and dining room. Outside there was a small garden in which my brothers had laid some paving flags and planted a few shrubs and flowers. The family had painted the walls, put up light fittings and generally worked hard so that everything was ready for my arrival.

Both I and my furniture arrived and the family helped me to unpack and settle in, then when that was done they left and returned to their homes. I was alone in what suddenly felt like a strange country.

I think it was at that point that reality struck. I was back living in Holland in a totally new place but unlike my adventures of the past I was not a young girl or even a young woman any more, I was a widow in my sixties. Lelystad was a "new town" and as such it was home to many refugees, immigrants and gypsies. There were about forty different languages spoken, the people came from a multitude of different countries and cultures and often rival gangs of gypsies fought openly in the streets.

I realised my family all had their own lives to lead in other parts of Holland. My brother Jan and sister Ellie always spent six months in Spain during the winter months, my brother Henk who lived the other side of Holland was often away in his caravan and suddenly I knew that I had swapped one form of loneliness for another. Thankfully, one of my nephews, Kees, his wife Annelies and daughter Mirjam lived not too far away and they proved a wonderful help to me. When their second daughter, Marjolein was born I would have the joy of being present at her birth.

Lelystad was in itself a lovely new town with a big shopping centre and pleasant pedestrian area and fountains. It also had a good local market where in months to come I would treat myself to some fresh herring each Saturday, but for now, I was unaware of these things and just felt very isolated and homesick for England.

My family encouraged me to sign up with a local doctor as soon as possible. His name was Dr. Hardy and he was exceptionally kind and supportive. The pain in my back was by now almost unbearable and I could hardly walk. Part of my leg and foot was also paralysed. Dr. Hardy arranged for me to be admitted to a neurological unit where they asked me lots of questions and did various tests.

The doctors thought they could certainly ease my pain and thought there was a good chance they could get me walking again. I was terrified of the anaesthetic and told them what had happened in England. They promised they would use a riles tube and I would be safe. The operation went ahead and was successful. Months of physiotherapy again lay ahead of me but I learnt to walk again although for a while I had to wear an old fashioned calliper on my leg.

Gradually I became more mobile and able to look after myself again. Someone began taking me to an evangelical church called The Ark. It was a modern building and a wonderful church. There were so many people wanting to attend on Sunday morning that they had to have two services. The preaching was good and after a while I got to know more of the people and if I could get someone to take me I also went to the weekly Bible study.

My first Christmas back in Holland promised to be bleak. I would be spending it alone. Then someone in the church told me that need not be the case. The church would be open all day and after the morning service anyone on their own was invited to stay for lunch, entertainment and then later, some tea. I thought it was a truly wonderful idea and thanked God for those people who put their own Christmas celebrations on hold to ensure people like me were not alone. It turned out to be a very happy day.

One couple I became close to in Lelystad were Sandie and Wim. They came from South Africa, were committed Christians and we felt we had a lot in common. Sandie loved speaking English which was great, and her husband often helped me if there was something needed fixing in the bungalow. I would tell them about England and they would tell me about South Africa where her mother still lives today.

In some ways I was getting used to living in Holland again but I missed England and my friends there so much. My mobility was still not brilliant and my brother Jan suggested I buy a motor scooter. I was due to go and see Dr. Hardy for injections in my knees and shoulder joints so I decided to ask his opinion on the subject. He thought it was a great idea but insisted

I get one that was low enough for my feet to comfortably reach the ground, and one that had an automatic starter and did not require kick starting. He understood my loneliness and knew that with a scooter I could lead a more independent life and get out more.

A few weeks later I was the proud owner of a red crash helmet and a green 49cc motor scooter! It had been adapted to prevent it going faster than 25mph and had an automatic start and a special stand which just pushed down. Due to the speed restriction I was allowed to go on the many cycle paths, which were scary enough to begin with, but I soon gained confidence and my scooter became a lifeline and an opening to freedom and independence. I could now go and do my own local shopping, browse around the market, take myself to church or visit my nephew and his family. It also meant that rather than having to wait for people to do things for me I could help others, visit those in the church who were elderly or unable to get out and perhaps collect some shopping for them.

Sometimes my brother Henk came to visit, bringing plants for my garden and if they were in the country Jan and Ellie occasionally came but family visits were rare. My nephew and family were the only ones I saw regularly. More and more I began to long for England. I found myself constantly listening to the English radio and television, writing countless letters to English friends and often wanting to speak English far more than Dutch. In retrospect, since I had already spent more than half my life in England, I suppose such feelings were not really surprising.

The postman regularly bought letters from England and most weeks there was one from Irene. I looked forward to those so much. She seemed to have a gift for cheering me up, recounting amusing tales of life in Formby and all the little incidents that made up her life with her husband and boys.

I had many things to be thankful for. I had a warm, comfortable bungalow for which the rent was reasonable. The cost of living in Lelystad was much less than in Ainsdale. My mobility had improved and I had a good doctor who was always ready to listen and support me. I belonged to a good church. What more could I want? The answer was always the same.

England! Despite everything good that I had I still longed for England - English food, English conversation and English ways.

One day I received a letter from Irene telling me that she and her husband Alan were planning to visit Amsterdam to see the Dutch bulb fields, something they had always wanted to do. They enquired if it would be possible to visit me during their stay and how far Lelystad was from Amsterdam? I was so excited I could hardly get my fingers on the typewriter fast enough to reply - yes, yes, yes! Arrangements were made and I sent them instructions of how to get the train from Amsterdam. I was almost counting the days to them coming.

Finally they arrived. My nephew Kees took me to the station to meet them. It was the first time anyone from England had come to see me and I was overcome with so many emotions. Seeing them stepping down from that train is imprinted on my memory. I hugged them so hard I think they must have thought a bear had escaped from the local zoo.

We went back to my bungalow for coffee and cakes and Kees stayed talking with us for a while. Later, I took Alan and Irene to a nearby restaurant but despite me wanting to treat them Alan insisted they treat me. It was wonderful to say grace in English before we began to eat and although I have no idea which foods we ordered I know they tasted good. I remember how wonderful it was to see their familiar faces again and I know I talked non-stop! After the meal we returned briefly to the bungalow for more coffee before they had to catch the train back to Amsterdam. Whilst we sat talking I began telling them how homesick I was for England and how much I missed it. Alan suddenly said,

"If you ever want to come back for a holiday, you can always stay with us, especially if it is during term time when the boys are away at university".

I was overwhelmed by his kind offer and soon after when I had to see them board the train I sobbed uncontrollably. I felt my link with England was again being broken and I was alone once more.

The following week a letter arrived from Irene saying how much they had enjoyed their brief stay in Holland and seeing me again and she reiterated the invitation to visit them. I made up my mind I would take up their offer.

I booked my flights and wrote to Irene saying I would visit for three weeks towards the end of September. Not wanting them to get fed up with me being around all the time I also contacted other friends and made arrangements to see them at the same time.

The weeks sped by as I now had something to look forward to. It never occurred to me that really Alan and Irene did not know me particularly well. Irene had responded to my request for people to write to me but until then I had just been a lady in the church they had recently begun attending. For the first time I began to have doubts regarding the wisdom of my decision.

Back in England, Irene was also beginning to wonder what she had let herself in for. She too, realised she knew little of this Dutch woman who was about to descend on her home for three whole weeks!

Finally, September arrived and Kees took me to the airport. At Manchester, Alan and Irene were waiting for me and hugged me warmly. They took me to their car and on the journey to Formby I think I must have talked non-stop (what a surprise) because as I stepped out of the car on their drive I overheard Irene whisper to her husband,

"Well, at least we don't have to worry if we'll have enough to talk about for three weeks. Johanna talks enough for all of us"

They took me into their home and welcomed me. Irene took me upstairs to what would be my bedroom, saying on the way that she hoped I would not mind sharing. My heart sank. I should have trusted her - I was to share with a lovely teddy bear!

To this day, that "little room" is still mine. It is the place where I sometimes stay overnight if we have been out late or returning from holiday. It is the place I am cared for if I am unwell and above all it is the place where I feel loved, safe and secure.

That evening we enjoyed a lovely meal together, lingering at the table and chatting easily. The following day Alan left early for work and later Irene too left for her part time job. I spent the day visiting friends in the area, which was to be my pattern for the rest of the holiday.

In the evenings we would sometimes play games but more often than not we would just talk, and it was not just one-sided! Something just "clicked" between us. I recounted many of the stories told in this book and often had them laughing as I described various incidents, especially those during my nursing and midwifery days. We would still be talking at midnight when Alan would "give in" and go to bed but often Irene and I would stay talking until four or five in the morning. For someone who likes her sleep this was unheard of for her.

At the weekends Alan took us out visiting different places and it was nothing unusual for all three of us to stop in our tracks, doubled over with laughter much to the amusement of passers by.

Two weeks had passed and one day Irene surprised me by saying,

"Do you think you could spare some time during the day for me?"

I was flabbergasted. I had been so concerned not to "crowd" them that I was going out every day visiting other people but now she was saying she wanted to spend more time with me.

The final week of my stay we spent more time getting to know each other. The bond between us had grown quickly but strongly. We had shared so many joys, disappointments, laughter and tears. The lack of sleep was beginning to show on Irene but still she felt we had so little time left that she did not want to waste it on sleep. She said she could catch up when I left.

All too soon the three weeks had come to an end and I had to return to Holland. It was a subdued trio who journeyed to Manchester airport that day and when the time came to say our goodbyes there were tears all round.

On the flight back I tried desperately but not very successfully to quell the tears and sadness I felt would overwhelm me. Little did I know that in the car returning to Formby Irene was having the same battle. That evening, Irene was still upset and Alan suggested she pick up the phone, ring me, and invite me back for Christmas. It was the most wonderful phone call I had ever received. I felt like dancing! Sometimes "thank you" is the most inadequate phrase in the whole wide world.

I could hardly wait to return to England and now, instead of weekly letters Irene and I were writing several times a week and we often spoke with each other on the telephone, never seeming to run out of things to say to each other.

Soon I was packing my case once again and looking forward to spending Christmas with the Powells. The family were all going away to Gran Canaria on the 27th December but I would be able to share in the festivities with them before they went. I had little idea at that time the work and effort Irene and probably many other English housewives put in to making Christmas special for their families.

I arrived the week before Christmas and Irene told me she had left some of the preparations for me to join in. I endeavoured to help make flower arrangements although it was something I had never done before. We made a good team making the traditional mince pies. Irene made the pastry and rolled it out and I put in the mincemeat and placed the lids on top. This is something we still do together each year. She had already made several bun loaves, something I had never even heard of and the Christmas cake was ready for icing. Irene performed this task but allowed me to put on the decorations. When I saw the variety of snowmen, Father Christmas, robins, holly, children on sleds etc. I wanted to put them all on rather than choose one or two. I don't think the cake was decorated quite as tastefully as usual that year! Finally, Irene was making some "petit fours" some of which were peppermint creams. Irene has cool hands (and a warm heart!) whereas my hands are always warm. She deftly took a spoonful of the peppermint mixture, rolled it in her hands, flattened it and a peppermint cream was made. I tried to do the same. Suddenly this mixture took on a whole new life of its own. It stuck to my fingers and when I tried to separate them the mixture just elongated into strands of sticky mess. The more I tried to extricate myself the more sticky I became. Irene fell about laughing!

Decorating the tree was a highlight of the preparations and I was amazed that she colour co-ordinated the tree. That year it was to be red and gold. It was a revelation to me as I was used to putting everything on in no particular order and with no thought to size, shape or colour, but I must admit it looked beautiful when finished.

These things were to show me the type of person Irene was - always giving attention to detail and doing things properly no matter how much effort it may entail. In many ways we are totally different. To this day, she is methodical and tidy and I am...... not!

However, they say opposites attract and although I know that she sometimes thinks I live in chaos it does not detract from the wonderful bond we still share.

Christmas Day arrived. After church the presents were opened. I had never seen so many. Soon the lounge was covered with discarded wrapping paper as the six of us unwrapped our parcels. Then it was time for lunch. The turkey was cooked to perfection as were all the accompaniments and I tasted brandy sauce for the first time. It was an English Christmas unlike any other I had ever known and I loved every minute of it.

Once again there was a tearful farewell at the airport and although our time together had been busy, if not hectic, it had been wonderful and I could not begin to thank them enough for having me. I returned to Holland to spend New Year on my own.

Having been amidst the company and fun of the family my solitary life in Holland seemed more difficult than ever to cope with but I tried hard to make the best of it. I knew that if it had not been for my spinal problems I would never have returned to Holland but now I was there I told myself to make the best of it and get on with life. At least now I knew I could visit England occasionally for a holiday but I missed them all so much.

Irene and I began telephoning each other frequently, spending ages chatting. Sometimes in an endeavour to keep the calls short we would buy telephone cards and use public call boxes but invariably we were cut off and either went to buy another card or returned home to continue the conversation from there.

In February 1994 Irene decided to visit me in Holland for one week. She had never travelled on her own before and was nervous about the whole experience, convinced she would end up on a flight to Outer Mongolia! However, she arrived safely and although Kees and I did not manage to find her immediately in the airport she remained calm telling herself we would turn up eventually, which of course we did.

At home I had planned our meals and what we would do each day, wanting to spend as much time together as possible. I took her to the market where she tasted hot syrup pancakes, quite different to those made in England. We went around the shops and visited several other nearby towns. In the evenings we sat and chatted. It was the first time she had ever been away from her family and she treasured the time to be herself and not just "Alan's wife" and the "boys mother". It was also the first time she felt as though she was not ruled by the clock, having to have meals ready by a certain time, or having all the responsibility for keeping everything running smoothly in the home. She relaxed completely and it did her good. For my part, I was more than happy to repay some of her kindness and allow her to be the one being looked after for a change. The time spent together in Holland was special.

After she returned home life went on as usual but I began thinking about a promise I had made to God some time ago. Before leaving England I had become more aware of the significance of believer's baptism. I felt it was Biblical and something Christians ought to do as a witness to others of their faith in Jesus. However, at that time I was physically unable to contemplate this but I promised God that if ever I was able to walk again I would follow His command to be baptised by full immersion. I knew that time had now come and so I contacted the pastor at the Elim church in Southport. The next Baptismal Service was to be held on Easter Sunday. I prayed about it and felt sure this was what God wanted me to do.

Once again Alan and Irene offered to let me stay with them and I returned to England for the occasion. People being baptised by immersion normally stand in the baptistry pool and the minister, after asking them to proclaim their faith in Jesus, slowly tilts them backwards and immerses them completely in the water. I was unsure what effect this would have on my back and so it was agreed the pastor would place a chair in the pool and he and one of the elders would together tilt me backwards with the chair giving extra support to my spine.

So it was that on 3rd April 1994, with Irene beside me and helping me in and out of the pool I witnessed to a packed church that Jesus Christ had died for my sins and that He was my Lord and Saviour. It was a wonderful moment and I felt the blessing of God fall afresh upon me. He alone had guided and protected my life, been with me through all its trials and all its joys and now I was able to show how much He meant to me.

That evening Irene gave me beautiful leather bound Bible as a reminder of that very special day. It is something I will always treasure and it sits beside my bed ready for me to read each day.

Once again I returned to Holland. I was getting quite used to all this travelling but leaving Alan and Irene never became any easier and I still longed to be living back in England but thought it was an impossible dream.

The months passed and in Formby something amazing was about to happen. One Saturday morning Alan went out to post a letter. He was gone for ages and Irene began to wonder where on earth he could be. Eventually he returned and handed her some papers. Glancing at them she could see that they were estate agent details of various properties in Formby.

"What on earth have you got these for?" she asked.

"I thought one might be suitable for Johanna. It would be cheaper to move her here than pay for all the phone calls!"

They talked it over and decided that with the money Irene had been left when her mother died some years previously, they could afford a small property for me without having to borrow too much on mortgage. If it made me feel better they could charge a nominal rent. They also discussed it with their sons who thought it was a good idea.

The following day I received a mysterious phone call asking me to come over for a week, as they wanted to show me something. They would say no more but I could tell by Irene's voice that she was excited about something. Yet another flight was booked and I arrived in June, just a few months after my baptism, wondering what on earth it could be that they wanted to show me.

Nothing, absolutely nothing, could have prepared me for their suggestion. They explained that they knew how homesick I was for England and as they had the means to help they would love to make it possible for me to return. They had short-listed several properties and wanted me to view them during the week and decide which one I would like. I am rarely lost for words but that was certainly one occasion when I was speechless!

Irene took me to visit them all. Two were part of sheltered housing schemes but somehow I could not see myself in such places at that time and there was nowhere I could keep my scooter! We looked at several flats and then we went to see a bungalow. It was perfect even though it needed some work doing to it. It had a reasonable size living room, small kitchen and two bedrooms. There were gardens front and back and a garage where I could keep my precious scooter - the lifeline to my independence. The property needed re-wiring, a new kitchen, central heating and a shower in place of the bath but between us we could afford to have these things attended to. It was where I wanted to be. It was far enough away from the Powells to give them space and their own lives, yet close enough to know they would be there for me should I need them.

Alan and Irene told me to think and pray about it. They were right of course; it was a huge step to take for all of us. Part of me just wanted to say, "yes" straight away but I promised them I would carefully consider all the pros and cons. I knew the family in Holland would be furious but I could not help the longing in my heart. I had prayed for the past few years that somehow God would find a way for me to return to England and now thanks to these dear friends He had provided that way.

So it was that I returned to Holland that June with fresh hope in my heart. Words could never express the joy and gratitude I felt. An offer was submitted and accepted and the legal process of buying the bungalow began. When the keys were finally handed over workmen went in and did the various improvements. All that remained was the decorating and although someone was booked to do the work they left it until I arrived so that I could choose the wallpaper.

Back in Holland I had the unenviable task of telling my brothers and sisters that I had decided to return to live in England. There reactions were mixed. Some were angry and thought I was making a great mistake, warning me that they would not help again if I changed my mind. Others were more sympathetic, understanding my longing for the country where I had spent more than half of my life and where I now had such dear friends who meant the world to me.

The next three months were paradoxically the longest but also the shortest I have ever known. Some days it felt as though I would never get there and September seemed so far away and yet other days when I was in a frenzy of packing I thought the time was speeding by all too quickly and I would never be ready.

Sadly, during this time my sister Leni became ill with cancer. She suffered a lot of pain and the cancer spread to different parts of her body. A few weeks before I left for England she passed away quietly. It was an abrupt reminder that none of us lives forever and as the eldest child of the family I felt her loss keenly.

Despite the fact that he was still grieving for his mother my nephew and his family helped enormously with all the packing. I collected boxes each time I went to the supermarket and we boxed up all my books, souvenirs, ornaments and crockery leaving out only essential every day items. The week before the move Irene came over to assist with the final packing and arrangements. Her first reaction when she came in and saw thirty two boxes already packed was to say,

"This will never all fit into the bungalow at home".

She was very nearly proved right!

She set to methodically marking all the boxes, writing on them which room they were destined for and whether the contents were breakable. She helped pack the remaining things and generally got me organised - something she's been doing ever since!

The rules governing the property in Holland were such that even if a tenant had made improvements to the property they had to be taken out and everything returned to its original state. It was perhaps the most stupid rule I have ever come across but rules were rules. Consequently, my lovely garden had to have its paving stones and plants removed, the expensive flooring in the kitchen had to be taken up, light fittings taken down and various other things put back to basics. Every tiny hole in the walls where pictures had been hung had to be filled in and when the kitchen flooring had been taken up the floor had to be re-cemented! Someone from the council came to inspect that everything was as it should be and if they found anything amiss, even a tiny hole not filled in a fine would be issued. Thankfully my nephew and his brother-in-law took charge and did all these things for me.

Finally everything was finished and packed up. We waited for the furniture van to arrive and when it did we received an enormous shock. I had used the same firm who moved me from England. They did part removals meaning that the van could be shared between more than one customer. When it arrived it was more than half full. I had already given them a detailed account of the items for removal but it now seemed either I had underestimated the amount of goods I had or the previous customer had too much. The men looked in amazement at all the boxes plus my furniture and when Kees told them I had a motor scooter to go as well they said there was no way everything would fit in the van. I started to panic and Irene did her best to calm me down. Kees eventually persuaded the men to at least try to fit everything in.

I watched helplessly as all my worldly goods were pushed and squeezed into every available space. Amazingly everything went in....except my scooter. The removal men shook their heads. It was just not possible. There did not seem to be an inch to spare. I began to get upset. I could not leave my scooter, it represented freedom and independence. Kees took one look at me and another at the removal men, and speaking in Dutch, told them in no uncertain terms that his aunt was not going to England without her scooter. They took out some of the furniture, put it back in a different way and finally they dared to lift in my scooter. It sort of fitted! Kees is well over six feet tall and he was not about to be beaten. Putting his shoulder to the doors he pushed with all his might and soon the other men were joining him. Gradually the doors closed and the locks were quickly put into place. I heaved a tearful sigh of relief.

That night Irene and I stayed in a hotel where it was good to relax after the stress of the day. The following morning we had a leisurely breakfast and a last look around the town of Lelystad before Kees took us to the airport for our early evening flight.

Some of my relatives came to see us off and although there was an element of sadness at leaving them I had no doubts that I was doing the right thing. We boarded our flight and were soon looking down as the lights of Amsterdam twinkled in the distance. I had left Holland and felt with absolute certainty that I was at last going "home" to England. The day was September 23rd 1994 and a whole new beginning lay ahead of me.

CHAPTER NINETEEN

Stepping down from the aircraft on to English soil had never felt so good. I almost wanted to kiss the ground. At long last I was back where I belonged and when Irene turned to me and gave me a hug, saying, "welcome home" that is exactly how it felt. Home.

Alan was waiting for us as we came through into the arrivals hall and on the journey to Formby we told him about the events of the past few days including the saga of the removal van. He laughed. I spent the night at their home but we were all up early the next morning as the furniture was due to arrive at 10 a.m.

Gradually everything was carried into the bungalow and I began to suspect Irene may have been right in thinking it would not all fit in. Thank goodness we had a garage. All my books and less important items were stored there until we had more time to unpack them. Over the next two weeks, whilst I stayed at Irene's we chose wallpaper and the decorator began his work. We went to the bungalow each day and began sorting through boxes, hanging curtains and trying to find a place for everything. I think that was when Irene first discovered I rarely throw anything away!

When the decorating was complete Alan made shelves for the spare room whilst Irene and I sorted out all the books. Many were in different languages and in an attempt to have them in some sort of order Irene divided them between English and Foreign, leaving me to gather those in the same language together. Until that time I do not think I fully realised how many different ones I had - Dutch, German, Spanish, Italian, French, English - all languages I had learnt over the years.

Finally, everything was unpacked and in its right place. Curtains and pictures were hung, the bed made and with a big bunch of flowers and a welcome home card from Irene and Alan I was ready to spend my first night in my little bungalow. I thanked them for all their hard work and for bringing me home.

That night, going from room to room, admiring all their work, the new kitchen and bathroom, the cosy central heating and everything around me I thanked God with a heart full of happiness.

Some months later when my brother Jan told me that I ought to arrange my affairs in England as he would not understand our legal system I went with Irene and Alan to a solicitor and had papers drawn up saying that they would act as my legal next of kin. In effect, they have adopted me and Alan often introduces me as his adopted waif and stray! Twelve years later and I am still grateful for all that they have done and still do for me.

A few weeks after my return Irene and Alan celebrated their Silver Wedding with a small party in their home for family and friends. Suddenly a voice called to me from across the room, "I know you. You delivered my children".

The voice was that of one of Irene's cousins and when I looked at her I remembered her very well. She had been one of my patients in Litherland all those years ago. Another surprise was in store when the husband of another cousin turned out to be one of the bus drivers John had known and who had often popped into the shop in Southport. It is certainly a small world.

Some days after that party, David, Irene's youngest son, (well, the younger of the twins by twelve minutes!) was admitted to hospital for an operation on his spine. The day of the operation was in fact the actual day of their Silver Wedding - not quite what they had planned for that date! Instead of celebrating in Rome they sat anxiously waiting in Leeds General Infirmary. Like myself, his operation was considered to be successful but he had a lot of physiotherapy ahead of him and problems with his back are something he has had to learn to live with.

As their anniversary holiday in Rome had been cancelled, sometime in November Alan suggested the three of us go on holiday. It seemed a good idea - we all felt in need of a rest after the events of the past month or two. We booked a last minute deal on teletext and set off for Portugal the next week.

We stayed in an apartment and enjoyed the rest and the sunshine. Alan hired a car and some days we went exploring. We had all been to the area before and so it was good to re-visit old haunts and familiar places and Alan took me to some of the places I had been on John's retirement trip. In the evenings we sat playing cards, chatting or quietly reading. It was good to relax and that holiday was to be the first of many which all three or just Irene and I shared together.

Irene and I developed the habit of speaking with each other at the beginning and end of each day, something we still do now. I ring her each morning and she rings me last thing at night - just to ensure I am safe and well. Sometimes it is good to be able to repay love with love and as the years and lack of mobility catch up with me at least I know I can still pray and be a listening ear for those I care about.

The year after my return to England Irene took me to Llandudno for a few days holiday. We stayed in a small hotel on the sea front and each morning we were awakened by a seagull tapping on our window. Presumably previous guests had fed him. That first morning we went down to breakfast, and in my usual cheery, (perhaps noisy) way I entered the dining room where other guests were quietly enjoying their meal and called,

"Good morning everyone. Isn't it a beautiful day? Did you all have a good night's sleep? What are you all going to do today?"

Irene cringed. Despite spending half my life in England I was still not used to the great British reserve and Irene was certainly not used to this noisy, often outspoken Dutch woman! It took quite a long time for us to realise that there are definite cultural differences between the British and their Continental counterparts. Some times I would infuriate her because I was unafraid to loudly voice my opinion or complain about bad service. Some times she would infuriate me when she was so reserved, and accepting of things, including standing patiently in queues! Time would "iron out" these differences and with a little give and take we became accustomed to each others different ways.

However, despite such minor things the holiday was a great success and the people in the dining room were very friendly! We took the tram up the Great Orme, visited the butterfly park in Conway and viewed the smallest house in Great Britain. We walked along the seafront and the pier and drove out into the surrounding towns, hills and valleys enjoying the lovely scenery. Llandudno was the place Irene had spent her childhood holidays and it has remained one of her favourite places and after subsequent visits it now has fond memories for me too.

In 1992 Alan had begun working for a Danish firm and was soon dramatically expanding the business but with such success came a cost. A year or so after I returned to England his "empire" consisted of thirty four factories in the U.K. and a further twenty four scattered throughout Denmark, Germany and Norway. Ensuring they all ran smoothly meant Alan was away three or four nights each week and so it was good that I was around to keep Irene company and sometimes stay overnight. It was not long before Alan suggested Irene and I go away somewhere for a week as he was away so much and so we turned again to the Teletext to see what was on offer at a reasonable price.

We found a holiday in Zante, (or Zakinthos to give it its Greek name). It was somewhere neither of us had ever been to. The self-catering accommodation sounded reasonable and it was close to the beach, shops and restaurants. It seemed ideal so we rang the travel agent and booked it, but just before she rang off Irene asked in which brochure we could find the accommodation. She was unprepared for the answer,

"Club 18-30".

"Oh! We don't quite fit into that category", I heard her say.

The lady on the other end of the phone reassured her that early in May it would not be a problem. The young people did not go until much later in the season. We decided to chance it. Irene's boys thought it was hilarious, telling their friends, "Guess what? Mum and Johanna are going on a Club 18-30 holiday". They couldn't wait to hear all about it!

The day of departure arrived and Alan took us to Manchester airport. Joining the queue at the checkout desk we were dismayed. The only people aged over twenty five were ourselves. Alan wished us luck and left us to it.

We arrived very late at night when it was pitch dark. Street lighting was something they obviously had not managed to get around to right by the complex. We groped our way to the

247

apartment, fortunately on the ground floor. We were too tired to notice what all the youngsters were doing we just grabbed our nightclothes and went to sleep.

The following day we awoke to brilliant sunshine and a sparkling pool just outside our bedroom. We spent the morning relaxing and about eleven o'clock our fellow guests began to emerge. Despite any misgivings we may have had they were a friendly bunch and happy to talk with us and tell us about their lives and loves! Soon the pattern for the days and nights began to take shape.

The "young ones" would go out drinking about 9 p.m. and the first lot would arrive back about 2 a.m. make some noise for a few minutes and then all would be quiet again. The next lot would come back about 4 a.m. shout their goodbyes and then presumably fall comatose into bed. We had the pool to ourselves until they aroused themselves mid morning - often sporting headaches for which they would come to me for a paracetamol! They were just a group of young people having a good time and during the day they were happy to chat and sleep by the pool. However, if any of them were going to the local supermarket they always asked us if we wanted any water or supplies bringing back.

Irene and I had a great time. The weather was perfect and we took a trip around the island and used the local bus to visit other towns. There were plenty of restaurants nearby and soon we found one that was to become our favourite. They served the traditional slowly cooked lamb called kleftico, wrapped in foil and set alight. We have often had kleftico in other Greek Islands but never quite as succulent or served in the same way.

Two days before we were due to leave Irene badly hurt her back and could barely move. Then these youngsters really surprised us. My back was not so good and Irene usually did my packing as well as her own and we wondered how we would cope. It was a bit like the blind leading the blind. We need not have worried. Seeing the problem two of the young girls came in and packed everything for us and the next day their boyfriends carried all our luggage, got Irene a wheelchair and generally did everything for us. We never had to touch our luggage until it was handed over to Alan at Manchester. Despite Irene's injury it had been a great holiday, made all the better by the laughter we shared with those young people and their practical help when we needed it most. We will never forget them.

Irene and I continued to take regular holidays together several times each year. I had always loved travelling and seeing new places and I now had the opportunity to visit places I had only ever heard or dreamt of.

One such place was Florida. I had heard so much about it but never thought I would actually ever get to go there. Yet again Irene and Alan made a dream come true. We were away in Anglesey at the time and suddenly Irene said,

"You know, everyone should go to Disneyworld once in their life. How would you like to come with us at Christmas?"

I couldn't believe it. I was so excited. That night in bed I kept shouting, "I'm going to see Mickey Mouse". They should have got me to be in the current T.V. commercial! Hearing my excitement Irene and Alan probably wondered what they were letting themselves in for.

A couple of days after Christmas in 1995 we set off. Two of the boys and a girlfriend were coming as well and so there were six of us and we had rented a house complete with indoor pool. I had never travelled so far before but even the lengthy check-in procedure followed by the long flight could not deter my enthusiasm.

Alan had booked a people carrier for the two weeks and we collected it at the airport and set off. The first thing we noticed as we drove into the estate was all the garden Christmas decorations. In recent years these have become more popular here in England but at that time we had never seen anything like it. All the gardens had giant Father Christmas, snowmen, reindeers and such. They seemed to have as many lights on the outside of the homes as on the inside.

We went into our "house". It was huge. I was soon to realise that most things are oversized in America! There was a beautifully appointed kitchen, lounge, several bathrooms and bedrooms and the master bedroom had a walk in "dressing room" bigger than any of the bedrooms. There would be no shortage of storage space. The swimming pool was fabulous and almost as warm as a bath. Not ideal for strenuous exercise but wonderful for relaxing after a hard day at the theme parks.

The Powells had already been to Disneyworld once before and knew that if we were to see everything I would have to go in a wheelchair to cover the distances. This also had the added bonus of allowing us to go to the front of the queue on all the rides. Graham, Irene's eldest son was great at pushing me around, especially when he gave me the odd "wheelie"!

Everything was amazing to me and I loved it all. I was enthralled by the entrance, across the lake towards the fairy castle and impressed by the courteous and helpful staff everywhere. I loved the picturesque rides and thought the "scary" rides were great too. I was fascinated by all the different "countries" in the Epcot centre; feeling as though I had really visited Canada, China and other far away places. The shows were brilliant, the parades exciting and the fireworks just spectacular.

Irene had everything well organised so that we had one busy day in the theme parks from early morning until late at night and the next day was spent more leisurely, perhaps exploring the local shops, enjoying a game of crazy golf on the most amazing course I had ever seen or visiting places like Kennedy Space Centre, Sea World or Busch Gardens.

We ate out sometimes for breakfast, going to a place where for just a couple of pounds you could eat as much as you wanted. I had never seen so much food or so many Americans eating so much! In the evenings we went to one of the many restaurants where again food was cheap, nicely prepared and tasted delicious.

One day, at Busch Gardens which at that time was mainly a safari park with just a few rides, the family were having a rest whilst they sat eating enormous ice creams. David and his girlfriend had finished theirs and were eager to go and look at one of the rides, suggesting I go with them. Off we went with the others promising to catch us up soon. We got to the ride and always loving an adventure I went on with them. The rest of the party eventually came over and Irene nearly had a heart attack on the spot. I was nowhere to be seen and then she realised that was because I was already doing loop de loop on the ride! Back then, such rides that turned complete revolutions had not appeared in England and Irene watched aghast as I plummeted up and over, round and round. I loved every minute of it but got told off in no uncertain terms when I landed.

"How could you be so stupid? Do you want to injure your spine again and be in a wheelchair for the rest of your life?"

I guess she was just worried and doing her "mother hen" bit!

Maybe, just maybe, at sixty nine years I should have known better.

Two other memorable days were at Kennedy Space Centre where I was amazed at the sheer size of these rockets which go into space and then at Sea World where I saw for the first time dolphins and killer whales jumping high out of the water and was able to stroke and feed ray fish.

Our time in America was almost at an end but on the final day we went to a new place replicating China. It was wonderful. The shows where acrobats and jugglers performed were amazing but apart from those the area was just a quiet and peaceful haven of beautiful gardens. After all the business of the previous days it was so good to drink in the stillness and tranquillity. It had been an unforgettable holiday and one I wouldn't have missed for the world. I was so grateful to be able to share in such experiences with the Powell family and words alone are insufficient to express just how much it meant to me.

Back home our Formby Elim church had joined with another fellowship and we found it difficult to embrace the new style of service. Consequently, despite the added distance we began attending a church in Aintree some miles away. It was not an ideal situation as the distance made it more difficult to become involved. However, several years later when I became dangerously ill the prayers and support of this fellowship were tremendous.

Our life continued with normal everyday things - housework, gardening, shopping and suchlike but these were interspersed with days out, visits to markets, garden centres and in the evenings, the theatre.

Alan and Irene had always been great lovers of live theatre and even before they were married they had season tickets at the Liverpool Playhouse. Now they began introducing me to a variety of different productions.

In some ways the most memorable was a play called "Her Benny" which was staged at the Liverpool Empire. It was wonderful and I felt as though I was part of it all, feeling how Benny felt and his anguish at not being able to save his little sister. The Christian message in the play was also powerfully portrayed and Irene bought me a copy of the book, which I eagerly read. Suddenly I wanted to change the title from **Her** Benny to **My** Benny.

Another production, Twopence to Cross the Mersey, was also a favourite. I could so readily identify with the characters, their suffering, poverty and desolation and began to realise the power of the theatre to transport you into the lives of the characters portrayed.

One Christmas Irene took me to a pantomime. I had no idea what such a thing was and asked her to explain it to me before we went. It did not seem to make a lot of sense. Apparently, no matter which story was being told, certain elements were always the same. The leading male parts would be played by women, there would be at least one man dressed very flamboyantly as a large lady, someone would get booed and hissed every time they came on stage and there would be lots of audience participation shouting out such things as "He's behind you" or "oh! Yes he is". I thought I must have been going to a mad house! Needless to say it was great and I soon got the hang of it all and was shouting loudly with the best of them.

Over the years we have seen many different productions, from the big musicals like Les Miserables and Phantom of the Opera to the older but still wonderful musicals like Oklahoma and My Fair Lady and also the distinctive style of Gilbert and Sullivan. We go regularly to see plays both at Southport and Formby and I look forward to these evenings so much. I feel as though a whole new world has opened up to me and each performance is different and special in its own way. I have a great admiration for all the actor's skills and especially their memory to learn their lines. Sometimes I wish I was twenty years younger as I would love to take part and have a go at "treading the boards" myself!

Another "different" form of entertainment that Irene has taken me to a few times, is the old style music hall in the Floral

Hall at Southport. Although Irene jokes she is probably the youngest person there, it is a great afternoon and I have a lovely time joining in the singing of the old songs. Years ago John and I used to go to the Floral Hall to watch the wrestling and we both loved cheering our personal favourites. It is amazing to think of two such different events being held in the same place!

Irene is very good at keeping my "diary" and in addition to keeping up with all our theatre bookings and holidays she also keeps a note of my varied and all too numerous appointments with doctors, hospitals, dentists and opticians - quite a full time job at times and juggling them all so that they don't clash is not always easy.

As I get older my memory is not as sharp as it used to be but there are certain events that are impossible to forget. In 1996 I celebrated my seventieth birthday and what a celebration it was! As far as I was concerned it was just an ordinary Sunday and Irene collected me and took me to church. On Sundays I always have lunch and spend the day with them so after church we returned to her house as usual. When I went through to the dining room I received a big surprise. The table was laden with wonderful food and a big cake in the middle. Out in the garden were tables, chairs, sun umbrellas, balloons and streamers. Everywhere looked so festive and suddenly, from the back lounge came all my friends singing Happy Birthday. I just burst into tears! I don't think that was quite the reaction they all expected but I was just so overcome that anyone would go to so much trouble for me.

It was a perfect day. The sun was shining, the food was delicious and I was surrounded by people who loved me. What more could one ask for? I had so many cards one of the Powell boys clipped them to the washing line! I kept saying over and over, "I can't believe it". It was a never-to-be-forgotten day. Later that month whilst Irene and Alan were away on holiday I went to Holland and my nephew and his family gave me another celebration and took me to their caravan for a day in the country.

When I think back over my life I can recall so many times when God has blessed me and enabled me to appreciate the beauty of His wonderful creation. I remember one time when Alan and Irene took me up Mount Snowdon in North Wales. Of course I was unable to climb so we took the little train to the top - well, almost the top. We were so lucky as it was a beautiful, clear, sunny day and the views were spectacular. Leaving me to admire the scenery Alan and Irene climbed the remaining short distance to the very top. Soon they were back with me and told me that I couldn't possibly come all this way up and not reach the very top. They had "sussed" out the best way and with one each side of me they encouraged, (with a little pulling and pushing) until I too had reached the summit. I can now truly say I have climbed to the very top of Mount Snowdon!

I have always loved travelling and during the years I have been back in England I have enjoyed many holidays especially those with Irene in the Greek Islands. I love the white and blue painted houses and churches, the abundance of flowers, especially in the springtime and of course the delicious Greek food.

One year Irene and I went to the island of Crete. It was a week after we had celebrated Easter in England but we were in for a surprise. The Cretans had not yet celebrated Easter and we would be able to join in their festivities. We were staying in self-catering accommodation and had made good friends with several other couples and families in the small complex of apartments. Our holiday rep. was a young man full of enthusiasm for this was his first job abroad. He wanted to make everything perfect for us during our stay and nothing was too much trouble for him. He told us about the traditional Easter service and meal and asked if we would like to experience it for ourselves. We all agreed it was a good idea. Mostly, everything went according to plan.

On Easter morning most of the group walked to the tiny church at the top of the hill (the rep. gave me a lift in his car) where the priest was to officiate at a special service for us which involved the giving out of real palm branches. Unfortunately rumour had it that the priest had been drinking the night before and forgotten all about us. Whatever the reason, he did not appear and we came back down the hill again. The views from the top had been superb and the church had been open so it had not been totally unproductive.

Back at our apartments a large awning had been erected to shade us from the sun and tables had been placed in a square shape with chairs all around. To one side a lamb was slowly being roasted on a spit over an open fire. When all was ready a traditional Greek toast was made and we enjoyed delicious baked potatoes, salad and roast lamb accompanied by various Greek side salads and of course plenty of wine. Afterwards we were all given a painted hard-boiled egg and the tradition was that each person banged their egg with that of the next person. When your egg cracked you were out of the competition and those remaining continued until finally only the strongest, uncracked egg remained. I suppose it was a bit like our conker contests. It was certainly different to the chocolate eggs we had eaten at home.

Local traditions have always interested me and so at the beginning of December Irene and I have sometimes travelled to Germany to the Christmas markets. We have been to the ones in Cologne, Berlin and Dusseldorf and I'm not sure if it was purely because Cologne was the first but it definitely seemed to be the best although each has its own unique quality.

We travelled to Cologne and arrived at our hotel just opposite the famous cathedral and main market. That first experience of the market was unforgettable. There was so much to see but perhaps even greater than that was the aroma. It is indescribable. The smell of sausages cooking over open fires, onions, mushrooms, potatoes and garlic sauces too. Then there was the chocolate…. melted and poured over fresh fruit, kebab style. If you've never tasted fresh strawberries, pineapple, banana and grapes dipped in delicious chocolate you've never lived! Then there was the hot gluwein - the local fruity but very alcoholic hot punch. Some stalls also sold a hot toddy containing advocat. Well, you have to try all these things for the sake of tradition don't you?

The "stalls" are not in the least like our market stalls. Instead, they are like little wooden garden houses complete with twinkling fairy lights all around the roofs. In daylight they are pretty but in the dark of the evening they become like a magical fairyland.

The typical nativity scene is unlike those here at home. Yes, there are the usual statues of Mary, Joseph and baby Jesus in His cradle but in Germany they are in a real stable with hay and real live sheep, goats and donkeys.

Periodically throughout the day and evening Father Christmas walks through the market greeting people and throwing handfuls of sweets from his large sack to the excited children.

To complete the magic, carol singers proclaim the real message of Christmas and bell ringers too add to the atmosphere as they perform traditional and well-loved carols.

All this, and I haven't even mentioned the things for sale on the stalls. These too are special. There are lots of traditional wooden toys, hand made with such amazing detail. There are wooden decorations for the Christmas tree too. Then there are the glass balls - similar to those we hang on our trees but these are beautifully decorated and hand painted. Some are small but others have a diameter of perhaps eight inches and it is easy to just stand in awe at the beauty and craftsmanship involved in their making. Other stalls sell hand knitted gloves, scarves and hats and of course there are hundreds of different candles of every size, shape and colour imaginable, many again intricately carved. Need I say more? I think you've got the idea that we loved every minute.

Whilst in Cologne we visited the cathedral and a chocolate factory. We walked along the banks of the river and shopped 'till we dropped! The main stores were tastefully decorated for Christmas with many of them having animated displays in their windows. We were amazed that everything we bought was beautifully gift wrapped at no extra charge and the "ready to buy" gift wrapped presents were amazing - even tiny boxes of chocolates or a bar of soap were all wrapped and decorated with ribbon, a Santa, robin or such. Whilst accepting that there is so much more to Christmas than all these trappings it was a wonderful time, which we thoroughly enjoyed.

One year we went to Berlin to enjoy the Christmas markets but we also experienced a little more of the place itself. It was humbling to go to the museum at Check Point Charlie and see how many people, desperate to cross from East to West, had been prepared to squeeze themselves into minute spaces within boxes, pianos and all manner of items in the hope of gaining their freedom. There were the stories too of those who did not make it.

Another year we went to Dusseldorf where we stayed in

the "garden room" of a small hotel. It was very inexpensive but proved to be one of the best hotels we have ever stayed in. The owner obviously had a flair for interior decorating and every room was different, ours being cream and soft green - very restful. Nothing was too much trouble for him and he personally brought us in a tray of tea and home made cakes each evening when we returned. The breakfast table held every food imaginable. I felt I had a landed in Heaven when I found I could have smoked salmon - a treat I love but find too expensive to buy.

The Christmas markets in Dusseldorf were different to the previous places and consisted of not one or two main markets but stalls lining all the main shopping areas. Whilst there we took a train one day to a nearby town, which had the feel of an olde worlde village and that too had a small market. Nearby was a castle in beautiful grounds with a huge lake, which was frozen solid. The temperature was several degrees below freezing and didn't we know it!

All these have been wonderful times. Times which I can recall with happiness and thankfulness that God has given me such a good friend to share them with.

During the past years my mobility has decreased and I have had to use a rollator to help me get around. Sometimes it can be a nuisance and I get fed up with being unable to walk without it but then I remind myself it is better than a wheelchair. At the time I returned to England I had to use a wheelchair if I was out for the day or needed to walk a reasonable distance.

On one occasion we were in Lincoln and poor Alan was puffing his way up a steep street - I thought he was going to need the wheelchair more than me by the time we reached the top. Another occasion Irene and I were shopping in Southport and passed by some shelves displaying handbags. There was not much room for the wheelchair to pass and Irene miscalculated the width. The chair knocked the shelves and an avalanche of bags scattered everywhere. For a split second Irene, red with embarrassment, considered whether she should begin gathering up all the bags or make a quick exit. I won't tell you which option she chose! Having the rollator is definitely better than a wheelchair.

However, even with the rollator life is not always smooth.

Once, on holiday with Irene I insisted I would be able to take it on an escalator. I had done it before and had no problems. This time was different. I'm not sure what happened but suddenly I was on my back, legs flying in the air, the rollator on top of me, the stairs still moving and Irene shouting for help whilst rushing past me to push the emergency button at the end. When the escalator stopped there was then the problem of trying to get my less than featherweight body back into an upright position. Not an easy task. I emerged from my ordeal with little more than my pride hurt but Irene was a nervous wreck! I have also discovered that rollators simply do not move over cobbled streets and unexpected holes in the pavements have also caused me to take a tumble on more than one occasion - the rollator suddenly stops in the hole and I am propelled forward. It's a bit like watching the dance of the sugar plum fairy.

A few years ago I discovered the "Dial-a-Ride" service, which offers a door-to-door service for disabled people in the local area. There are strict booking rules but provided I can remember to ring at the appropriate time I am sometimes able to use the service to take me to Southport on Saturdays. It is great and gives me a feeling of independence. The drivers are helpful and it means I can browse through bookshops or supermarkets at my own pace. Recently, having had my purse stolen on such an occasion I felt my confidence was shattered but with encouragement from Irene I have ventured forth once more, determined not to be beaten. When you have been confined to a wheelchair or dependent on other people sometimes even little ways in which you can be independent become even more important to you.

Sometimes I wish my mobility was better as I miss being able to visit people who are ill or housebound. Last year I had to give up my motor scooter. It was a difficult decision to make as I saw it as my way of being able to go out on my own. I had not used it much in recent years and eventually had to accept that my reactions were not quite as sharp as they had been and I no longer had the power in my hands to control the steering. Knowing these things with my head was one thing but accepting them in my heart was another. It was like losing a trusted friend when I finally saw it being taken away.

Several years ago Alan was replacing the computers in one of his offices and the old ones were no longer required. He brought one home for me. I was well into my seventies and had never used a computer in my life. I did not even know how to switch it on. However, I was thrilled to have it and determined to learn how to use it. My family in Holland all used computers and e-mailed each other and I saw no reason why I shouldn't be able to do the same.

Alan and his son Graham taught me a few basics and I borrowed books from the library and taught myself the rest. Whilst not professing to be an expert I can now confidently e-mail and use the internet. It has proved to be a real blessing. My hands are not so good at holding a pen and writing legibly any more so I can type away to my hearts content and e-mails to Holland are so much cheaper than telephone calls. Some times when I check my computer and find there are no e-mails waiting for me I feel quite disappointed!

I discovered that my service provider had different payment rates depending on when or how often I used the internet. There was no way I was going to pay more than necessary so I signed up for their cheapest "Night Owl" rate which is only £4 per month. It means I can only be connected to the internet between 10p.m. and 6a.m. but I'm often still awake into the early hours so that was not really a problem.

My brother Henk often sent me e-mails and soon my sister Ellie was going to the local old people's home where for a mere 5 euros per year she could have unlimited access and tuition on their computers. Soon she too was e-mailing me and as in recent years she has spent a lot of time travelling all over the world she has amazed me by finding internet cafes in the most unusual and unexpected places and has been able to send me almost daily accounts of the places and things she has seen. It is great to be able to keep in touch this way and I've felt able to share those experiences with her. Sadly, during the past twelve months she has become seriously ill and can no longer communicate.

Via the internet I also read parts of the Dutch newspapers each day and keep abreast of what is happening over there. My family send me sermons from their churches, photographs and music and I can appreciate all these on my computer. It is wonderful, fills my evenings and keeps me out of mischief - well, sometimes!

CHAPTER TWENTY

Irene and I continued to visit Muti. She always welcomed us with a huge smile, grabbing our faces and giving us a big hug. As we spoke in German Irene would take a book and read whilst we chattered away. Gradually over the years we noticed Muti was eating less and less. Often we would visit and I would ask Irene to check the cupboards in the kitchen whilst she made coffee. Many times there was only bread and perhaps a little cheese. Whilst remaining ever cheerful Muti would say she was just waiting for St. Peter to come for her to take her to Heaven to join her beloved Joseph. We suspected that she deliberately did not eat to try to hasten that day.

She lived very frugally. I had arranged for a home help to visit once a week and she did any shopping Muti needed but she never asked for much. A few chicken wings (she insisted there was enough meat on each one for a meal), some bread and tins of evaporated milk, which she used in her coffee. I think the only time she had a cooked meal was when her son or daughter visited. She insisted on saving her money under the carpet and when her son came he always took the money back with him. I opened a bank account for her instead.

She continued to watch television even though she understood none of the language but she would ask me questions sometimes about the things she had seen. Sometimes Irene would play snakes and ladders or ludo with her. She loved to win and was not averse to cheating if it meant she got her player home or missed going down a snake! No matter how much or how little we did for her she was always grateful. We tried to persuade her to come out with us in the car but she had become afraid to go beyond the security of her home and in her way she was very contented with her life and never gave any indication of being lonely. Her simple way of living, her acceptance of life as it was and her joy and pleasure at even the smallest attention were an inspiration and blessing to us.

She developed cataracts on both eyes and after she had

them removed she was like an excited child at Christmas. Suddenly she could see things clearly again. She no longer needed to wear glasses and was amazed she could see the houses on the opposite side of the street. She sat in her chair by the window watching the birds and the people pass by. She was able to see flowers in her garden opening in the sunshine and one day she saw a rainbow and her joy knew no bounds. Oh, if only we could all capture afresh that joy in simple every day things.

Each time we left she would say, in Polish, something, roughly translated as goodbye, come back soon. I'm not quite sure how it happened but somehow she persuaded Irene to say a similar phrase - "dowyzena pane preziez" (apologies for what is undoubtedly a totally inaccurate spelling!) Phonetically it was probably something like doveyjenia panya pritsize but obviously Irene's pronunciation must have left a lot to be desired as each time she said it Muti would fall about laughing and she would hug her more fiercely than ever.

Her walking deteriorated and after having a couple of falls she had to use a walking frame to move around the house. A bed was moved into the living room, a telephone installed by her chair but still she insisted on living alone. Her daughter, Gusta was very good and visited as often as possible, cleaning the house from top to bottom each time and trying to persuade her mother to go and live with her in Germany. Each time, Muti refused. She wanted to be buried in Southport next to Joseph.

Amazingly Muti still did her own washing, by hand, in the bath. She saw no need for "new fangled washing machines". Clothes had always been washed by hand, scrubbed clean, rinsed and hung on a rope over the bath and she saw no reason to change her ways.

In the year 2000 Muti suffered a stroke. She was admitted to Southport Hospital where she stayed for many weeks. Always tiny, she lost even more weight and seemed to shrink before our eyes. The staff were unable to encourage her to eat and I can still see in my mind Irene encouraging her to eat just one more spoonful, using every trick she had no doubt used with her children many years before. It always worked and she would laugh as Irene got her way but we could not be there all the time.

Eventually the staff told us it would be impossible for

Muti to return home. She must be placed into a nursing home. Armed with a list of homes in the area that had vacancies, Irene and I went to check them out. We were unimpressed with several of them. Finally we found one where we felt she would be cared for with love. The difficulty of language was always going to be a problem. Despite her twenty years in England Muti had still not learned to speak English. No one spoke Polish but in this home one of the staff could speak a little German and the Matron assured us they would be patient and find ways of understanding her.

Having collected some clothes, pictures and personal possessions from her house we made her new room, next to the Matron's office, as homely as we could and moved her into the nursing home. In typical Muti fashion she accepted it all graciously and was thrilled to see her familiar pictures and ornaments. We need not have worried about communication. Her smile won over all the staff and she became their favourite, in fact sometimes we wondered if there was ever a time when one of the staff were not popping in to give her a hug and check she was alright. In a world without words - hugs, smiles and a reassuring arm around the shoulder became the order of the day. We made a list of essential German words - cold, hot, hungry, thirsty, pain etc. and wrote them phonetically so the staff could know her basic needs but it soon became apparent that with all the love and care she received and her happy, contented disposition, the lack of verbal communication was unimportant.

We visited regularly, as did one or two other people who spoke a little German but she was happy and contented as always and we knew she was well cared for. Her daughter visited and was happy with all that we had done for Muti.

The following year, Muti began to deteriorate. There was nothing specific, her body was just wearing out. She was spending more and more time in bed but despite the fact that bodily she was becoming more and more frail her mind remained as sharp as ever. We visited one afternoon and I had taken a small bottle of advocat, her favourite drink. Her eyes lit up when she saw it and I poured some into a small glass. She drank it, licked the glass and even ran her finger around the inside ensuring she hadn't missed any! Her next favourite drink was lemonade but the staff were anxious she didn't drink too much of this as she was becoming dehydrated and they wanted her to drink more water. We tried giving her water but she wanted the lemonade. Irene thought she could outsmart her and picking up the lemonade bottle, she walked behind Muti, poured a little lemonade into a glass and topped it up with water. Despite her frailty Muti was not to be fooled. She told me it did not taste right!

I think we all knew that Muti's life was nearing its end and on her last visit Gusta, Muti's daughter had left a very special candle. In Poland, when someone is about to die this candle has to be lit and Gusta was most insistent that this should be done. I explained this to the Matron and staff and they assured me it would be lit at the appropriate time.

In March 2001 at the age of ninety five, Muti peacefully passed away. The Matron rang me, and Irene and I immediately went to the home. She had been a dear and very special lady and we would both miss her enormously. On arrival at the home the Matron took us up to see her. She lay peacefully in bed with just the merest hint of a smile on her lips. Leaving the room, we noticed the candle. There was just about an inch left. Matron explained that they had lit the candle as requested and she herself had checked on Muti every fifteen minutes throughout the night when each time the candle was burning brightly. When she found Muti had slipped peacefully away she also found the candle had gone out. There was no logical explanation. Gusta later explained that this was normal.

I rang Gusta and broke the news to her. She asked me to attend to the funeral arrangements and she would come with her husband as soon as possible. We contacted funeral directors, arranged the various legal formalities and arranged a service in a local Catholic church. We collected Muti's Bible and Rosary thinking Gusta would want these. When I telephoned her to tell her the time and date of the funeral and mentioned we had the rosary beads she said they must be placed in her mother's hands and buried with her. I'm not sure if this was a Polish or Catholic custom but we took the beads to the undertakers and Gusta was happy.

The day of the funeral arrived. Gusta's brother was

staying at Muti's house and as brother and sister did not get on with each other the nursing home kindly gave Gusta and her husband a room for a couple of nights. I sat behind Gusta ready to translate the English as necessary but it was a traditional service and they seemed to understand what was happening. At the graveside I could not believe brother and sister said not a word to each other, barely acknowledging each other's presence with little more than a glance. I thought of their mother and how she had literally covered their bodies with her own to protect them during the war, her love for them which knew no bounds and yet now at her funeral they would not speak to each other. This brought almost as much sadness as her passing from us.

After the funeral Irene took Gusta and her husband home to her house. We had lunch together and then took them back to the nursing home. The following day they would have the long journey overland to Germany, as they could not afford the airfare. I am still in touch with them by telephone and they still regularly send cards at Christmas and Easter, always asking after "Frau Irena" and thanking us for the care we gave her mother. My answer is always the same - it was not difficult. It was a pleasure and our privilege to have known her.

CHAPTER TWENTY ONE

The year 2002 is one that will not be forgotten easily although some of the details are forever lost to my memory and the blanks are filled in by Irene.

There was nothing to suppose it would be any different to other years as we toasted each other on New Year's Eve and made plans for holidays, alterations to Irene's house and a reunion she was organising for friends who had all been at the Baptist church where she and Alan had first met and subsequently married. March and April were going to be busy times - that was when the alterations were happening, the reunion was to take place and after that at the end of April Irene and I planned to return to Holland and visit the bulb fields and Keukenhof Gardens together. Irene is not known to do any thing in half measures!

At one time she had plumbers, plasterers, joiners and decorators all working on different things in different rooms but still she continued planning the final arrangements for the reunion, daily adding to the mounting list of people attending, checking with the hotel and caterers, conjuring up games, mounting displays of photographs, working out the thanksgiving service and typing out the service sheets. Despite all this she still found time for me and was concerned by the severe pain I was experiencing in my head and over my right eye.

She took me to the doctor who prescribed some pills. They did nothing for the pain and as she was worried about me I went to stay at her house. A few more days passed and still the pain persisted. Another trip to the doctor who then prescribed different pills. It was the day before the reunion and Irene was busy checking everything, including the workmen, whilst making twenty flower arrangements for the tables. I was trying to help but found it difficult to concentrate on anything as the pain in my head worsened.

The following day Irene was reluctant to leave me but I assured her I would be alright and sent her on her way to enjoy the reunion. That night the pain worsened and Irene took me to the hospital the following morning. After several hours I was sent home. They said there was nothing wrong with me and headaches were considered to be neither an accident nor an emergency! I was told to take some extra paracetamol.

Without labouring the point, sufficient to say that during the following week I went three more times to the local doctors and three times to the hospital. The pain was unbearable and I was literally crying out in agony. The response from the hospital was still that I had a bad headache. To be fair, on Irene's insistence they did eventually do some blood tests and x- ray but nothing of any significance showed up. Towards the end of the week Irene noticed some tiny blisters above my eye and a return visit to the doctor confirmed I had shingles. The doctor put me on the specified medication but it was to prove too little, too late.

During that week I had fallen numerous times, especially during the night and Alan and Irene had to try and lift me back on my feet again. No mean feat. Doctors had been told of this but no one had paid any attention. Now, two days after being diagnosed with shingles I was getting worse, not better. My co-ordination was going, I was falling almost every time I got up and I began talking even more nonsense than usual! Apparently Alan had suddenly become a goat herder making feta cheese!

Once again the doctor was called out but the answer was that I was just tired after all the lack of sleep due to the pain. Irene was told, "Don't look so worried. She'll be fine. She just needs a good sleep. Trust me." Those words almost cost me my life.

The following day Irene again voiced her anxieties wondering if I had suffered a stroke but district nurses who brought a commode and cot sides for the bed again reiterated the doctors words and thought I was just tired. "Just let her sleep" was their advice. By the next day when Irene eventually got someone to take notice and an on-call doctor, appalled by the events of the past ten days rang for an emergency ambulance I was unconscious and diagnosed with encephalitis. The shingles virus had attacked my brain. At the hospital I was taken to intensive care where the doctors told Alan and Irene that at the most, I had only a few days to live.

I can only imagine the effect that news must have had on them. Over a period of ten days there had been only one day, the day of the reunion, when I had not been seen by one or other person of the medical profession and yet no one had been prepared to listen and act appropriately.

Alan and Irene returned home stunned and faced the task of telephoning my family in Holland. Fortunately they also told people in church who supported them in prayer.

It seems that my salt levels had fallen dangerously low and priority was given to raise these back to normal levels. Irene was told that if this was successful it would raise my level of awareness but it would not change the ultimate outcome and prognosis. She spent every day by my bedside and Alan joined her when he came home from work.

Against all the odds, but I have no doubt as a result of prayer, I regained consciousness. My nephew and two brothers came over from Holland. They stayed a couple of days and returned home wondering if I would ever be able to live independently again. By then, the doctors had reviewed their initial prognosis and decided I would probably live, but how severely my brain was damaged was an unknown quantity. The doctor **hoped** I would be able to walk and talk.

Irene tells me she went home and prayed angrily to God telling Him that if He was going to spare my life He'd better make a good job of it and not leave me unable to walk, talk or function independently. He miraculously answered her prayer.

It seems Irene and two friends from church were sitting by my bedside. I had showed no signs of "coming round". Shirley offered Val and Irene a polo mint and apparently a voice from the bed suddenly said, "where's mine?" Shirley nearly fell off her chair and the three of them burst out laughing. My next comment was nearly as good as the first - "What's so funny?" I was immediately enveloped in hugs all round as they tearfully but joyfully welcomed me back and explained to me what had happened. They had thought I wasn't going to make it when all the time all I really needed was a polo mint! Many prayers of thanks and praise were raised that night. Our God is a great God!

That was just the beginning. I had to learn to walk and talk again and my memory was not too good. Not only could I not recall anything of the past few weeks, but even when I was told about it I had difficulty in retaining the information. After a while I was moved to a ward and slowly began to improve. Countless numbers of "Get Well" cards flowed in. Sometimes it takes something bad to make us realise the good things we have in life and friends are perhaps the most precious gift of all. Friends and people from church visited regularly enabling Irene to have a few hours at home. We were both sustained by their love, support, encouragement and prayers.

Steadily I made progress. My right eye was permanently turned in towards my nose and I had double vision, which made for interesting manoeuvres when it came to reaching for things or putting things down on tables. I would invariably miss on both counts! Although these sometimes became frustrations I gradually began to realise the seriousness of my illness and how fortunate I was not only to be alive but to be almost fully restored. I had so much to thank God for.

However, as I grew stronger my impatience increased and I was anxious to leave hospital. The specialist wanted me to stay longer but when I told him I could go and stay with Irene (without asking her, I should add in all honesty) he agreed that as long as she was there to care for me he would allow me to leave. It proved to be another big mistake.

The day for my departure arrived and Irene came to collect me. On the way home I had to attend a different hospital to have my eyes checked as the virus had obviously left some permanent damage. Whilst waiting to see the consultant I experienced the first of many post herpetic pain attacks. I had thought the pain in my head prior to my hospitalisation was extremely severe, but nothing compared to the pain which now shot through my eye and head. I literally screamed and writhed in agony as Irene watched helplessly and shouted for a nurse.

A doctor was called and gradually the pain began to abate. I was informed that this type of pain is not uncommon after a serious attack of shingles and that it could come unexpectedly, or be present for most of the time to a greater or lesser extent for anything up to two or three years. Occasionally it may never go. Some patients suffered dull pain over a long period, others, like myself would suffer acute and extremely severe bouts in short, sharp episodes which may last anything between a few minutes and an hour.

I had thought the worst was behind me but now I was to experience this new terror. Over the next couple of months whilst still staying with Irene and Alan I would suffer so many of these attacks. One minute I would be fine, the next I would be screaming with pain, thrashing about and fighting off anyone trying to comfort or hold me. I wanted to give up. It was hard for Irene to watch, unable to make it better.

Various painkillers were prescribed but nothing helped. I was waiting for an appointment with a pain specialist and one day, during a routine check up at the eye hospital the doctor, reading through my notes and I suspect, feeling that the system had already badly let me down, offered to contact the pain specialist personally and arrange for me to be seen immediately.

The specialist was very understanding and seemed to know exactly the severity of the pain and how I felt. He prescribed some tablets and also some special liquid anaesthetic, which could be applied directly to the area of pain. It was not a miracle cure but it worked wonders and certainly made the pain bearable. Life was again worth living.

Over the next twelve months, with regular exercises, my eye gradually returned to its normal position and I could see ahead and not just the side of my nose! The double vision improved and with special lenses in my glasses I now see only one of everything for most of the time. I'm a lot slower in thought and actions but maybe this is down to old age!

By October of that year I was well enough to go away for a few days. The proposed visit to the bulb fields had of course been cancelled but that year Holland was hosting an autumn flower festival - Floriade - and as much to boost my confidence as anything else Irene booked for us to fly to Amsterdam for a few days. I was terrified something would go wrong in my head or eyes despite the fact that the doctors had said I was fit to travel. However, all was well and we enjoyed the beautiful floral displays and took time to relax, soaking up the atmosphere and thanking God for eyes to see the beauty and colour of the flowers, ears to hear the sound of the wind rustling in the trees and to experience the joy of just being alive. Our God is a great God!

CHAPTER TWENTY TWO

In 2003 Irene had yet another surprise in store for me, and one which I was not too sure I was looking forward to. A few years previously she and Alan had gone on a cruise to Alaska, which they had thoroughly enjoyed. Since then they had cruised the Adriatic and now she suggested we go on a cruise together. I had many misgivings. I had enjoyed a cruise on the Rhine but that was just a river. I had travelled over the sea to Holland numerous times and although I had been fine I had seen countless numbers of people ill. I had no wish to spend a whole week being seasick! Then there was the question of dress. I had heard most people who went on cruises had to dress up in special evening clothes. I was definitely not someone who did "posh". I had visions too of all these "posh" people with their airs and graces and me feeling like the proverbial fish out of water. Then of course there was the cost. Surely cruises were very expensive?

Irene laughed at my fears and said that not all cruises cost the earth, nor did they all have "formal dress" for evenings and in her experience most of the passengers were just ordinary folk like ourselves and I would fit in fine. She assured me I was unlikely to be seasick, as the ships were large and well stabilised. Experience would show the latter did not necessarily mean they would not roll in bad weather! Eventually she convinced me and we set off to the travel agents where we were lucky to find a week cruising the Mediterranean followed by a week on half board accommodation at a hotel in Majorca. The cost was no more than we normally paid for a two week holiday. We booked it and I tried to put my doubts to the back of my mind.

As the time for our departure approached so my anxieties increased. I had so many "what ifs…" I could write a book just on those alone! We were to fly out to Palma, Majorca and then transfer to our ship - the Island Escape. Irene had packed my suitcase as usual and Alan took us to the airport. By that point I was both nervous and excited and I'm not sure which feeling was the stronger.

We landed at Palma airport, collected our luggage, were met by a representative and escorted to the coach that would take us the short distance to the ship. As we drew up at the dock I caught my breath. The ship looked enormous, far bigger than I had expected and much bigger than anything I had ever seen before.

We were greeted, told our luggage would be brought directly to us in a short while and then escorted to our cabin. It was wonderful. It was spacious, with twin beds, a sofa, dressing table and stool, plenty of storage and room to move about and a small shower room and toilet. It was nicely decorated and furnished and had a lovely big picture window. I had imagined a small, dark room not something like this. Irene laughed, as I stood transfixed.

Sometimes when I think back to that week I think my mouth must have been agape half the time. Having unpacked and freshened up we went to explore the rest of the ship. There were long carpeted corridors with cabins each side. The reception area, lounges and dining rooms were all beautifully decorated and furnished. Pictures adorned the walls. There were lifts to all the floors. It was just like being in a beautiful hotel. I could not believe all this was inside a ship. There were theatres, shops, gymnasium, hairdresser and even a swimming pool and jacuzzi. One of the restaurants was open twenty four hours so at any time, day or night you could go and get a cup of tea or coffee, some home made cake or biscuits or even a full meal if you were so inclined. There were outside decks with sun loungers and near to one of the restaurants, tables and chairs were also outside so you could enjoy breakfast and lunch in the sunshine. It was almost too much to take in.

Later that night the ship left Palma. Above us fairy lights twinkled the length of the ship, a band played and we watched as the buildings and shoreline of Palma receded into the distance. I almost had to pinch myself to make sure it was all real - I was actually on a cruise ship. It was something I could never have imagined in my wildest dreams and fears forgotten, I was looking forward to seeing all the different places on our itinerary and enjoying the whole experience of cruising. I was seventy seven years of age and about to prove you are never to old to learn or try something new.

Over the next seven days I soon became used to sailing overnight and awakening each morning to a new destination. Sometimes we went on an organised excursion; sometimes we just took ourselves ashore and explored the local area. We stopped at ports in Malta, Italy, Spain and France.

In Italy we took a taxi to Sorrento and I had to use my almost forgotten Italian to explain to the driver where we wanted to go, what we wanted to see and do, and most importantly to negotiate how much it would cost. The scenery was magnificent and we loved browsing in the tiny shops down the pretty narrow streets.

In France we went to a market and Irene persuaded me to buy a pair of black evening trousers ready for future cruises! I tried them on over my shorts and decided at the equivalent to £5 I could afford to be extravagant!

In Barcelona we boarded a "hop on hop off" tour bus and explored that beautiful city, marvelling at the intricate and colourful architecture of Gaudi. If the Temple de la Sagrada Familia ever gets finished, it too will be wonderful but we were a little amazed to pay an entrance fee and then find ourselves in the middle of a building site! It was however, quite an impressive building site and the structures already complete were amazing, totally symmetrical and intricate.

On board ship everything was fantastic. The crew could not be more helpful. The cabin steward changed bedding and towels so frequently it must have been like painting the Forth Bridge. Some nights we would return to the cabin to find our towels had been fashioned into swans, rabbits or such and were displayed on the beds. One night my pair of reading glasses had even been placed on one such rabbit. These things always delighted us and brought a smile to our faces.

We chose to eat in the buffet restaurant rather than the more formal waiter service dining room and the waiters were only too happy to carry my plate and escort me around the vast variety of food. They also took delight in "parking my Ferrari" as they called my rollator.

In the evenings we enjoyed fantastic professional shows with dazzling costumes and wonderful singing. Elsewhere on the ship in various lounges and bars cabaret entertainers sang or played music. Sometimes we treated ourselves to the "Cocktail of the Day" - some were nicer than others but as neither of us is a connoisseur of such things we just enjoyed the experience.

It was a very friendly ship and everyone was happy to chat about their various experiences and what they had done each day. Virtually everyone changed into some smarter clothes for the evening but there was no formal night when people wore evening dress and I felt completely at home with everyone we met. All my worries about how "posh" it was going to be had been unfounded.

I had found my "sea legs" almost immediately although I confess finding my way around the ship was not quite so easy. It was just so big! I had even managed to get into my life jacket for the emergency drill on the first day. By the end of seven days I felt as though I was a veteran sailor (ancient mariner?) and could not wait for the next year, hoping that Irene would be willing to take me on another cruise. I was hooked.

Since that first time Irene and I have enjoyed several other cruises. Each one has been special. I have seen Rome with all its famous landmarks, visited tiny, unspoilt Greek islands, with towns perched almost precariously on top of mountains and in Madeira I even came down the slightly perilous "basket run". This, for any one who does not know, involves sitting in what is basically a basket on skis, which is then pulled at an alarming speed down a long, steeply cobbled street. There are no brakes and the basket is guided (I use the term loosely) by two men holding ropes who alternate between standing on the back, running alongside or pulling back on the ropes in a somewhat vain attempt to curb the increasing speed. It sounds crazy and it is but then what else is there for a nearly eighty year old to do in Madeira?

Last year Irene found another cruise with what appeared to be an ideal itinerary taking in some of the smaller Greek Islands. There was just one slight problem. This particular cruise had set times for dinner, allocated tables and during the course of the week there would be two "formal" dinners requiring appropriate dress. I was unsure but once again Irene used her powers of persuasion. We managed to find a long black skirt and

I already had several nice tops and the evening trousers bought in France so we decided these would fit the bill. With an inexpensive pair of gold shoes and matching handbag I began to feel like the Queen, only more nervous. Watch out, Cinderella was coming!

Again my fears were unfounded and we had a wonderful cruise. Amongst our favourite places were Kefalonia, Mykonos, Zakynthos and the incredibly beautiful Santorini, which is perched on the top of a mountain. Everywhere was so pretty and quiet. The blue and white houses and churches glistened in the sunlight. It was like stepping back in time and we felt so peaceful sitting in tiny open air cafes, often right on the edge of the sea and just admiring the tranquillity and simple beauty all around us. It was definite therapy for body, mind and spirit! Watch out Shirley Valentine we may be joining you!

Since moving back to England, several of my family from Holland have been able to visit me and stay with Irene and Alan. When my nephew Kees and his family came, Alan hired a people carrier to enable us all to travel together as we visited local places and further afield into North Wales and the Yorkshire Dales. My brother Henk enjoyed a wonderful day in the Lake District as Stephen, one of Irene's sons, showed us many of the local beauty spots and the spectacular scenery where he now lives. At such times I feel so lucky to have not just my own family, but my 'adopted' Powell family too.

Looking back on the past twelve years and the numerous holidays I have been able to take, I almost feel as though I could write a travel book (only joking!). I have been tremendously privileged to have seen so many places and when I think back to my impoverished childhood it hardly seems possible that I could ever have enjoyed so many wonderful experiences. I thank God for each and every one of them.

CHAPTER TWENTY THREE

We had been attending the Baptist church in Aintree for about ten years but sadly for about two years things had not been going well. Different ideas had been introduced which many of the members were unhappy with. As a consequence, a large number of the congregation left, most of whom stayed together, forming a separate fellowship. We had a decision to make. Should we go with the new fellowship or take the opportunity to find a church nearer home? Irene had always believed Christians should be involved in their local church and with my lessening mobility it seemed a sensible option for me too. We decided to try some churches in Formby and pray that God would guide us to where He wanted us to be.

A few months before this time Alan's mother had died and the vicar of St. Luke's had conducted the funeral service with which we were very pleased. Afterwards we had spoken to her and been assured of a warm welcome at St. Luke's.

Neither Irene nor myself were familiar with the Anglican style of worship and were therefore a little in fear and trepidation on the first Sunday morning we attended St. Lukes. We were welcomed at the door and surprised to be singing lively hymns and lots of the choruses with which we were familiar. We had not expected to find a music group at the front! Our previous church had met in a school hall and although we had never considered it before we suddenly realised how much we had missed hearing the wonderful sounds of real organ music. It was good to hear the Gospel preached and also over the next few weeks to feel we were being spiritually fed once again.

Seeing the vicar and the choir in their robes took a bit of getting used to as did the going forward for Communion, but the most difficult thing was the responses and read prayers. The free churches - Baptist, Methodist, Salvation Army have no set prayers or orders of service. We prayed God would help us make the right decision.

Now, almost two years later I think we can say we feel we

belong and there is a wonderful added bonus that Alan now attends with us.

During our time at St. Lukes I have been thankful for the love and care shown to me. When Alan and Irene are away on holiday it is good to know people from church are there for me should I need them and several have called or visited to ensure I am coping on my own. Recently, when my purse was stolen I was amazed by the kindness and concern of so many people. It is in such ways that God's people show His love.

In November 2005 I was asked to give a short talk in church about how God had led and protected me throughout my life, especially during the war years in Holland. There were so many memories it was difficult to know what to include and what to leave out. I did my best and presumably that must have been enough for afterwards over coffee numerous people asked me further questions or said how much they had enjoyed and indeed been touched by my words. Several wanted to know when the next instalment would be given or even suggested I should write a book! It was not the first time such sentiments had been expressed.

Several years ago Irene had thought about writing my story. I had made some tape recordings telling of events in my life and she had begun making notes from them. However, other pressures and lack of time meant that it went no further. Now people were again suggesting that my story should be written. God works in wondrous ways and one thing I have learned in my life is that His timing is always right.

In September 2005 Alan retired from work and this was to have great bearing on the writing of my story. As more and more people suggested writing a book Irene asked Alan if he thought she should really try to do it. His answer was "yes". Furthermore he was prepared to support her in any way and if that meant taking over some of the household chores and taking me to various appointments to give her the extra time then he was more than willing to do so. God had provided the right time and made it possible.

In January 2006 "the book" was begun! A new computer was bought and Irene set herself up in a spare bedroom, which quickly became her office. I have been busy making tapes,

277

prompted at times by Irene's list of headings. She then listens to the tapes, makes notes and somehow transcribes it all into what we hope is a readable and enjoyable book.

I cannot quite believe that a book is being written about me - Johanna, the eldest daughter of a poor Dutch family. How could I have ever imagined that people would want to know about my life - the ups and downs, the laughter and tears?

I think back to my childhood days and remember all the hardship but perhaps even more than the regular beatings and lack of food I think the one event which still hurts the most is being forced to abandon the place I had won at the senior school because my parents said they could not afford it. Education is a wonderful gift. We should embrace it and take advantage of it no matter what our age or circumstance.

The next biggest regret is having to give up midwifery. It took me a long time to realise that God could still use me in different ways but it was a hard lesson to learn. Even today when I see on the television a baby being born the feelings still bubble to the surface.

Losing John and moving back to Holland were difficult times too. In Lelystad I was so lonely. As Christians, we know that God is with us always, that He never leaves us. That is true and I have proved it throughout my life. However, that does not mean that there are not times when despite the head knowledge that He is with us our hearts feel empty and we feel alone. Those are the times to remember the famous "Footprints" message. It is when we are struggling and think we cannot see God by our side that He is in fact carrying us in His arms. How true are His words: "I will never leave you or forsake you."

Sometimes I wish I had less pain, that my legs would walk better, that my arms were stronger, and that my hands would grip things instead of dropping them. I wish I could hear, see and remember the way I used to do. I wish I didn't have to take all the tablets I do to keep me "ticking over" especially the steroids that make me gain so much weight. Then I stop and think of all God's blessings and feel ashamed at my negative thoughts.

At the present time my dear sister Ellie is still seriously ill and again in hospital. Having suffered strokes, brain haemorrhages, and fits during the past nine months she is once again unable to communicate. It is hard sometimes when God does not answer our prayers when and how we would wish but we have to keep on believing that "all things work together for good for those who trust in Him". I am thankful that others are praying with me for Ellie and I place her in His hands.

In a couple of months I shall, God willing, be celebrating my eightieth birthday. I am amazed I have made it this far. On days when life seems a struggle I look at the flowers on my table, my computer on my desk, shelves filled with books and all these in a warm and comfortable bungalow which is mine for as long as I need it. I look out the window to my garden with its spring flowers in all their glory - the brightly dancing daffodils, the jewel centred primulas and I know that I have much to be thankful for. God's blessings are new every morning.

I have lived a truly wonderful life and God has allowed me to see many beautiful places and to be a help to many people. For the opportunities I had in serving Him in the Salvation Army both in Holland and Germany I am indeed thankful. They were wonderful, if humbling times.

My nursing and midwifery days I can also count as blessings. Nothing can for me, compare to the wonder of bringing a new life into the world. It was a great privilege and joy.

I was married to a wonderful man, a true "scouser" who had a terrific sense of humour and with whom I was able to share a large part of my life. He supported me in my work and encouraged me to be "myself". I thank God for him.

Finally, what would I do without my dear friends Irene and Alan? They rescued me from loneliness in Holland, provided me with a home and have continued to care for me in a million and one ways during these past twelve years. Each Sunday as I enjoy my lunch and tea with them I am grateful that I can feel part of their family. Only when you have lived alone can you fully understand how good it is to sit down and share a meal with someone. I thank God for them each and every day

Looking back over nearly eighty years I've asked myself what lessons I have learnt. The first that springs to mind is that I have learnt to be grateful for food and never to waste it. We prayed so hard during the war for even a few crumbs. I have learnt that earthly possessions are of little importance. You can't take them with you when this life is over. I have learnt to appreciate family and friends for these are the true treasures in this life. Finally I have learnt to put my trust in a God who will never let me down.

The old hymn says, "count your blessings, name them one by one, and it will surprise you what the Lord has done".

Those words are so true and the more I start to count my blessings the more blessings I remember. Our God is a great God and throughout my life He has been and still is, beside me every step of the way - through laughter and tears.

POSTSCRIPT

On June 16th 2006, I celebrated my 80th birthday. Irene and Alan took me to Llangollen in North Wales where we had a wonderful time and I was truly spoilt!

Soon after our return, my brothers Jan and Henk came on a surprise visit and it was great to see them again.

My dear sister, Ellie, is now out of hospital and slowly making good progress. I have so many reasons to be thankful.